The Challenge of Diversity

The Challenge of Diversity

HARPER & ROW, PUBLISHERS

by *Richard E. Engler, Jr.*

The American war is over; but that is far from being the case with the American revolution. On the contrary, nothing but the first act of the great drama is closed.
　　—Dr. Benjamin Rush, Philadelphia, 1789

New York, Evanston, and London

To the memory of

JOSE GARZA, OF BENAVIDES, TEXAS

. . . who contributed to the American Revolution

FIRST EDITION

LIBRARY OF CONGRESS CATALOG CARD NUMBER: 64–12707

K-O

Contents

Preface

This book is concerned with how people, almost unwittingly, evolve patterns of social institutions and cultural values. The major chapters describe eight communities in different regions of the United States where men and women accepted the challenge of a physical frontier and developed somewhat different modes of social accommodation as they pursued their individual ambitions and the goals of their groups.

The book speaks to current controversies over minority rights through the crucial concept of "role." For whatever the economic and political power exerted by social movements, and whatever the legal decisions of courts, it is implied here that increased human dignity can ensue only as new roles in a free society are made available to those who have had limited opportunities because of their ethnic characteristics. These roles may take different forms, considering the varied histories and present social contexts of people in different regions and localities, but they must in the final analysis be based on a belief in the value of the individual. The majority of these roles must be enacted in local communities where men recreate their institutions.

Because the stories are presented as representative models,* names of communities and of individuals directly involved in local affairs rarely appear in the narrative. However, many footnote citations refer to communities by name. Contemporary interviews were obtained during a study of local welfare services in different parts of the country. This narrows what is intended as a general analysis of American life by restricting the formal contacts the author—and other researchers—had. But impressions of these settings were expanded by informal experiences in the course of living in the communities for a period of months.

---

* "Model" here does not imply "best" but "characteristic pattern."

A major assumption of the thesis is that as men attempt to effect change in their society, they must be aware of the social and cultural forces that deflect and transform rational plans when the deeds of legislators are translated into human institutions.

The immediate impetus for this book came from a study of child welfare services conducted in 1957–1959 through auspices of the Child Welfare League of America with a grant from the Marshall Field Foundation. The resulting report was published as *Children in Need of Parents* (Henry S. Maas and Richard E. Engler, Jr., New York: Columbia University Press, 1959). Subsequently, I felt impelled to build on that study. The inclusion of historical materials located in the Library of Congress made possible a more complete story of American Society.

Henry Maas of the University of California at Berkeley gave permission to use interviews from the original study, which was planned and conducted by him. Others who collaborated on that project were Zelma Felten, Margaret Purvine, Meredith Friedman, and Arnold Lyslo. Joe Reid, executive director of the Child Welfare League, gave encouragement, and Zelma Felten went out of her way to arrange for additional interviews. Acknowledgment must also go to the people in communities around the country who shared their feelings in interviews with the study teams.

Joseph Kohn was a sounding-board for ideas while the manuscript was being prepared. Mary Catherine Voss and Jean Seay helped with retyping and put up with the author's need to air frustrations. John Macrae of Harper & Row gave the manuscript a hearing, offered many suggestions, and then worked diligently to see the book through to its final form.

I wish to thank friends who shared, in widely separated parts of the United States, the warmth of a family circle when I was moving about the country. I am also indebted to men at the Postal Terminal Annex in Los Angeles—Pink Dangerfield, Guy Hatago, and Odell Barber—who supplied needed incentive.

Finally, acknowledgment must be given for primary motivations: a young President, John F. Kennedy, who turned men to unfinished tasks; parents who taught that one should care about one's country and about people.

R. E. E.

Introduction

Here at last is something in the doings of man that corresponds with the broadcast doings of the day and night. Here is not merely a nation but a teeming nation of nations.

—Walt Whitman[1]*

A student from England attending a university in the United States recently appraised characteristics of this country he found most disconcerting. He maintained that freedom and democracy could flourish only where an inherent unity is clearly manifest in a society. For this young man the sense of "being an Englishman" was almost a racial identification. He was hard put to discover the things-in-common holding together the American people.

Perhaps men from most countries that call themselves free and democratic would adopt this same position. The unity built around a crown or around a sense of blood kinship, preserved in tradition, is characteristic of most stable Western nations advocating freedom and government by the people. But the promise of America—the unfinished society—has been that it is a pluralism of groups and individuals who seek to discover grounds for unity.

* Superscripts refer to the Notes at the end of this volume.

And once achieved, such unity promotes further differences that renew the vitality of a social experiment.

The diversity within our society has made a persistent contribution to human freedom. Between the Atlantic and the Pacific on the North American continent freedom advanced as people pushed back a frontier, accepting physical challenges that posed new social problems calling for different patterns of institutions. And within America's national borders today there remain distinctive individuals, groups, and communities still engaged in winning their freedom. These conditions exist wherever democracy has not faltered and the revolution of the forefathers is continued.

This domestic experience should place Americans in a good position to comprehend major problems of today's world. For a world growing smaller through technology is not moving consistently toward uniformity. The great pride of new nations highlights the phenomenon of diversity. But old nations too, sophisticated and mature, are asserting strong identifications with institutions developed through particular experiences of their people in history. And within nations the loyalties that make men human are revealed again as identifications such as those with region, local community, ethnic group, profession, family, and are seen finally in unique assertions of pride in talent and possessions by the individual.

Reinhold Niebuhr expresses the faith of the "cause" of pluralism in the world:

> . . . We believe that history is a vast drama or series of dramas, in which individuals, communities, classes, races and cultures are engaged in winning their freedom from the limits and necessities of nature, even in exploiting and misusing their freedom in contest with other individuals and communities, in elaborating theme upon theme and dramatic configuration upon configuration. . . .[2]

No simple dogma, he notes—like the Marxist morality play where history is a contest between good and evil factions—does justice to the multiplicity of human strivings.

To the proponents of human freedom, the signs of diversity give cause for rejoicing. They indicate that standardization and regimentation meet resistance at every social level. And they give warning, too, that a perfect order belongs to another realm than the historical condition of man. Certainly the heritage they share leaves Americans with difficulties in discovering grounds for unity. But energies that bring tensions also give impetus to the continuing search for a better social order.

Initially, the arrangements set down in the American Constitution reflected the realities of an agricultural society with growing commercial interests in its larger cities. These conditions helped to shape the attitudes of the Founding Fathers. But the experiment moved upon ideas that provided broad and changing goals for each new generation.[3] Basic to the unfolding process was the *idea* that human beings could and should be responsible for initiating governments, assuming sovereignty for the people as a body and delegating this sovereignty to chosen representatives.[4] The social corollary of this political imperative was that people would develop different and changing patterns of social accommodation as they communicated with one another over problems of promoting the general welfare and achieving individual dignity.

From this standpoint, Jefferson's Declaration of Independence seems a clearer trumpet for American society than the Constitution.[5] For the Declaration opened the way to the quest of more perfect unions across the American continent. The germinal ideas can be variously expressed in the institutions of human communities. The crucial ones are broad in scope.

There is the idea of the human individual as the primary element of history. There is the idea of equality in intrinsic worth of these individuals. Then the idea of freedom is linked to this concept of the individual who is benefited by a condition unfettered by rigid constraints. The implication that compromise and controversy are important indicates willingness to continue the dialogue between individuals about means for effecting their welfare. Finally, the linking of individuals in communities is expressed in the idea of the people—a body of sovereign citizens who conduct a forum for social experimentation. For it is in communication with one another that free individuals and groups refine hopes and aspirations and weave their varied goals into institutions.

What attitudes and orientations emanated from these ideas amid the physical conditions of this continent?

A simplified outline can help to present a story of theme and variation in American life.* The social orientation that went with the idea and the conditions of freedom was one of achievement; that is, a man could *achieve* dignity, self-realization, and his position in human communities and need not be anchored to a position *ascribed* for him by past social conditions or by his heredity. This orientation was basic to the American ideal. It helped to generate the restlessness that reserved center stage for the "discontents."

Independence of the individual, as he accepted responsibility for shaping his own destiny, was also a challenge and a possibility of continuing frontier conditions. However, if independence was an ideal as the individual escaped from hereditary bondage, wherever men broke with old orthodoxies they soon formed other bonds of *interdependence.* This was true of separatist groups of settlers, tied together by religious and political ideals, who came from the Old World to found colonies in the New. It was true of groups breaking off from colonies to found other communities after coming to the New World. It was true of pioneer groups seeking land and fortune and more freedom through the passes and across the plains leading farther west. Separatists, settlers, pioneers, adventurers achieved new linkages around common interests amid the perils of the American continent.

There were other conditions influencing the expression of basic values where social renewal continued. Relationships between individuals were largely *personal* and *specific.* The American social world was small—the numbers of men's associates were few —and in small groups it was the specific individual, struggling to create his own identity, who was "experienced" in human intercourse.

Writing in the early nineteenth century, Tocqueville described the characteristic American social scene as a European saw it:

In America, where the privileges of birth never existed, and where riches confer no peculiar rights on their possessors, men unacquainted

* See Appendix II for definitions of concepts and for a scheme classifying—in terms of these concepts—the communities described in the book.

with each other are very ready to frequent the same places and find neither peril nor advantage in the free interchange of their thoughts. If they meet by accident they neither seek nor avoid intercourse; their manner is therefore natural, frank, and open. . . .

Those who went before are soon forgotten; of those who will come after no one has any idea: the interest of man is confined to those in close propinquity to himself.[6]

Through his experience of specific persons in his social world one individual granted inalienable rights to another. And through perceptions of his own dignity in such relationships, a man sought to insure *his* rights.

Even today, Americans live their lives in particular physical settings where they seek to provide shelter for themselves and their families, to work, and to communicate with each other. In effect, the search for the kind of human relationships once provided by local communities* seems symptomatic of frustrations among many Americans today. Basic social psychology of identity and socialization involves people communicating with people. This process begins in the family circle and radiates outward to other social encounters.[7] A local community, where common problems of the general welfare were confronted immediately, once provided a firm bridge between the intimate, private, and the broader, public, commitments in American life.

It was in the local community that the democratic experiment was carried on by people grappling with conditions that required concerted action. Many of these settings became focal points for a pattern of culture that infused wide areas. In any case, wherever a community endured it left institutions that conditioned the behavior of anyone who came to live there.[8] But most important, history shows that even where communities were impermanent and transitory, the people had been able to form and maintain ties to one another for a time.

Some of these persistent patterns have been chosen for this discussion of strains of diversity that flavor American life today.

---

* "Community" is used in this book to *denote* local geographical areas—physical settings considered manageable for comparative analysis as cultures and "communication systems." However, throughout these essays the term "community" also *connotes* any human grouping as a communication system. (See Appendix II.)

An effort has been made to clarify the arrangements of populations and to determine the significant "names" in local cultures.[9] A look at history and at current social conditions indicates something of the nature of encounters between groups and individuals in the systems. This helps to point up both the opportunities and the problems of human dignity in different contexts of America's "unfinished society."

These essays emphasize that the continuing revolution has been carried on where men had a common stake in their situations and asserted their individual value and identity while recognizing the worth of others. The process persisted while institutions were created and then were defended by men as part of themselves. The revolution can flourish only as the germinal ideas remain relevant to men's experience.[10] In the past new vitality appeared as people achieved new identities, building communities in a land with an open frontier.[11]

The thesis presented here stresses movement and diversity as vital to the American heritage. It stresses that the concern for new social answers and "more perfect unions" cuts through differences to underlying values. It says that without a commitment to these values, and the exploration of new ways to express them in community institutions, the shots at Lexington become only a fading echo—in America and, perhaps, around the world.

PART I. *Movement Toward Segmented Societies*

1

A Crowded Coast: New Bedford

We . . . doe by these presents solemnly and mu-
tualy in the presence of God, and one of another,
. . . combine our selves togeather into a civill body
politick, for our better ordering and preservation
. . . ; and by vertue hereof to enacte . . . such just
and equall lawes . . . and offices . . . as shall be
thought most meete and convenient for the generall
good of the Colonie. . . .

—*Mayflower Compact, 1620*[1]

"They Came . . . as Strangers"

The leaders of the little band had reason to hesitate at debarka-
tion. The voyage had been long and hard. Winter was at hand.
And the newcomers who had joined their ranks since the group
had left Holland included many whose motives and feelings were
not those of the majority. The common bonds of "fear of God"
and "mutual love and respect for one another" did not embrace
all those who waited to settle a desolate coastland.

There had been trouble during the voyage, largely from among
adventurers who had joined in England at the instigation of the
commercial backers of the proposed colony in Virginia. In
Holland there had been much discussion and debate, in the weeks
and months of negotiation before the trip, about the propriety
of risking to "break the course of communitie" by accepting
strangers into the little religious colony. But the representative
who wrote from England of the progress of negotiations argued:
"Venturs are made by all sorts of men, and we must labour to
give them all contente, if we can. . . ."[2]

Mutinous speeches caused concern even in midocean. When the landfall which was decided upon as the site for settlement was determined to be far north of the area defined by the charter, the murmurings of lawlessness appeared more threatening. One of the colonists later recorded the discontent of these men who said that "when they came a shore they would use their owne libertie; for none had power to command them."[3] The simple compact drawn up was the first formal act by which a small community of like-minded people took account of the challenge that diversity presents to joint human ventures.

The hard core of the group had more than worldly interests to guide them. Their spokesman later said: ". . . most important of all was their hope to lay some good foundation for the kingdom of Christ in remote parts of the world. They had a great desire to be the steppingstones for others to carry out so great a work." Leaving the creaturely comforts was not easy even for such a people as this: "But," he said, "they knew that they were pilgrims and looked not back, but lifted up their eyes to the heavens and their spirits were quieted."[4] The formation of a "civill body politick" was an accommodation to physical and social realities; for when men of great faith face terrestrial matters, they see, inevitably, an imperfect world.

During those first months, all who had come saw little around them that was comforting. "The whole country," recorded their chronicler, "full of woods and thickets, had a wild and savage look"; while, "If they looked behind them, there was the mighty ocean which they had passed."[5] Before the winter was over, fully half had died. Of the fifty remaining, only six or seven were sound of health at the height of the winter's travail. "These six or seven . . . spared no pains, night nor day," reported the chronicler. "With abundance of toil and hazard of their own health, they got wood, made fires, cooked food, made beds, washed filthy clothes, . . . did all the homely and necessary tasks. . . ." All "was done willingly and cheerfully, without any grudging in the least, showing their true love unto their friends and brethren."[6]

Perhaps the early suffering was partly responsible for the successful beginning of the venture. For sickness dampened rebellious spirits and permitted the selfless example of the few to be experienced by the many. The survivors carried on. Many years later a famous participant* in the experiment begun by this Mayflower band reflected on their initial condition: "They came not even as English subjects, but as strangers, long exiled from her borders by the tyranny of her laws . . . , subject to no law but that which they consented to impose upon themselves."[7]

On a rocky coastland, holding the threshold of a continent, they now faced away from the past and toward an uncertain future. In the things of this world, there was little to sustain them except their mutual support and the still-unknown power of the ideas by which they lived.

Together and Apart

From the moment of landing, these people were destined to be both "together" and "apart." At first the *common* ties predominated. "In those hard and difficult beginings," their chronicler said, "they found some discontents and murmurings arise amongst some"; but these dissensions were overcome by the wisdom and patience of the Governor and by the "better part, which clave faithfully together in the maine."[8]

Each colonist was to work for seven years and give all his profits to the merchant company in London during that time in return for the money needed to start the plantation. At the end of this period the houses, land, goods, and money would be divided "fairly" among the merchants and settlers. In addition, the necessities for survival within the colony made the provision of a common store, to which all contributed, a first concern of the colonists as they extracted life from their physical surroundings.

The Separatists' beliefs in their ultimate mission as children of God also wove strands of mutuality around their community. The principles for which they had suffered exile and banishment from orthodoxies in the Old World led toward the rejection of ultimate, human authority over a congregation of Christian believers. For higher authority, their guidance came from God working through the Holy Spirit and interpreting His Word to His children. A church, for them, was an autonomous group of believers who met to share the light coming to them from above. And in the con-

* John Quincy Adams.

ditions of the New World, membership in the association of believers also determined, initially, the boundaries of citizenship in the body politic.

The individual conscience was of prime value to these people. The individual must strive to tune in on God's truth and discover a "calling" in God's plan. A group of His children also sought to blend their consciences in this same search for their collective "mission." Thus, a sense of equality before ultimate authority pervaded the association of believers. With allowance for differences in formal civic functions and duties, this same equality was manifest in the civil body.

There were also forces in this community that strained the bonds which would tend to hold any particular group of people together. These forces countered efforts of men to specify a "final" blueprint for a society in this world. For here was a people intended for the breaking of orthodoxies, even those developing in their own midst. The new continent provided room for restless energies and for new beginnings. The "calling" of an individual conscience brought the man of faith to grips with this world in his preparation for the next. Energies were directed both to overcoming nature—God's testing-ground of the human spirit—and toward controlling oneself in a spiritual association with one's fellow believers.

The chronicler of the Plymouth venture described developments after the first decade:

. . . the people of the plantation begane to grow in their outward estats, by rea[son] of the flowing of many people into the cuntrie. . . . And no man now thought he could live, except he had catle and a great deale of ground to keep them. . . . By which means they were scatered all over the bay, quickly, and the towne, in which they lived compactly till now, was left very thine, and in a short time almost desolate.[9]

At the same time that the civil society was undergoing stress, the most intimate inner association was endangered; for "the church must also be devided, and those that had lived so long together in Christian and comfortable fellowship must now part and suffer many divissions."[10] The Governor permitted some to form new congregations as the extent of habitation expanded. But the requests increased: "And others still . . . break away under one pretence or other," the Governor reported, "thinking their own conceived necessitie, and the example of others, a warrante sufficiente for them."[11] An effort was made to draw people back to the central community. Good farms were given out to special persons who would promise to live at Plymouth.

The growth of population alone brought increased diversity that threatened the dominant unity around one church and one belief. The coastal land west and south of the first settlement soon became a haven for malcontents and dissenters. Into this area Roger Williams withdrew, extending the doctrine of religious freedom and separation of church and state as he broke with New World orthodoxies. Although he was considered, during a brief stay at Plymouth, "a man godly and zealous" and "exercised his gifts" for a time and was admitted to membership in the church, he "begane to fall into some strang oppinions," it was said, "and from opinion to practise."[12]

The people who scattered westward along the coastland below the cape were much in tune with Roger Williams' doctrines. The outlines of a theocracy—a blending of civil and religious authority —were being clearly defined in New England colonies.[13] Baptists and particularly Quakers, who had come to the colonies and remained nonconformist in the midst of tightening regulations, found their lot becoming more difficult. Whippings and banishments of nonconformists were occurring in Plymouth. And so Baptists and Quakers, and others who felt the pinch of civil and religious authority wherever populations were densely congregated, pressed on to become separatists and dissenters in the New World.

The open westward region of the coastland into which men of conscience moved was purchased from Massasoit and his son Wamsutta in 1652. Included among the names on the deed were Plymouth stalwarts William Bradford, Captain Standish, and John Alden. But none of these men moved to occupy his new holdings.[14]

An early explorer, in 1602, left a record of this part of the mainland: ". . . replenished with fair fields and with fragrant flowers, also meadows, and hedged in with stately groves, being furnished also with pleasant brooks and beautified with two main rivers."[15] Colonists had already moved to the area prior to 1652. Industrious farmers and fishermen from the Plymouth colony came in increasing numbers, and a town was incorporated in 1664, sending a representative to the Plymouth Court.

People who had scattered across the new township made little effort to congregate closely together. Perhaps they feared the pressures toward conformity which close association might bring. But in 1674 a town meeting was held at which a deputy, a grand juryman, a constable, six surveyors, and a clerk were chosen. The township tendered a wary allegiance to Plymouth; however, it continued to balk at paying taxes for the support of an "official" ministry and for building church meetinghouses. Otherwise, the lessons of democracy learned in the New World were put into practice locally. A proclamation of 1674 stated that "all the town meetings do begin at ten of the clock and to continue until the moderator duly relieved the town, not exceeding four of the clock." A fine was imposed for failure to appear at the town meeting.[16]

The people of the sparsely settled township had just begun to form the human associations of a community when their territory was devastated in an Indian uprising. The western coastland felt the fullest measure of the terror of "King Philip's War." Increase Mather recorded in Boston that this new coastal township "did they burn with fire and barbarously murdered both men and women; stripping the slain whether men or women, and leaving them in the open field as naked as in the day wherein they were born."[17]

It was several years before any effort was made to reorganize the township. Demoralization was so complete that taxes were suspended for many years. Men who had accepted the risks of freedom did not rush to return to the protective but constraining folds of Plymouth and other population centers, however. The authorities at Plymouth looked upon the destruction of the township as a punishment for the errant ways of the freedom-seekers in the wilderness. A Court order of 1675, referring to the township, stated:

This Court . . . do therefore order that in the rebuilding and re-

settling thereof, that they so order it as to live compact together . . .
as they may be in a capacity both to defend themselves from the
assault of an enemy, and the better to attend the public worship of
God and the ministry of the word of God, whose carelessness to obtain and to attend unto we fear may have been a provocation of
God. . . .[18]

The Court further admonished the township to obtain "an able,
faithful dispenser of the word of God amongst them"—indicating
that only a minister appointed and approved by the Plymouth
authorities would suffice to meet this need.

Still the stubborn dissenters refused to bow to authorities. The
dictates of conscience did not indicate to the majority that an
"official" church or minister needed to be provided, and the township as reorganized continued to resist payment of taxes for this
purpose. In 1686, an order was passed that a meetinghouse be
built. But neither the desire nor the necessity for close association
—for living "compact together"—was present in this coastal wilderness for many decades. The Baptist preacher-proprietor who
represented the town at Plymouth Court for six years found himself in constant trouble with Plymouth authorities. On one occasion the General Court fined him 10 shillings "for breaking
the Sabbath by unnecessary travelling thereon."[19] The demands
of serving a far-flung congregation which did not have even a
meetinghouse apparently caused this encroachment on the moral
standards of the stable, established, town dwellers who dominated
the Plymouth Court.

Even the more liberal tone of the new Province Charter which
came to Massachusetts in 1692 (when Puritanism and the Epis-
copacy achieved an accommodation in the Old World) did not
alter the dissenting proclivities of the coastland separatists or their
position in the now consolidated "province" of Plymouth and
Massachusetts Bay. Massachusetts as a whole was tied more
closely to the king, and all laws passed were subject to revision
by the king; but the experiences of seventy years of self-government had already set a pattern for the New World institutions
which the settlers had created. The new charter stated that
liberty of conscience was assured "to all but Papists," and that
church membership was no longer to be the qualification for
citizenship.[20]

However, the Puritan church and Puritan principles were still in the ascendancy. The old ministers had lost little of the influence they had come to wield in New England communities. So the dissenters in the coastland township continued their fight against the imposition of state religion. Finally, in 1723, the Quakers of the town—who as tax assessors had refused to collect the tax for maintenance of ministers—were joined by Baptists in a successful appeal to the king to overrule an Act of 1692 for the "Settlement of and Support of Ministers and Schoolmasters." During the period of the long, stubborn fight, more than one dissenting tax assessor suffered jail rather than compromise a principle.

The sparse records of a century of diffuse and separated settlement in this community of the coastland leave the bare imprints of a people who remained more apart than together. But they do show some of the issues which quickened the conscience of men who still had slight reason for close and interdependent association but some desire for face-to-face discussion:

1704: A schoolmaster was chosen at town meeting.

1716: The Quaker Monthly Meeting recorded: ". . . it is concluded by ye most of ye meeting that it would be most agreeable to our holy profession to forbear for time to come to be in any way concerned in purchasing any slaves."

1722: Town meeting took important action bearing upon the case of the Quakers in their appeal to the home government.

1730: Town meeting went on record against "ardent spirits."

1741: Town meeing voted "whether it be the town's mind to come under the government of Rhode Island, and it passed in the affirmative by a clear vote." (However, the break with Massachusetts government did not occur.)[21]

In 1758, it was recorded that the township furnished soldiers for the French and Indian War. But a postscript to the payroll record of 1757 for the regiment raised in this county said of the little township of dissenters: "The four companies in the town . . . are deficient, and the biggest part of them are Quaquers."[22]

At this time the community was approaching a period when changing circumstances would enhance conditions for a people to live more "compact together." Soon forces which unify would begin to take precedence over those which divide. But dissent is not easily eradicated once it takes root in individual consciences. It does not quickly disappear; not in one generation—not in many.

Dramas of Enterprise and Independence

The men and women who populated the northern coastlands were truly a religious "elite." At the time that the confederation of their colonies was formed (1643) they proclaimed: ". . . we all came into these parts of America . . . to advance the kingdom of our Lord Jesus Christ, and to enjoy the liberties of the gospel *in purity, with peace. . . .*"[23] Edmund Burke said that their spirit and attitude was the real protestantism of the Protestant religion. And it was an attitude that prized equality. Carried to its logical extremity, their doctrine found no basis for human inequality before God. True, "liberty" could often seem a hollow ideal within communities which these people formed; but nonconformists *did* survive and *could* move to areas where they might at least attempt to remain independent in the midst of human affairs that pressed men toward interdependence.

The separatists did not attempt to bring Old World marks of rank and privilege to the New. Starting as equals, they set about achieving mastery over nature and approval for their efforts by the Almighty. In the course of their strivings some achieved preeminence in the new communities they helped to create. One historian has noted that few pioneers attached the designation "gentleman" to their names on passenger lists and on church and other records, although in some cases the title later appeared when a person had been in public office in New England. The great majority were "the plain, untitled people, bred to industry and economy, trained to professions, merchandise, trades, husbandry or service."[24]

For most of a century the dwellers among the "fair fields . . . with pleasant brooks" of the township of separatists were farmers and fishermen. A traveler's journal described the township in 1761: ". . . a spacious town; twenty miles will carry you through it. Rocks and oaks are over the whole town."[25] Farmers wrestled with this soil, while the major figure in the area remained a grain millowner. In 1760, this principal landowner sold one acre of his

800-acre homestead estate—a section having frontage on the major river—to a seafarer who wanted to build ships. A new village began to grow beside the river near the bay. Mechanics, shipbuilders, blockmakers, and blacksmiths immigrated to this spot, to congregate in new forms of enterprise that combined resources of the land and the sea. These men began the transformation of a diffuse agricultural settlement into a center of commerce.

Mechanics who sought an outlet for their talents would have found limited opportunity had it not been for a visionary Quaker who came to the coastland at this time. The Quaker merchant had already developed the whaling industry on the Island of Nantucket. He came to the mainland in 1765 with his capital. Acquiring choice frontage on the west bank of the river, he began to establish a business that soon accomplished what a century of exhortation to live "compact together" had failed to accomplish.

A description of the newly developing port town of 1765 declares that the waterfront street of the west-bank village contained "five houses, a blockmaker's shop and the buildings of William Macomber, cordwainer. . . ."[26] The whole township (including developments on east and west sides of the river) reported both agricultural and industrial assets in 1768. Sixteen thousand feet of wharves and 2,933 tons of "vessels of every kind" bore witness to the new directions in which the community was facing.[27] A tax record for 1771 shows that seventy-one men were assessed as owners of shipping, and that "20 of these and one other owned the wharfage." However, most of the inhabitants of the township still tilled their land and cared for their livestock in addition to working at a trade. No great fortunes had been accumulated as yet among these independent Yankees, although, it was said, forty-three of them "at least . . . had sums of money from £4 to £4000 in trading stock or at interest."[28]

New people with new interests, as well as older residents with new interests, were forming a bustling community centered around interdependent industries. Ships were built for whaling and to carry other commercial cargo. Wharves were constructed. A ropewalk and candle factory were built. Men made the tools for shipfitting in shops along the waterfront; other men labored to fill the land, make streets, dig wells. The community grew in population and soon was to find its fortunes linked with those of a larger range of interests on the American continent.

The first ship built in this port town was to carry a cargo of tea which the citizens of Boston, defying the Tea Tax, did not wish to see unloaded on their wharves. The son of the original entrepreneur of whaling was the managing owner of this ship. As Quaker merchants, his family had found a congenial atmosphere in the coastland community for the development of their business. They were largely concerned with immediate challenges to their fortitude and ingenuity; and while entering into the local processes of community building, they appeared relatively unencumbered by broader political issues. But the young Quaker shipowner found his business caught in the middle of growing social and political passions.

A description of the "eventful Thursday" of December 16, 1773, in Boston, pictures the dilemma of the merchant as he sought to extricate his cargo from the impasse created by a recalcitrant Royal Governor and a purposeful colonial public. A throng of nearly 7,000 persons gathered at the Old South Meetinghouse in Boston to determine whether opposition to the landing of the tea would continue. The merchant appeared to report on the failure of his appeal at the Custom House for a clearance to leave the port with his tea-laden ship. "Immediate action was necessary," the account explains, "as the twenty days allowed for clearance terminated that night. Then the revenue officials could take possession, and . . . land the tea." The assembly voted unanimously that the tea should not be landed. The Quaker merchant was instructed to apply directly to the Royal Governor for a pass to proceed from the harbor with his vessel for London. The final refusal precipitated the act of open rebellion—the Tea Party—which cost a merchant his cargo* and gave to a people a symbol of defiant independence.[29]

The port town of seafaring merchants and mechanics was also animated by the sentiments that were unifying diverse colonies along the narrow strip of coastland. The issues which brought opposition to the distant Crown and the formation of citizen-patriot groups in Charleston and Philadelphia, New York and

---

* The merchant was later reimbursed, in part (according to the account), by the Crown for his loss.

Boston were the focus of local interest and local action too. At a town meeting in January, 1774, a pledge was taken to abandon tea drinking until the "unjust act" was repealed. Minutemen companies were formed, to be ready at a moment's notice to join with other colonial brethren in defending their rights against the king. While the Quaker merchants of the fast-growing port town had a large stake in maintaining commerce and thus avoiding outright hostilities (which they could not approve, in conscience), the mechanics and artisans were among the leaders in the township in the identification with a new freedom cause.

A town meeting of July, 1774, passed a resolution of majority sentiments. The resolution expressed regret at the necessity for taking a part "which at first appears unfriendly with respect our manufacturing brethren and friends in Great Britain and Ireland," but explained that the action to be taken "will have the greatest tendency of anything in our power to save both them and us from Bondage and Slavery." The resolution spelled out new identifications of the people:

. . . we unite with our American Brethren and Resolve that we will not purchase any goods manufactured in Great Britain and Ireland which shall be imported from thence after this day . . . that we will not purchase any foreign teas whatever, that we will not export any flaxseed to any foreign market, that we do acquiesce in the need and necessity of raising our proportion of money to pay the Congress. . . .[30]

On the 21st of April, 1775, just two days after the engagements at Lexington and Concord Bridge, three companies of Minutemen marched from the township for camp at an assembly area near south Boston. The call was for five days of service; but the companies were soon enrolled in a "regiment of foot of the army of the United Colonies of North America." At least two companies saw service at Bunker Hill in June. During the course of hostilities, some five hundred men were furnished for the armies by the township. Six other companies were raised in 1778 and 1779 to serve in different regiments of Massachusetts militia.[31]

In spite of the unifying energies directed against an external enemy, the specific character of the township continued to influence its citizens involved in the drama of Revolution. A record of a local census of male population from ages sixteen to sixty, taken in 1777, indicates that three classifications were used in counting manpower available for the war effort. The census recorded 1,008 "Popular," 248 "Quakers," and 30 "Blacks" in the township for that year. Thus, in these years, the Quaker population was not in the majority, although Quakers were among the most influential and well-to-do citizens.

It cannot be said that members of the Society of Friends were completely out of sympathy with the colonial struggle for independence. What they could not condone were the more open signs of belligerent patriotism. A popular poem of the time, written by a resident of the settlement on the east bank of the river where hostility toward the supermerchants of the west bank was not hidden, ridiculed the "men of peace—meek and sleek . . . on their Consciences written—non-resistance."[32] But long before the war was over the people on both sides of the river had felt the wrath of the enemy. Men of the community had been more at home fighting the British on the sea than in regiments of foot. And the secluded harbor, with its maritime supplies, wharves, and other facilities, as well as its readily available supply of crewmen, became a favorite rendezvous for Yankee privateers.

In the month following the engagement at Lexington a band of local adventurers engineered the first successful colonial naval engagement, in the waters off Nantucket. A party of volunteers—militiamen from local Minute companies—set out and recaptured, on fog-shrouded waters, two prize ships seized by the British: "The prisoners were soon disarmed and [the Yankee ship] was at anchor before 'meeting time.' "[33] Other accounts relate that John Paul Jones' ship *Providence* had many local men in her crew. After one encounter with a British brig-of-war, when Jones brought his prize into the local harbor, it was said that "the blood of the killed and wounded was running down the sides of the brig. . . ."[34]

In 1778, the British took revenge on the port town which had harbored the vessels and the men who preyed on British shipping so successfully. The waterfront on both sides of the river was flamed, and stores and houses were sacked and burned. Only token resistance could be offered by a small militia contingent. In three days—while most of the populace fled to the woods or farther up the river—warehouses were destroyed, as were sailing ships, armed ships, and smaller sloops and schooners. Also, eleven houses, twenty shops, and one ropewalk were burned.[35]

Commerce in whaling was stopped completely by the war. After the British raid, the entire community was prostrate for several years, although its sons still served in the War for Independence. At the town meeting of March, 1780, a committee was chosen to supply the families of soldiers during the ensuing year. As hostilities came to a close, the same stubborn character of the coastland individualists—rock-solid when directed toward affairs of conscience and public responsibility and relentless when directed toward private gain—was again revealed among the people.

Thus, the first ship to arrive off London on the day of the signing of the treaty of peace—the first ship to display the American flag in those waters—was a local vessel with a cargo of whale oil to sell. And a local monthly meeting of Quakers prepared a petition for the selectmen requesting that "no more publications of political or military matters be set up or posted up on their meeting houses," since such publications were disagreeable and were "such as their religious principles enjoin them to have no concern with."[36]

The Concentration of Things Shared

Shortly after the close of the Revolution a new township was incorporated on the banks of the river. The boundaries excluded some of the agricultural areas extending westward and concentrated the township at the mouth of the river. The census of 1790 gave the population of this township as 3,313; in 1800 it was 4,361; and in 1810, 5,651.

A newspaper began publication in the west-bank village of the township in 1792. A regular mail run to Boston by stage was established. The schedule called for three trips a week, and the fare between terminals was "three dollars and fifty cents. . . ."[37]

Interests remained fixed largely on the sea and on affairs of the sea, and here new issues of rights and independence arose. American shipping began to encounter rough sailing on oceans controlled by a British navy that was maintaining a blockade against Napoleon and insisting upon the "right of search" at sea. In June of 1812 President Madison asked for—and received from Congress by a considerably less than unanimous vote—a declaration of war against England. In the West and South, where frontiersmen sought to expand the nation's boundaries, the "War Hawks" held forth. But in New England coastal towns, where population looked to the sea and still retained some of that sense of kinship with "manufacturing brethren and friends in Great Britain," sentiments were less than favorable toward "Madison's War."

The local newspaper said in an editorial:

The awful calamity is at length officially announced. . . . Never have we seen dismay so generally and forcibly depicted on the features of our fellow citizens. . . . The hand of enterprise is withered, and the heart sickened, the hardearned treasures of industry are dissolved, and the business of life seems to pause in awful suspense.[38]

The meetinghouse where citizens from several villages gathered was a scene of bitterness and rancor in that year of 1812. One description of a meeting leaves a taste of local dialogues. A question under discussion had provoked such interest and temper that the people adjourned from the town house to the open green, where the debate was continued. As a vote was taken on the issue, people divided on either side of the road. One captain of privateering fame pointed jauntily to his followers and shouted, "I began alone on this question, and now, you see, I have a respectable company." To that an opposing orator from the Quaker village repiled, "Yes, and old Cloven-foot commenced his career alone, and he's got a respectable following, too."[39]

That year the village on the east bank of the river was incorporated as a separate town, formed its own town meeting, and adopted a resolution to back the war effort. The seaport community dominated by the Quaker village on the west bank now closed ranks around its commercial interests. In the first three months of war, eight vessels belonging to the port were captured by the enemy with a loss of cargo valued at $218,000. Once again, members of the Society of Friends refused to pay taxes for war purposes.

Many people moved inland from the shore areas and the

islands off Cape Cod. The coastal blockade was so tight that most commerce proceeded overland. The salty seafarers reported on these developments in the local newspaper in 1813:

A convoy of wagons, with families and household furniture, from Nantucket, left Falmouth on September 19, 1813, for Ohio. They were to touch at Sandwich for some others to join the fleet. The farms of Nantucket men were formerly on the ocean, but Madison's war has obliged them to take their land tacks on board and pass the mountains.[40]

News of the Treaty of Ghent received by rider from Boston on February 21, 1815, brought this comment in the local newspaper: "So sudden and total was the revolution of feeling that age forgets its gravity and poverty its sorrows. A despondency awoke to joy and resignation kindled into rapture."[41]

By the close of the unpopular war the stage was set for the development of institutions with which all the participants in this community were vitally identified, although at first glance such might not appear to be the case. The census of 1820 showed a drop in population to about 4,000; and a description of the town for 1815 indicated that shops and shipyards were closed, the port itself was shut, and citizens wandered about the streets in enforced idleness. But beneath the frustrations of the war years burned a vital energy in these people.

The years of population decline permitted a commercial elite to draw together and prepare a new assault on nature. A part of this was to be seen in the great schism in the Society of Friends. Many defectors, who joined the Unitarian church, were among the wealthiest and best educated of the citizenry. One prominent citizen expressed his feelings about what was to him the growing irrelevance of the Quaker meeting in the community where a new orthodoxy was apparently taking shape: "Formerly little was said about doctrines," he wrote; ". . . now whole discourses of an hour and a half in length are almost entirely occupied in enforcing theological dogmas, which even the orthodox of other denominations have in a great measure abandoned for more practical objects in everyday life."[42]

A great change was occurring as the groundwork was laid for the community's most prosperous era. Fashionable parties with music and dancing became the vogue in the best families. "The customs of our metropolis were introduced," wrote a prominent citizen, "and one of our late leading merchants who had been strict in the use of the 'plain language' and dress, after a winter spent in Boston, returned home with a fashionable blue coat and gilt buttons, and used frequently in his conversation with his friends the then fashionable exclamation of surprise, 'Good God, sir!' dropping altogether his Quaker phraseology and habits."[43]

The diary of a young man of breeding reveals the world of 1823 as seen in one of the more prosperous mercantile families. It was a world infused with two major areas of concern: matters relating to weather, ships, and cargo; and matters relating to God and church and intimate social fellowship. He wrote:

Reformations and Revivals, as they are called, seem to be the order of the day.

Sunday—a pleasant day. The *Persia* commenced discharging her cargo, which made some stir being the first day in the week. Many considered it wicked. . . .

. . . Mr. Maffit [evangelist] again in town. His second appearance . . . does not seem to cause as much excitement as was manifested at his first. . . .

The large quantity of Spermi oil expected this summer from the Japan fishery . . . is the general topic of conversation. . . .

Town meeting day—held in the Friends old meeting house. There was a great excitement on the subject of money for the support of schools. . . .

News received this morning of the Declaration of War by France against Spain. . . . This intelligence has caused business to revive and the prospect seems very good for our obtaining a freight for the *Sophia* today. . . .

A young man from near Poughkeepsie . . . preached a long sermon in the morning. . . . In the afternoon I went to hear him. . . . His sentiments were completely what is called New Light. . . .

. . . The ship *Europa* and Brig *Juno* sailed this morning for the southward. . . .

[After changing churches]: I was very much pleased with the service . . . believing that the moral lectures and instruction which I shall receive . . . will be of more advantage to me than to attend the Friends' meeting. . . .[44]

Between 1830 and 1860,* the population of the community increased threefold to 22,300. Shipbuilding was at its height in 1835. Locally cut timber was used. During the peak year of whaling (1857), 329 locally owned ships were engaged in the business.[45]

In the 1850s, the community was known as the wealthiest city, per capita, in New England. The town was estimated to have forty-six "wealthy" men in those years, while "many of the men who were then rated at $100,000 and $200,000 were millionaires at the time of their death."[46] And through the "good years" the sperm whale industry engaged the attention of all the population.

The involvement of these people with their whale fishery shows how institutions relating to this commerce of the sea were truly an extension of the personalities of those who participated. A prominent citizen in later years set down his boyhood impressions:

. . . In those days the boys who could not tell the names of all the whaleships sailing out of the river and could not distinguish the private signals of the whaling merchants were thought to be deficient in intelligence or wanting in loyalty to the town . . . the boy who first carried to the captain's wife the news that her husband's ship was coming into the harbor received a silver dollar.[47]

Whaling vessels usually were owned by a company of men, each man owning a share, or "lay." Lays might be broken down to quarters, eighths, sixteenths, even thirty-seconds or smaller fractions. At times the captain was the shipowner, but even then, ships' officers and crewmen were paid in shares of the profit from the voyage. The practice of buying lays in a voyage became common throughout the community, among those who never ventured on the sea as well as among the seafaring gentry. For the young men in the community—and for those who flocked there from the hinterlands—the rugged captains of the vessels were the heroes to be emulated. "We had hardly a home that was not interested in their [the whaling voyages'] successful termination," reminisced the local newspaper in an anniversary issue; "there were so many fathers and sons and husbands and brothers and sweethearts away on these long campaigns against the leviathans. . . . Somehow, the business was regarded as a sort of lottery, with large prizes and mournful blanks."[48]

* The port community was incorporated as a city in 1847.

News of arrivals was gathered by a marine news collector and reporter of the newspaper staff. He would board inbound vessels in the lower harbor and question the master on his catch and also for news of other vessels. The marine reporter brought this information to the merchants' reading room near the docks, where he transcribed it in an open book kept for the purpose (following, scrupulously, a rule not to answer verbal interrogations). The contents of the book were then read by those who gathered daily to discuss the fortunes of voyages upon which so many depended. People of small means took their chances in the great enterprise along with people of greater resources, and the rewards of a successful investment were not only increased ownership and holdings, but opportunities for greater degrees of involvement in the valued institutions of a community. Another facet of the common involvement came into focus in this period. A newspaper item of 1851 presents a commentary on a local attitude:

Extradition Extraordinary. We are pleased to announce that a very large number of fugitive slaves, aided by many of our most wealthy and respectable citizens, have left for Canada and parts unknown, and that more are in the way of departure. The utmost sympathy and liberality prevails toward this class of our inhabitants.[49]

Slavery was particularly distasteful to these people of conscience who could accept human inequality only in the things which men might achieve. It was natural that the town of seafaring merchants with Quaker roots should become a major station on the "underground railroad." One local historian said: "In the early years of the century [nineteenth] there was hardly a house in the place which had not given shelter and succor to a fugitive slave."[50] The cause of abolition was thundered from local pulpits even before William Lloyd Garrison carried it to the heights from his Boston church.

The community was the home of a number of Negroes before the Civil War, some of them fugitive slaves but others descended from families that had been on the local scene since colonial times. One citizen reminisced: "We had Negroes in almost every branch of business." At least one Negro had been a venerated sea captain of early days "who commanded a handsome ship with a white owner and a white crew." On one occasion, the citizen recalled, the colored people of the town had pooled their money and purchased a whaling brig and manned it mainly with Negroes. But the ship made a broken voyage "and the speculation . . . came to grief," he said, "as the small speculations were apt to do."[51]

Thus, it was not just the cause of Union that brought men flocking to the national colors in 1861: there was an even deeper moral fervor beneath the local patriotism. Noted Quaker families —firm in the past in their principles of nonviolence—contributed sons to the Union armies. In the months and years of the Civil War, local companies were mustered for service in some ten different Massachusetts regiments, while the community spent over $125,000 for the families of volunteers in those years. Local physicians offered their services free to families represented in the City Guards. In 1863, state aid was directed to be paid to families "of colored citizens who shall be mustered into the service of the United States."[52] One local company was a part of a regiment of colored Massachusetts Volunteers.

On an evening in the fall of 1864, when news of Lincoln's re-election over McClellan was announced, a local minister recorded in his diary: "The bells are now ringing and guns are firing. . . . Rockets are flying and the largest procession is moving through the streets I ever saw here before." For this man of God the great cause of the war was not "union" but "slavery." He wrote: "This may be called the great revival of Reformation. The slaves are, or will be, free, and the nation has repented of her sin of slavery which is the cause of this awful war. . . ."[53]

There could be no doubt of local patriotism in the cause of abolition and union; yet, an episode of the first year of the war is characteristic of the conflicting attitudes of these men of conscience and commerce. One of the earliest Union plans for blockade of the Confederacy called for the sinking of a number of stone-filled ships across the channels of important rebel harbors. Twenty-four of the forty-five ships of the "Stone Fleet" were bought and fitted in the local port. The community supplied many of the sea captains who carried out the daring mission. But the records show that local merchants were able to unload on the federal government many aging ships of a declining industry; and it was further recorded that farmers pulled down their stone walls and sold the stone as cargo for the fleet, while "the highways were gleaned of cobble stones and refuse granite . . ." for similar purposes.[54]*

In the first month after Lee's surrender, and in the midst of horror at Lincoln's assassination, few local pulpits and congregations throbbed with "charity for all." The minister who wrote in his diary that "the nation has repented of her sin of slavery," recorded in May, 1865, that he thought the government should do with Jeff Davis what Daniel Webster did with his scythe: "Hang him on a tree." When this remark was repeated in a sermon, "it set the people to stamping. . . . All appeared to say Amen."[55]

Even before the Civil War the most valued activities in this social system were changing. The great stone fleet, formed at the start of the war, was in part a requiem to the good years. There had always been broken voyages and less fortunate backers; now there were greatly lessened demands for the products of a broken industry. The first to be affected were those of small means. Then the human groupings of the society came to be more clearly segmented: new activities created new clusters of groups in community life.

The Appearance of Things Dividing

As long as the separatists of the northern coastland remained relatively scattered, their contacts and associations with one another were on the order of confrontations between equals. Their situation was much like that later described by Tocqueville who wrote that in America those who went before were soon forgotten; only the present aspect of a man is important as he meets his fellows face to face. Once a community centered around activities that brought a growing population closer together in daily contacts, the conditions for inequalities to be more readily perceived were present.

It is not easy for people to consider each person they encounter as an equally valuable human. The problem is compounded as a

---

* Local records provide no evidence of mutual exploitation on a personal, human basis in the community, given the opportunities and deprivations of war time. The record indicates the contrary; but the relationship of a people to an abstraction—"the government"—was a different matter.

community grows so that the number of persons to whom one must, somehow, relate oneself becomes unmanageable. One solution is to draw a tighter circle around an inner group of associates with whom one has most in common. For example, one commentator said that the Quakers sometimes denominated those not included within their "sacred inclosure" as "the world's people," but he hastened to add, "yet not with that exclusiveness as might from the phraseology appear to be the case."[56] Another answer is to divide, mentally, one's social world into identifiable groupings to which most persons can be assigned.

Both types of answers were applied, to a degree, by most people in the community as their world of "others" became more complex. At first, however, even as merchants were joined by mechanics and artisans, most participants still were also farmers; and the whaling industry which they were building together absorbed the talents of most of the people. There were many values to be shared—in achievement.

From the earliest days of the commercial township the pursuit of private gain accentuated the insulation of the rich from the poor. Those who were achieving success could, and would, look out for themselves. And they reached back to keep those who were slipping from falling completely. But they did little more. Thus, a town meeting in 1789 appointed a committee "to inquire into the number of poor children in . . . town necessary to send to school at the expense of said town." It was then voted "to choose a committee of eight persons to lay out the same sum [$200] on those most needy."[57] The public school was placed under a branch of the department for the support of the poor.

A stronger and broader public school system was not forthcoming until 1821. The Quakers built their own schoolhouse in 1798, and a sectarian Friends' Academy appeared in 1810. The Congregationalists also provided a privately financed school for their own people.

In the third decade of the nineteenth century the young merchant-diarist reflected some of the social attitudes that were crystallized by then in different parts of a growing population:

Town meeting day. A considerable opposition to the old town officers, but the old town clerk, treasurer and collector of taxes was reelected and other officers to the satisfaction of the better and more respectable part of the inhabitants were elected in opposition to . . . the needy Shaylers that have come into the town the year or two past.

[On a later occasion]: . . . There was great excitement on the subject of money for the support of schools. . . . It was the wish of the lower with some of the middling class of the inhabitants of the town . . . to have all the children of the Town to be educated together at the public expense in town schools, but they found the town too aristocratic to carry a thing of this kind into operation.[58]

By that year, however (1823), town schools of a higher caliber were being provided: at issue, according to the diarist, was whether an additional $1,200 should be raised for schools to add to the $1,400 already in the town treasury for that purpose. The additional sum was voted down that year. But ten years later the school fund was $5,000; and in 1841 it had increased to over $15,000.

Throughout this period various elements of native New England population were moving into the community. Arriving at different times and with different means, at first the newcomers *were* often considered "needy Shaylers" and of the "lower" or "middling" classes by the older "aristocratic" elements. But newcomers, too, had come to achieve success and to participate in the commercial institutions around which the whole community rallied. They, too, were drawn to the sea and its wealth and adventure. Many participated and voted in town meeting as responsible citizens, but nevertheless the social system was manifesting symptoms of indigestion.

The industry that sent local vessels all over the globe also carried the reputation of the whaling community over great distances. Young men from the farms and the inland towns and cities found their way to the wharves in search of adventure and fortune. And as the ships returned from their long voyages they brought back, along with their cargo, men who were native to other climes and cultures. A large transient element appeared in the local population. A startling contrast was apparent between a rather austere respectability at the core of community life and a cosmopolitanism born of broad travels.

In early decades of the whaling boom a number of respectable citizens took measures to protect their community from the backwash common to port towns. The hull of an old whaler docked

on the river had been converted into a brothel. The streets near
"the Ark," as it was called, were considered unsafe at night, and
several murders in the vicinity had shocked the town. On two
different occasions—once in 1826 and again in 1829—aroused
citizens took the law into their own hands and descended on the
site to destroy the Ark.

After the first Ark was burned, a vigilance committee was
formed to prevent further mob action. The citizens corrected their
own abuse of the law. One local commentator pointed out: "The
same men who in their wrath destroyed the first Ark, joined a
vigilance committee to prevent further outbreaks." He added:
"The list of 110 citizens who formed this vigilance committee is
interesting: they were the representative men of their time."[59] The
similar mob action of 1829 followed a "reign of terror" from
"odious characters" from the second Ark.[60] In 1830 a town meeting
again selected a committee of vigilance to prevent "the further
destruction of property by riotous assemblages."

The following year a church, known as "the Bethel," was built
for the specific purpose of looking out for the welfare of homeless
sailors. The minister was expected to devote nearly all his time to
the problems of the sailors. A registry office was included to provide information for distant friends and relatives.

The diary of the chaplain at the Bethel during the height of the
whaling trade (1844–59) shows awareness of the problems of
those who were not truly "in and of" the community. He wrote
on one occasion, in 1852: "Toward night I was called upon to
visit a sailor. . . . On inquiry of what physician they had, was
told he did not have any. They had no money to pay for one and
no means to pay for medicine if they had a physician." In 1855
he wrote: "I am more and more convinced that any man who will
be a true friend to the sailor and look out honestly for his temporal
welfare will be unpopular with most of this trading community."[61]

The chaplain at the Bethel was not alone in his concern for
the exploitation of the transients. Local boarding-house keepers,
often called "sharkers" or "land sharks," would advance money on
the sailors' shares from voyages and act as shipping agents as well
as landlords of the boarding houses. With a law still in effect for
imprisoning debtors, the local prison was overpopulated. Thus,
one who wrote ". . . From the Prison" in 1840 maintained that

there was more imprisonment for debt in that town than in all the rest of the state, excluding Boston. " 'They are only sailors,' is the too frequent remark," he wrote. He described the County Jail as a great tavern, where hundreds of the sons of farmers ended their travels as victims of callous laws and callous men. "Ignorant of the modes of deception practiced upon the young," he continued, ". . . they find, before they are ready to embark, that they are in debt" and must sign their names to any ship on any voyoge. Such indebtedness and near slavery might be perpetuated over many years and many voyages. The "voice from the prison" suggested some answers: "There must be a boarding-house, where the sailor may feel that he is a human being. . . . He must have for friends and protectors the owners of the ships. . . ." And if imprisonment for debt were abolished, he concluded, "a different aspect will pervade all the institutions which are threatened with premature decay."[62]

The decay of the whaling trade may not have been premature, but it was inevitable in a world of changing technology. As the uses for whale oil declined, whalebone continued to be in demand. But gradually the fleets decreased in size.

There was a human side to this decline of the great institution that some New Englanders saw as the "deterioration of the seamen," as ambitious farm boys were replaced by "improvident and indifferent" debtors. Apparently the Yankee, if he avoided the pitfalls of indebtedness, was always set upon becoming an owner or a master. It became difficult even in the early days to sign on full crews before leaving port. Records show that many ships set out with no more than a captain, a complement of officers, and a bare skeleton crew (perhaps from among the growing "debtor class"). The many hands needed were obtained at routine ports of call.

The Sandwich Islands of the Pacific and the Azores and Cape Verde Islands of the Atlantic were favorite recruiting spots for the Whalers. One local citizen recalled that in his boyhood the whaleships "brought back . . . not a few tattooed natives" from Pacific islands.[63] The Portuguese and "Cape Verders" who first visited the community as sailors and boarded in its boarding houses, began to make it their home also. In later years of the nineteenth century they were joined, increasingly, by others from

Portugal and the Portuguese islands—women as well as men—and took up family life in this community which was usually both entry-point and stopping-place for them in the New World.

As the whaling industry declined, other developments were further transforming the community. New England had long caught the fever of industry—of cotton mills and machine shops. The proud whaling town was slow to adopt these forms of enterprise; but in 1849 the first cotton mill began operation. This mill was begun by a local businessman who had been employed in a small southern cotton mill and decided, in planning a venture for himself, to return north to raise funds and test the feasibility of the port town for a mill. Most of the leading men in the community subscribed for shares, albeit seldom more than ten shares per man. This first corporation built other mills until by 1882 it had six of the fifteen mills then in operation.

The early years of the 1870s were dismal ones for the community. Population had decreased by several thousands during and following the Civil War. A former editor of the local newspaper reminisced on those years: "In spite of the courage of the leading ship-owners, it was clearly evident that whaling had seen its best days, and the inevitable decay was accelerated by the two great Arctic ocean disasters which occurred in this period."[64] At that time little economic benefit was expected from the developing mill industry.

However, contrary to gloomy expectations, the decades following 1880 were years of spectacular growth. By 1890 population had jumped to nearly 41,000 and by 1900 stood at over 62,000. In 1910, the community had become a thickly populated city of more than 96,000 persons.

Who were these people? Many young Yankee boys were moving on, some going West, others seeking opportunity in the still larger eastern cities which developed in those years of the industrial-urban revolution. The population figures for this New England state are the key to the new character of the port-town community. The census of 1880 showed that 25 per cent of the population of Massachusetts was foreign born. The largest contingents were of Irish, French Canadian, English, and Canadian stock. Then, in the 1880s, the tide of emigration shifted toward southeastern Europe, and Italians and other eastern Europeans began to fill the manufacturing towns and cities of the state.

In the port town where the mills had been grudgingly accepted as a substitute for whaling, the heterogeneous elements of this tremendous population growth persisted as distinctive segments of a society. Natural features of the countryside—the river, the harbor, swamps and hills—facilitated the division of the town into a south end, a north end, a west end (away from the harbor), and a central area still close to docks and commerce. Both north and south ends were the scenes of the building of new mills and the congregation in multiple-family dwelling units of the workers who ran the machines. New population elements began to cluster in ethnic neighborhoods.

By the mid-1880s the community transition to the activities of the mills was well advanced. Cotton-mill operatives predominated among male workers and also in the occupations of the many women working outside the home.[65] In 1906, the mills emloyed over 18,000 workers.[66]

A commentary on the changed face and character of the community, written just before the turn of the century, provides a local impression of the new segments of population:

> But still the new comers formed a class apart from the old inhabitants . . . they were natives of other countries and their ideas, manners and modes of life differed in many particulars . . . the factory people have been to many of the old inhabitants an alien race, of whose life and struggles they knew as little as they did of those of the inhabitants of some far off country. . . .[67]

This commentator spoke of "fraternizing" and "breaking down barriers" between the groups, but he did not speak of intermingling or amalgamating. He also saw an increase in "understanding" and "toleration," brought about by the ebb and flow of fortunes which had caused some poor to rise and some rich to fall. Apparently most of this experience which bred mutual toleration and humility was among Yankees, or at least among Anglo elements, who adopted a less austere attitude toward "failure" amid the uncertainties of an urban-industrial society. But toleration was primarily an acceptance of difference, not an expectation of growth and development with subsequent realignment, or even disappearance, of ethnic groups.

A local newspaper early in the twentieth century reflected on the new symbols of a new era:

> Some of the names which were most familiar and prominent have disappeared. . . . Then there was talk of "lays"; now we hear about wage scales. Then the terminology of the whaling business was familiar to everybody; now, nine-tenths of the population would not know whether a bowhead was a whale or a whaleboat.[68]

In this changed atmosphere the opportunities for all to share, and at least to attempt to achieve "success" and new position through participation in a great, exciting venture, had disappeared. The coastland city had become the work place and crowded home of a people of many, separated faces.

Multiples of Social Insulation

At about the turn of the current century the people who conducted public affairs in this New England city still paid little heed to the unique, distinctive groups that were congregating in their community. Even the Portuguese and Cape Verdeans of the whaling days had earned much more attention when they were colorful participants in an honored institution. The newspaper's anniversary supplement of 1907 noted: "The stacks of great mills have replaced in the skyline the masts of ships." But most of this anniversary issue was devoted to the old whaling industry and to the lore of the sea.

Somewhere behind the stacks of great mills people labored, but away from work, away from the industrial center, people congregated in circles of association where they continued to share Old World languages and Old World customs. In these neighborhoods from one end of the long, narrow city to the other the private experiences of people were largely confined to those of their own kind, although from the hill overlooking the bay in the central area of town the inhabitants of the ethnic neighborhoods, these "factory workers," were remote shadows.

The physical conditions of the city contributed to the insulation of group from group. When the town was first incorporated in 1787 it was said to be made up of sections separated north and south "by the harbor and river, and east and west by the highway. . . ."[69] Because the cotton mills located in the north and south ends, the shops and stores which served the factory people also located there.

A three-paragraph description of the "French community," written by a French businessman, was included in a publication of the local *Journal of Commerce* in 1897. This was the only group singled out for specific recognition at that time. The French population was estimated then at "about 13,000." Particular notice was taken of "three parish schools." An "asylum" for young children whose mothers worked in the mills was also provided. One Frenchman was a successful banker. "Many are U.S. citizens," the account reported, adding: "All the French citizens keep with great care the language and the religion of their fathers, but they nearly all speak English, and are proud to be American citizens. They have amongst them doctors, merchants, justices of the peace, lawyers, overseers of the mills, real estate agents, etc."[70]

Today, the visitor who spends a little time in this community sees, inescapably, the continuing multiplicity here. He finds churches in which Masses are still conducted in French or in Portuguese. He notices a sign proclaiming the offices of a Portuguese-language newspaper—the largest in the country. Dotted throughout the neighborhoods of both north and south ends are meeting halls and social centers for "Cape Verdean Veterans" and "French Citizens," and squares like the one dedicated to "Lebanese War Veterans."

While there are those who speak of "classes," it would be a mistake to attempt to describe this social system as a series of social layers, because few people are conscious of their relative "position" in this entire community population. Ethnicity and "nationality" do provide strong labels for identifying a person, but, as the outsider realizes, there are many little subworlds and most people have experienced life in the community only within such a narrowed world.

Occupation and length of residence in the community do help the individual to identify himself as "above" or "below" some others. For the "middle majority" of people in the different ethnic groups the attitude is probably that reported by a Cape Verdean school principal: they see themselves as "better than those down by the shacks near the water, but not as good as the professional man." Perhaps only the "old-line Yankee" holds strongly to family name to anchor himself to a high position in the society.

The problem in understanding the whole was quickly pointed up by a Portuguese woman who worked as a stitcher in one of the needle plants. "I don't think you will ever find out much about this town," she said, "because whichever group of people you speak to will know of that group and no other." Her occupation was a common one among women in a population where nearly all women worked—a practice carried over from earliest times in the mills. Stitchers were among the highest paid operatives in one of the steadiest occupations in town; and since the men there considered that work "feminine," there were many Portuguese, French, and Italian homes in which the mother was the major breadwinner. This woman said: "We have classes of people here, and one class doesn't step out to find out what the others in the city are doing." She described "poorer sections" and "nicer sections" scattered throughout a community where, as she said, "housing is a real problem." She said: "I come from a family of immigrants. We have had to work to survive and have never been of the class of people who get into city activities—and those things aren't too important here."

The pastor of the largest local Portuguese church, in the north end of town, described the pride and attachment of his people to the Old Country: "We have the official Portuguese school sponsored by the Portuguese government in our parish. Only Portuguese is spoken there. The teachers are paid by the Portuguese government." He also commented on the French population: "You will often hear their young people speaking French to one another. Our people use English in their conversations when they are young; it's the older people that speak Portuguese. The French parochial school is taught in French. It is only recently that the French churches began to shift to English."

A majority of the people here—French and French-Canadians, Portuguese and Cape Verdeans—are Catholic. "We French-speaking people love our language," a French-Canadian attorney said, "and in most of our parishes all the sermons and announcements have been in French." He was asked if the French were isolated geographically from other groups in the community. "Like all the racial groups," he said, "we are separated by language background, social contacts, and close family acquaintances." Now, however, he feared a decline of the language he loved: "We spoke only French to the children at home until they were 3 or 4 years old, but today they speak the language with difficulty." This attorney had become active in a French social club for preserving the old culture and traditions.

A spokesman for the Protestant minority in the community was also a representative of the local American Negro minority. (The term "people of color" was applied locally to the dark-skinned Cape Verdeans, who were separated from the American Negroes by difference in religion as well as by their insistence on being designated "Caucasian" on all official records.) This Negro minister described the financial difficulties encountered by the Protestant interchurch council in pushing support of community-wide projects. "The Catholics," he said, "are always much more devoted to the policy of their church. If a project is Catholic, they will support it." The minister had worked on the Community Chest drive one year in the north end. The merchants he contacted that year were collecting to build a Catholic high school and said they had no money to spare for the Chest. "We have no nice recreational facilities for Protestant children," said the clergyman, "while there is a beautiful privately endowed center for Catholic children. And I have heard that a Protestant child must present a card from a Catholic parish—in other words, join the parish—in order to use those facilities."

It must be remembered that the Protestant people of conscience had required some prodding to expand their perspective on personal responsibilities in the affairs of this world. And in recent decades some of the richest parishioners of old Protestant churches had moved away from the central areas to homes along the inlets and beside the yachting harbor southwest of town. Current problems of fundraising had earlier counterparts. A Methodist minister of 1826 recorded in his diary the response of a local congregation when he announced he would be leaving to accept a call from a church in another town:

. . . it was thought best to take up a contribution for me, as a compensation, I suppose, for my labor for them night and day in the seven years past. $3.33 was contributed by the large meeting, and my numerous, and many of them rich, friends. . . . This sum will help pay my tolls over the bridge for seven years that I have labored for them more or less and attended funerals and meetings.[71]

A present-day editor of the local paper said that there was no stigma attached in this town to being a "hyphenated-American": "People here are proud of their nationality. One day a colleague of mine, from Delaware, read an article I wrote about a 'prominent Franco-American.' He said: 'Won't this man be offended at being labeled like that?' I told him that, on the contrary, people welcome such labels." There are over 450 clubs and organizations here with largely "national" memberships. "Even the British-Americans have their own societies," the editor said. "Several of our English have been decorated by the British government for service to Britain during the war. And some of our French people have been decorated by the French government, while one time the publisher of our Portuguese newspaper was a guest of the Portuguese government."

The English came as skilled spinners and weavers, from midland England, to work in the textile mills. The French and Portuguese who came to work the mills were, generally, less skilled. In earlier days, newspaper stories often reflected an attitude that the Portuguese were not quite on a par with other local citizens: "The paper might print an article saying, 'Two men and a Portugee drowned in the river' back in the old days," the editor said. "But there has never been a racial difficulty in this community; and we are proud of that."

It seemed that the great majority of the people, within their own little worlds, experienced the whole community in much the same way. That is, there were no sharp lines of conflict like those that would occur if groups were jostling for advantage. Ethnic groups were somewhat docile—"accustomed to less opulence," as one person phrased it. The visible symbols of change and open opportunity were not apparent. However, there were signs that antagonisms appeared between groups having the least advantages.

A Catholic priest who served a Cape Verdean parish said: "My Cape Verdeans tell me that they have always been the last ones hired and the first ones fired. But now Puerto Ricans are starting to move into the old neighborhoods down near the wharves and there is a lot of mutual dislike between these groups. You see the Puerto Ricans are about fifty years behind the Cape Verdeans. Some Verdeans are coming up in the world and are getting more education. They're not just the 'black Portuguee' of old any more."

One Cape Verdean who had made this transition through education was now principal of an elementary school on the south side, close to the waterfront. "When I was a boy," he said, "I can recall that whatever kids' fights we got into—you know, group against group—were with the American Negro kids. I guess we tried hard to distinguish ourselves from them. It wasn't until some of us left this community in war time and really experienced, in the South and elsewhere, what it was like to be a 'person of color' in this country that we began to identify at all with American Negroes." Now he was encouraging some of the brighter Cape Verdean young people to attend Negro universities, like Howard University in Washington, D.C. He maintained that most Verdean doctors and lawyers served clientele, locally, who were not Verdean. Professional status *did* provide for broader acceptance, as well as for a broadened perspective.

This young educator described how firm the insulations of ethnicity remained, however, outside the new public roles provided by some professions: "Recently I helped to get a bunch of Verdean girls, including my sister, to join a group down at the central YWCA. We ended up with a good, lively group—fifty girls; but all of them children of color. I had hoped to see these girls have a broadened experience with other girls in the community. When I asked my sister about it she said the Verdean girls felt more at ease together. They seemed to want it that way."

In all of this picture, where was the Yankee segment? Could it be identified?

There were growing numbers of people—products of intermarriages and of education—who were no longer so closely identified with old ethnic customs and traditions. These people would say of themselves: "I am 'American.'" There were just as many, however, among those escaping from the factories into professions and more active public roles who still remained closely identified, in their private lives, with the church and the language and the traditions of their fathers—and who knew well the history and the customs of the Old Country and would recount them to their children. Perhaps some among the former group—mostly Anglo-Protestants—could be called the "New Yankees."

There were even still a few who could qualify as Yankees of the old line and who performed an important function in this community. They were the true keepers of the oldest and most honored local traditions. One descendant of whaling skippers and Yankee merchants lived in a lovely home beside the yachting harbor. He said, without equivocation: "The mills were a mistake. We never should have turned the community into a mill town. It just doesn't fit our character." This man could trace his family history to the man who had brought the whaling industry to the mainland from the island of Nantucket. Now he lived in semiretirement, commuting to his downtown law office a few times a week.

The old Yankee was still active in town meeting in the village outside the port city. He was active, too, in the old historical society of this village. And his business downtown had retained some of the savor of the older enterprise: much of his legal practice dealt with maritime affairs and with problems of immigration of peoples from across the seas. When he spoke of the past, he spoke of the sea—of the exploits of kinsmen who had captained the whalers. There was nothing in the history of the textile mills that recalled past adventure like this.

The Yankee's son was a doctor who had returned to practice locally. There was no problem building a professional practice in these surroundings. It was only business opportunities that had withered in the years since the great whaling and textile booms; and most of the textile mills had been developed and owned by men who apparently had no deep stake in the community. Some had used up machinery as they had used labor in the sweatshop days, running full-out during the war years for maximum profit, then leaving the community and building new plants elsewhere. Locally, one heard a different emphasis on these matters depending on the informant: the labor unions forced the mills out with high wage demands, said some businessmen; the millowners always exploited the local factory people and had no concern for the community, said many laboring people.

It was true, at any rate, that factory work and the economic conditions of a crowded industrial city had contributed to the insulations separating group from group. They also had hastened the retreat of old Yankee leadership to areas where men preserved the past by shutting out the present. But now economic diversification was being sought, and there was evidence that this new diversity could help to foster an expansiveness in social outlook that would begin to break the crusts of the many little worlds.

Constraint, but Assurance, on a Crowded Coastland

Faint glimmerings of a new spirit appeared on the coastland in recent years. The new spirit was not the bland optimism of the businessmen who multiplied the mills and imported cheap labor to run them a half century ago. And it certainly was not the euphoric vigor of the days when this port symbolized adventure and fortune. But many people of diverse backgrounds were soberly contemplating the future of *their* community. They had no grandiose plans; but they did have a commitment to the whole, as well as to their own most cherished part of the whole. They were attempting to build for the future while retaining the assurance of personal identity which exists among people who maintain close ties to their groups.

The problems were basically economic; but they were also social-psychological.

Many textile jobs had disappeared following the Second World War. Only two major mills remained of the twenty-eight once in operation. However, commercial fishing (on the upswing), apparel manufacturing, a few electronics-parts plants, and a rubber factory were contributing to the diversification sought by local leadership. An industrial development fund was raised by subscriptions to purchase lands in the north end for an industrial park.

Population had been declining. From the peak of some 120,000 persons recorded for 1920, the census of 1950 showed only about 109,000 in the city, and that of 1960 only some 102,500. (The extended metropolitan area generally held its own in numbers in the most recent censuses.)

The decline did not indicate a *forced* exodus, for the city lost some residents who moved to outlying areas of "better living." In fact, it is surprising, in light of the economic facts, that so many stayed and rode out depressions and recessions, returned after wars, and sought new jobs locally when old ones disappeared. Somewhere amid the certainties and the constraint and limited opportunities of life in the coastland city one must seek the strengths and the weaknesses of "community" among these people.

A retired president of the city's oldest mill—which still was in operation—described changes he noted: "Working conditions are better today—cleaner, lighter, more comfortable." What of the future? "New industry is coming in. There is no question of it. We raised $600,000 for that purpose. The people here haven't changed. They just like better things to eat and wear and a greater variety of recreation. We have a good labor force. The English, the Poles, and the French are all good people. And the Portuguese have become skilled laborers." Note that people were still readily classified and identified by the labels of nationality.

The personnel manager of a leather goods company expressed his views on the present situation: "We have more diversified occupations here than before; but the real lack is in industries providing good jobs for men. There are a few now. But a survey showed recently that the percentage of working mothers per capita is higher here than in any other community in the country. And as for opportunities for achievement, there are not many jobs here where a man can make more than $10,000 unless he is a professional or owns his own business." Many people had migrated to California during lay-off and recession periods. But many also came back: "They didn't realize men were working 60 hours out there and that most of the money came from overtime in an aircraft plant."

This man indicated a crucial aspect of "constriction" among most population elements: "You must remember that the English and the Portuguese and the French who came, successively, to work in the mills were 'Old World' people who retained 'Old World' ideas. All three groups were more interested in seeing their children working and bringing in money than in having them go to school. My mother got as far as her freshman year in high school when her parents—they were English immigrants—pulled her out and put her to work at age 14. She kept 10 cents on the dollar earned, and her family took the rest." He said this pattern still existed, especially among the Portuguese.

What was the situation in education? "A lot of the French and

Portuguese are trying to better themselves; and more of the parents are interested in helping the kids get an education," answered the personnel manager, "but it is amazing how many young people I get in the course of the year who quit school early. They want a car or are forced to go to work to support the family. I try to encourage the bright ones to go to school at night." A clue to the problems faced by the public schools was contained in a statement made by the president of the local PTA (quoted by the newspaper editor): The community had the smallest number of PTA chapters (two) for a city of this size anywhere in the country.

However, an assistant superintendent of secondary schools explained that high school enrollment was on the increase, although dropouts were still numerous. The community operated a separate vocational high school. At grade eight, a child could choose: an academic high school, to go to work if he was sixteen years old, or the vocational high school. The superintendent's figures also showed that while in 1940, 35 per cent of the academic high school students took the college course, in 1958, 51 per cent registered for the college course. A local institute of technology had begun to grant a four-year college degree. A plan to bring a regional college to the coastland was also under consideration, which would be a factor in the efforts to expand local horizons.

This "shabby old lady" (as one citizen referred, lovingly, to the community) still encouraged restrictions which tended to keep people in their subworlds. As younger people moved away, those who continued to share activities with one another would tend, selectively, to be those sharing most the old ways and the older outlook. Where might leadership—committed to the community, but seeking to effect change and adaptation to the present—be found? An old Yankee said that one problem was that so much of local industry was controlled and owned by people who lived out of town. The newspaper editor said: "We are not yet far enough away from our international beginnings. The leaders we produced were primarily old-line Yankees that had been in the country three or four or five generations. Now this strain is all but gone—the remnants have retired from the city. It's not that the present leaders can't speak good English but that they lack perception and depth."

Yet it was from the struggling ranks of those who were beginning to transcend their particular nationality group that leadership could appear. For instance, the Cape Verdean school principal was now a leading spokesman for efforts to get the community's groups to talk to one another. And in spite of hesitancies and constraints, those who accepted a role in the public arena would find that stage well prepared. For generations of urban experiences had conditioned the participants in the relationships of the market place.

A local Episcopal minister, who had served a pastorate at one time in a very old southern community in the United States,* provided some insights on the local proclivity for "partial" human relationships. One of the contrasts he noted to the southern community was that here on the coastland more activities were concentrated outside of the home and the family circle. The coastland community had more of the characteristics of a market place: "Here everyone works," he said. "People here are more businesslike. In the South people made more of an effort to please, even if the effort was a false front. And there was more personal concern among individuals there."

It appeared that if a man had the incentive to achieve something for himself, the hand of tradition was not heavy enough to deter him. This was manifest in the ranks of professionals and political leaders on the crowded coastland. It was easier, to be sure, for him to assume a professional role if he did not have to fight so hard against the constraints of Old World tradition in his private associations. But once attained, whether by French or Portuguese or even Cape Verdean, a more active, transcending public role provided a new base for affirmation of the old value of human equality. True, achieved equality had not yet reached far into private social practices. Certain cultural labels and characteristics were limiting: "Colored families can come to tea or a church supper," the Episcopal minister said, "but not into your homes. There are instances where they come, but it's not a regular practice. In the South where I served, a Negro would attend a private affair—a wedding or a funeral, or something like that—as an individual member of the clan."

A local judge of Portuguese descent was recently appointed

* The community which is the subject of Chapter 2.

judge of the superior court of Massachusetts. When this judge spoke to interviewers of his practices as a juvenile judge, he spoke as a formal public agent attempting to express in his decisions the concern of an entire society for all of its children. The judge wore the formal hat of his profession easily.

The assistant school superintendent, an educator with a Ph.D. degree, was also secure in his public role and commented favorably on the quality of local educators. He offered another insight into the processes of self-identification and security for the professional: "I work on several levels here, and this is worth something to me. I lived in Boston and I know what that is like. I enjoy going down the street and meeting friends of long standing. The fellows on the garbage wagon say, 'Hi, Jim.' I'm a Lieutenant Colonel in the Air Force Reserve. When I go out to the Air Base I meet another set of people and I'm involved in other kinds of things. Call it provincial, but this living and working on several levels is important to me. It is the reason I stay in this community although I have a doctorate degree."

There was apparently a richness to life balanced by certainties and colored by diversity. The superintendent mentioned that the community had characteristics "that people in other places work twenty years to retire to." The person who had alternatives and some control over his vocation and avocations could live "at several levels," and avoid conformity. Even the more constrained and crowded elements of population had not degenerated into a social mass in which identity was lost. The thread of assured personal identity had persisted even through the years when the factory peoples appeared in the community, symbolized as a "mass" to community leaders, but always securely anchored in their smaller insulated worlds.

What was the intrinsic charm of this setting of the American experiment? Laying aside the economic "drabness" of a problem area that had many obstacles to overcome, many windows to open before the economy could accelerate and the social system expand, the surfaces of freedom here were an often unappreciated aspect of American society. Turned outward toward the world, this community system did not reflect an anonymous mass or a washed-out version of white-collar and middle-class America. Here one still finds men carving careers which link them closely to Old World strains that continue to enrich a country that proclaims itself a nation of immigrants. For example, a Portuguese-American public accountant is working to bring other Portuguese to this country, and he handles their immigration problems. From among these people efforts to expand the language curriculum in the public schools originate. A local Italian-American labor leader, visiting abroad recently for the first time in thirty years, wrote from Italy to his young grandson. In the letter, published in the community newspaper, he expressed the deep feelings of an immigrant grateful that America had been so good to him. It is from such a system that America still presents many vital human surfaces to other peoples in the world. The challenging task in the future will be to weave the variegated strands of group and individual identity more fully through the whole fabric of a society.

2

The Tideland Frontier: Charleston

I would have you in all the places where you shall touch to encourage men of Estates to remove into Carolina. But forbear to invite the poorer sort yet a while . . . it being substantiall men and theire Familyes, that must make the Plantation which will stock the country with Negroes, Cattle and other Necessarys.

—A Lord Proprietor, 1671[1]

Men of Property

The men who approached the threshold of a continent were moved by diverse ideas and constrained by varying circumstances. With the restoration of Charles II as the first parliamentary monarch of Great Britain, European man in the mid-seventeenth century began the new experiments of the "modern world."

England was still a world of dukes and earls, viscounts and barons; but men of title had learned to limit the powers of their monarchs. At the same time, the New World had begun to drain off not only dissenters and malcontents but the bold and daring among the untitled commercial classes of the growing cities. Attentions had turned increasingly to plans for the accumulation of wealth. The virgin lands of the New World presented possibilities of profit from commerce and from real estate.

The first overtures for a commercial venture along the southeastern coast of North America came from Barbadoes—in the islands of the West Indies—where a landed gentry had developed a plantation economy over a period of several decades. Those who had fled there from England or had been exiled by Cromwell re-established London contacts with friends who returned to court. But it was not the Barbadian planters who obtained a grant of lands from Charles. Instead, eight Lord Proprietors, bargainers in the inner circle of nobility, received a charter to all of the land of "Carolana" extending between the 36th and 31st parallels from one sea to the other. The promoter-politicians laid their plans. And prominent in their plans were men like the plantation owners of the West Indies: ". . . considerable men . . . able to make a Plantation . . . in a Condition to stock and furnish themselves . . . substantiall Men. . . ."[2]

The Lord Proprietors called upon John Locke to draw up a "Fundamental Constitution" for their proposed colony, and prepared to offer inducements to substantial men to go to Carolina to become "men of property" there. And there were willing colonists, who accepted the chance of a new beginning. But the society which was formed in the tidelands of Carolina did not follow, exactly, the outlines of the constitution prepared for the Proprietors that they might "avoid erecting a too numerous democracy." The constitution provided for a society in which rule and rank derived from property. It embodied the conception that individual rights were the rights of private property, and defined the initial terms on which the different ranks of colonists would be assigned their property and ascribed their rights.

New titles were to be created for the New World: "To every county there shall be three as ye hereditary nobility . . . who shall be called ye one a landgrave and ye other two cassiques." The Charter forbade the use of English titles such as "Duke" and "Earl."

Titles would be inherited: Whosoever "by right of inheritance shall come to be landgrave or cassique shall take ye name and armes of his predesessor in that dignity to be from thence forth ye name and armes of his family and their posterity."

A class of "leetmen," who would voluntarily bind themselves and their offspring for life as servants to the men of property, would be created: And no leetman or leetwoman would have liberty "to goe . . . from the land of his particular lord, and live anywhere else without licenses obtain'd from his said lord under hand and seale."

Rights of participation in legal process were prescribed as rights of property: "In ye Presinct Court no man shall be jury a man under Fifty acres of freehold. In ye County Court . . . no man shall be a jury man under three hundred acres of freehold, and in ye Proprietors Courts, no man shall be a jury man under five hundred acres of freehold."

The basis for participation in government would rest upon the stake in the community which one possessed by virtue of his property: "No man shall be chosen a member of Parliament who hath lesse than five hundred acres of freehold within ye presinct [for which he is chosen] nor shall any have a vote in choosing ye . . . member . . . [who has less than] . . . fifty acres of freehold within the said presinct."[3]

These were the outlines of a social order that a group of businessmen hoped to manipulate at long range. Advertisements for colonizers placed a premium on freemen who could bring servants with them as they undertook to plant along the south coast: The Proprietors offered to whoever should go "one hundred and fifty acres of land to him and his heires," and for every able manservant he or she should carry or send armed and provided ". . . one hundred and fifty acres of like measure."[4] From time to time further quantities of land would be given out by the drawing of lots. Even the servant would receive seventy-five acres of land after he had completed his term of servitude to a master.

This system, set in motion in a challenging environment, generated its own energies. A Proprietor urged an early governor to "dispose the poorer sort . . . to . . . become Leetmen which will be a very comfortable liveing as he may see by the conditions I propose to mind." There is no record, however, of any freeman voluntarily accepting the lifetime niche of "leetman," although some indentured themselves for a specified period. A stipulation in the Charter gave the colonial freemen the right to accept or refuse the constitution; and they availed themselves of this right so that the constitution was rejected in five forms over a period of thirty years and never became a legal document.

Thus, while the initial assignment of rank to various classes was emphasized in the prescriptions for the social order, it was the aspiration to become a man of property which dominated the attitudes and activities of people in the developing community.

Bonds of Plantation and Town

The first party of settlers in the colony consisted of seventeen masters with sixty-two servants, and thirteen unbound persons without servants.[5] Choosing an entrance into the coastal frontier where two rivers, flowing southeastward on either side of a narrow peninsula merged in a protected harbor, the party proceeded a short distance up the river to the west of the peninsula and made a settlement on the western bank.

In spite of the desires of the Proprietors, it is doubtful that many of these pioneers were from substantial families. The masters among them represented largely the trading classes of a commercial England. They responded to the same attractions which had helped to fill a ship on an unsuccessful expedition to the Carolina coast four years before. The inducements for that earlier attempt at colonization stressed the opportunities for the younger offspring who was not bequeathed "suitable fortune" by the inheritance laws of an old, established society. For the man barred from fortune and sufficient endowment in England, the avenues were open in a new continent, said the advertisements: "Here, with a few Servants and a small Stock a great Estate may be raised, although his Birth have not entitled him to any of the Land of his Ancestors, yet his Industry may supply him so, as to make him the head of as famous a family." There were opportunities, too, for those of even lesser rank: "Such as are . . . tormented with much care how to get worth to gain a Lively-hood, or that with their labour can hardly get a comfortable subsistence." Those who would indenture themselves need not "be troubled at the thoughts of being a Servant for four or five years," for once a servant had served his term, said the promoters, "he hath Land and Tools, and Clothes given him, and is in a way of advancement."[6]

These were incentives offered by and for a growing generation of capitalists. Men went out to plant and trade for profit, under auspices of sponsors in London who also attempted to manage *their* investments profitably. And the undertaking rested upon a faith that rational private enterprise should not be constrained by politics or religion. All were engaged in the business of "making the Plantation": they guarded the colony themselves and attempted to trade with the Indians, but worried little about saving heathen souls.

Colonists had been admonished to settle in towns. This plan was not solely for the benefits of mutual protection; the shrewd businessmen in England wished to control the flow of trade through central collecting points and did not wish to have individual plantation owners shipping from their own docks on the tidelands. Thus, the Proprietors restricted individual waterfront holdings, specifying that settlers were not to have a greater proportion of frontage of their land on the river than a fifth part of the depth of their property.

Soon the secretary of the colony wrote to the London promoters urging the allocation of a ship "to be wholly employed for three or four yeares in transporting of people and their goods to this place gratis."[7] When the ship was provided, it was dispatched to the West Indies, and a proclamation was displayed there to entice more gentlemen of Barbadoes, who had the needed wherewithal and experience in planting, to transfer their talents and their capital to Carolina. And as these men came in the first two or three years of settlement they brought, along with their tools and methods, slaves and titles, more than just experience in managing large manorial estates at a profit: they transplanted a way of life which impressed the other colonists with its gentility and aristocratic flavor. In gratitude and perhaps relief, the chief Proprietor wrote to the new Governor whom he had persuaded to leave the West Indies: "I am glad to hear soe many considerable men come from the Barbadoes for wee find by deare Experience that noe other are able to make a Plantation. . . . I am not very fond of more Company unlesse they be substantiall Men."[8]

But substantial men were hardly in the majority. The frontier attracted the ambitious and the adventuresome; and soon dissenters from religious orthodoxies in Europe as well as in America also joined the colony. The town settlement which the Proprietors desired was moved across the river to the narrow peninsula. This was to be the "Port Towne" on the river where the promoters would "oblige all shipps that come into that River to unload all theire goods and to take in all theire loading."[9] Both the plantations and the town began to fill with population, and the importance of the one aspect of life to the other in the community which developed, soon went beyond the natural economic ties that fashioned bonds between town and plantation, merchant and landowner.

In 1685, a minister of the gospel described the population of the community after the first fifteen years of settlement. He calculated that most of the some 2,500 inhabitants were "Dissenters," rather than of the Established Church of England (to which a majority of the Proprietors belonged). There were people of English, Irish, Scottish, and Dutch extraction, as well as a goodly number of French Huguenots. Although some had come "to better their condition in things temporal," said the minister, the majority of those dissenting from the English Church sought freedom to worship and "to escape bitter persecution."[10] This description indicates that the character of the community was changing. The leading religious elements recorded in 1686 were: English Churchmen; Scotch and Irish Presbyterians; Dutch and German Lutherans; French Calvinists; a few Irish Catholics; and a small contingent of Quakers. How could such diversity be contained in a setting where commerce and business, under the leadership of gentlemen of substance, were to dominate the lives of the people? What did these immigrants have in common, in addition to a belief in the right to dissent?

In spite of the statements by the local man of God which played down the lure of "things temporal," the challenge of opportunities for bettering one's condition was vital. Those who came to join the Barbadian planters were truly a "middle class": unanchored by inherited title or prestige to an aristocratic stratum in any society; and equally unwilling to accept a lower social position which promised them no hope of rising or of providing their children with opportunities to rise. Their quest for identity set energies in motion that could be unleashed only by people who had caught a new vision of themselves.

The tideland community developed around these energies. The Barbadian planters with their property in land and slaves were the nucleus of the system. They provided a social model for the "unlanded"; and the more prosperous merchants in the port town began to develop gentry characteristics of their own. The road to more independence and fuller citizenship—and, particularly, to a more secure identity in this new land—led through the acquisition of property. This, men set about doing, seeking both land and slaves. The Barbadian Slave Code was adopted early. It ordered punishment for killing slaves, but left their control and treatment otherwise to the master's caprice—much as the management of private property was left to the owner. As the merchants and tradesmen of the town—even mechanics and other small businessmen—vied for greater accumulation of wealth, the competition for slaves became as spirited as the competition for land. The Barbadian model of success was respected by those who came to form the community. New energies were added to the system by the people who had to strive to achieve the things the Barbadian planters already had.

Individual independence was an ideal on the tidelands. Plantation life in agrarian America epitomized private independence. As a student of the South has said, the plantation "tended to find its center in itself."[11] But commerce on the tidelands flowed through the port town, and plantation owners used the town for entertainment and fellowship as well as for business. Their public participations were an important aspect of their role in the community. From very earliest times these men owned handsome town houses in addition to their homes on the plantations. Most of the chief planters in those early days were also merchants, for until the great money crops—rice, indigo, and later cotton—were developed, trade with the Indians in the interior was a major source of wealth. A majority of the different groups arriving in the colony in the first decades settled in town, taking up occupations through which they hoped to acquire property. Others moved immediately onto the land but maintained their identification with their fellow churchmen in meetinghouses on the peninsula. There was a constant traffic between plantation and town; and while the plantation way of life provided the accepted social ideal for most participants in the community, the arrangements in town for living and working also began to symbolize a "proper" ordering of human relationships.

The community became a place of rendezvous in the New World for persecuted French Huguenots. They became the second most influential group in the colony. Their activities on the tideland illustrate the forces affecting all immigrants there. Some

Huguenots set to work as craftsmen in town—and subsequently became leading merchants—while others went upriver immediately to settle on the land bought with capital they brought with them. A description of the Huguenot plantation owners of early days pictures the conditions which wedded town and plantation into a community:

Their church was in . . . [town], thither they repaired every Sunday from their plantations. . . . They could be seen, profiting by the tide, arriving by families, in their canoes, at the public landing at the foot of Queen Street, preserving a religious silence, which was alone interrupted by the noise of their oars.[12]

Other groups also maintained a distinct identity in the town on the narrow peninsula. The Presbyterians built their meetinghouse there in 1685. By 1704, four houses of worship had been erected: the Huguenot Church; the First Baptist Church; the Episcopal Church; the White Meeting (Presbyterian and Congregational) Church. These structures served as public meeting places for groups that tended to keep their private lives to themselves. And this pattern, adopted by groups of newcomers, was completely in tune with the natural inclinations of the self-contained men of property on the plantations.

Movement and Consolidation on the Southern Frontier

The rivers and Indian trails reaching from the marshy low country of the coastal plain toward the Blue Ridge carried traders and trappers far into the interior of the continent. Many decades passed before communities of settlers were formed in these hinterlands; but the overland paths into the wilderness, skirting the southern Appalachians to the valley of the Tennessee and the plains of the Gulf, took the bold and the daring—and the eager businessman—as far as the Mississippi and beyond. The commerce generated by these men, far-reaching as it was, still found its focus in the port town on the tidelands. The governor of the colony boasted, in 1707, that the town "trades near 1000 miles into the Continent."[13]

This restless push to the back countries began early, inspired by the same motives that led men to acquire land and appropriate other forms of property. In later periods, the drive for interior lands for cotton growing would take men from the colony, with their slaves, to settle the land in Alabama and Mississippi. But for the early leaders in the interior trade there were also political motives. The southern colony stood alone and isolated—"in the chaps of the Spaniards"—and an aggressive approach amid these external conditions was deemed a wise course. The leader in the Indian trade went inland with stores of English goods and set up depots at many points along endless miles of trail. While other settlements on the slim Atlantic fringe of English colonial penetration stayed close to their coastal towns and villages, the southern colony developed a vast trade territory, linked to the one major port town. Men from the commercial venture on the tidelands seem first to have had a vision of the potential use and value of the unsettled American wilderness. Trade with the interior and the introduction of profitable rice-growing on coastal plantations generated independence of thought and action. But the consolidation of a system of life values which all except slaves shared continued in the vital center on the lowland peninsula.

A description of the community of the eighteenth century shows the contrast between processes of consolidation and movement. The town on the peninsula, says a student of this frontier, was "the one port town of the South: the residence of prosperous merchants and rice-planters, and the seat of a genteel if not yet a sophisticated society." But in the spring the tidewater capital began to take on the appearance of the remote frontier. "For . . . [it] was also the metropolis of the whole southern Indian country, and it was here that traders from the mountains and the Gulf plains paid their annual visits to civilization."[14]

A people who were creating a way of life fashioned in the conditions of the New World soon became more and more disenchanted with Proprietors who pulled strings from the courts and countinghouses in far-off London. When the Spanish threatened, and when fears developed of French encroachment from settlements along the Mississippi, the colonists received few signs of help from abroad. "They conclude they have no reason to depend upon the Proprietors for assistance," wrote His Majesty's Surveyor General for North America in 1699.[15]

Internal tensions, however, precipitated the final break with the absentee managers in England. These tensions began to develop between the Dissenters and the adherents of the Church of England. Although religious freedom was condoned and advocated, the Church of England was still the official, tax-supported church of the province. But men of other faiths had come in great numbers to the colony, and even in the last decade of the seventeenth century the office of governor was filled by three different men who were Dissenters.

Although the Huguenots had a form of worship similar to that of the other non-Church-of-England Protestants, they began to side in public affairs with the Churchmen of the official faith. The rapid entrance into the "property class" by successful Huguenot merchants and planters helped to shift their sympathies toward those of the Barbadian gentry. The result was that English, Scotch, and Irish Dissenters, although they claimed to be two-thirds of the population in 1706, began to lose ground in the balance of political power to the growing coalition of Churchmen and Huguenots.

The passage of a particularly odious bill in the colonial commons which seemed to threaten religious freedom of many of those who participated in government, caused the Dissenters to send an envoy to the Proprietors in London to lodge a protest. The protesters got little satisfaction from the Proprietors. However, a new governor was sent to the colony, and under his auspices the General Assembly was induced to establish a public school. The commissioners named in the act included Churchmen, Dissenters, and Huguenots. Thus, the community of individualistic traders was beginning to create interdependent public institutions. As one colonial descendant wrote of those days: "The religious and race differences were already healing."[16] But the conditions which fostered the independence of families and plantations and other small "worlds unto themselves" helped to perpetuate the identity of different groups and to keep significant aspects of life private.

The community was further unified and set in opposition to the neglectful Proprietors by pirate raids in 1718. Local leadership again provided the capital and manpower to put down the threats. And this time public unity was not dissipated until action had been taken to break the hold of the absentee landlords. A request was made by the citizens for free public lands for the use of the military garrisons. Other lands were also desired "in order to the effectual Securing and Well-Peopling the Frontieres of the Northward as well as to the Southward." With these requests went an appeal that "your Lordships will secure and preserve . . . [the People] in their Properties."[17]

Some years later the citizens set down their grievance of this earlier occasion: that the Proprietors "refused to part with the Uncultivated Lands, either for the Publicke or any Private Use but their own" although they had just before promised it in tracts to several hundred newcomers from Ireland. Further, "the Country had been put to the Expense of paying some Thousands of Pounds for their Passage to Carolina."[18] The Assembly met in 1719 to direct a resolution to the King: "That we cannot act as an Assembly, but as a Convention delegated by the people, to prevent the utter ruin of this government, if not the loss of the Province, till his Majesty's pleasure be known."[19] In 1721, the Proprietors' charter was rescinded by the Crown and a new governor with a Royal commission was sent to take charge.

Perhaps it was the ensuing political relationship to the Crown of George I that kept the external ties of the tideland colony so closely bound to England. Thereafter, governors were appointed by the King, while the Upper House was appointed by the governor and approved by the Crown. Only the Lower House was elected by the Freeholders among the people. By an act of 1721 a townsman was permitted to vote if he paid twenty shillings in taxes. But the town was ruled by a Commons Assembly dominated by planters from the plantations.

Native-born generations did not wish to establish a hereditary aristocracy as did some of their fathers; but they favored the aristocratic flavor in their society and wanted to perpetuate an atmosphere in which a man could achieve fuller rights of citizenship, proving in achievement that he was as good as the next man. And while the strongest families were entrenching themselves, demonstrating superiority at acquiring land and cornering markets for trade, the waves of immigration were beating less strongly on the tidelands. W. J. Cash has described towns like the port town of this period as "mere depots on the road to the markets of the world, mere adjuncts to the plantation," and not really "living entities in their own right, after the fashion of Boston and New

York and Philadelphia."[20] The melting-pot processes were not operating in this setting where groups remained separated and where people came to town to trade and meet others "of their own kind" while seeking avenues to moneyed independence.

Other groups did arrive, although none in such numbers as the Huguenots of an earlier day. Between 1730 and 1750 wars in the Palatinate brought many people from Switzerland, Holland, and Germany. Several Jewish families came in 1740 and by 1750 enough had settled to build a house of worship in the town. The motives of newcomers were those of a people seeking a new start. But the very processes of internal social movement and aspiration were operating now to consolidate a social system. The "strong" were becoming stronger and the "weak" weaker in the struggle for pre-eminence. And the accepted model of the successful man became more firm and set, for now it was truly a home-grown model, fashioned out of conditions in the New World. Rice had proved to be a wealth-producing crop in these lands irrigated by the tides. It afforded a steady income to those with sufficient land-holdings, and permitted time for the enjoyment of leisure. A genteel lady from the West Indies distinguished two social classes in 1742, calling one the "better sort" and the other the "poorer sort." The latter class she considered "indolent"—the people who had lost out in the drive for wealth and property and had slackened their efforts toward its attainment.[21]

In the years of consolidation both in plantation and town it was the Negro slave who contributed the largest numbers to the increase in population. He was valuable property: sought not only as a laborer, but as a sign of affluence. In 1737, the population of the colony totaled over 50,000; but an estimated 37,500 were Negro slaves. The town population in 1770 was estimated at 11,000, with over half of this number Negroes. Other figures indicate that the acquisition of slaves had become an important part of social and economic processes.

It might be expected that successful town merchants would acquire both land and slaves as they entrenched themselves in the aristocracy. Even the diligent overseer on the land could, if lucky, acquire capital, land, and slaves of his own. But figures show that the town mechanics and artisans were also caught up in this pattern for growth. The mechanics invested in land and speculated in town lots. Some built on their land and rented tenements or stores. Over one-half of the mechanics identified between 1760 and 1785 owned land either in town or country, and of 79 mechanics who left wills in that period, 37 mentioned ownership of slaves. Among 194 artisans identified in the census of 1790 as heads of families, 159 were slave holders.[22] Numerous, articulate, and leaders toward colonial rebellion, the artisans and mechanics bought land at such a rate that they were apparently absorbed into the agrarian society soon after the Revolution.

The "too numerous democracy" was avoided throughout the years of consolidation. The participants in the growing community all seemed to accept the claims and rights of property. None had voluntarily chosen the rank of leetman, but with Negro slaves to fill this role involuntarily, those able to achieve property status had in the Negro a symbol and a prop as well as an economic tool. The planter aristocracy continued in its pre-eminent position even after the town was incorporated in 1783 and artisans had begun to serve as city councilmen. For the planters were men of both plantation and town who had leisure to devote to politics and the arts.

A descendant of the planter gentry described the life of the successful people of property at the close of the eighteenth century, a pattern which continued for fifty years thereafter.

The family left town for the country right after the first frost in November, when the diseases of the semitropical lowlands were considered dormant. Until the end of January all the members remained on the plantation, carrying on the duties and participating in the social functions which continued to make this setting a separated world. "Christmas came in then," the description continued, "and was a great domestic festival for white and black. The Legislature always adjourned that the members might be at home at the sacred season." The entire household remained at home on the plantation until early May, unless there were young people—"especially grown-up girls"—in the family circle. "But if there were young people . . . the call of the 'gay season' brought them to town again, by the end of January."

The bright social occasions in the port town marked this place as the most festive and cultural center in all the American colonies. There were dances, philharmonic concerts and the races. Race Week and the Jockey Ball were the time of the town carnival, and all the planters came to town for this. "By the end of March," the chronicler described, "all were back in the country again." But as May and the approach of summer turned the pools and streams green and unhealthy, "the ladies were hurried off" to the comfortable town houses, built to catch the breezes from off the harbor, "and the gentlemen followed as soon as the work permitted."[23]

In households like this—particularly those persisting for several generations—the ordered arrangements of people and things were preserved. There was personal affection: "Old people lingered on and were given affectionate tendance; children were born and cared for." And there was continuity in relationships, even between people and their human property: "There were often three generations of house servants. . . . 'My servants next to my children,' the old ladies used to say."[24] From these ingredients the myths of a human community developed along with a political and economic order. And when history provides enough time and dramatic events, the shared memories of a people take on tremendous importance.

Unifying Drama and Separating Trauma

Shared experiences within a social system tend also to separate people from other social systems. The story of the tideland community reveals the strength of social forces that unify while they separate.

On many occasions the community had been unified by threats in the surrounding world. The French and the Spanish, often prodding the Indians to hostile action, were a constant menace to the Anglo-Saxon on the southern frontier. Pirate raids had also occasioned local organization to defeat and punish the outlaws of the coastlands. Events such as these precipitated the break with the remote Proprietors, who offered little or no protection to the colonists. But the internal solidification of community leadership was even more important on the tidelands. Old World identities were being lost in generations born in the New World. This was particularly true of men who became entrenched in the ranks of the propertied. *Gentlemen* of the community had time to devote to problems of government. One historian said of these men: "They were by education ever ready, with tongue or pen, to discourse elegantly and learnedly on subjects of statesmanship and the public interests. . . ."[25]

Three interested groups—referred to as "classes" in descriptions of this period—became discernible in *public* affairs. The mechanics, the merchants, and the planters ". . . met separately to discuss their politics," says one historian; and "each group considered itself distinct and made alliances, counter-alliances, and compromises as interests dictated."[26] The mechanics and artisans of the town were credited by a leading planter with being prime movers in the colonial rebellion. He stated that it was a blacksmith—one of the Sons of Liberty—who was ". . . the man who first moved the ball of revolution" in the community.[27] But it remained the planter gentry—embodiments of the community model for political leadership and the social ideal—who were chosen consistently to speak for the people in colonial councils.

By 1770, the inhabited territory of Carolina reached almost to the mountains. The last hostile Indian tribe had been subdued in the Cherokee War of 1761; the French in Canada and the West and the Spanish to the south had been suppressed and pacified by the British military victories of 1763. Backcountry lands had begun to fill with settlers moving southward from interior regions of Pennsylvania, Maryland, and Virginia. However, the low country remained the center of political power and social and cultural influence.

As discontent increased in the American colonies during the reign of George III, a natural focus for political leadership existed in the gentlemen on the tidelands. The Cherokee Indian War had given military experience and brought public notice to men with names that later became famous in the Revolution. But it was the tax policies of George III that brought leadership to the fore. The gentlemen had been schooled in the better universities of England where most of them had studied law. In effect, it was European education which produced the lawyer-gentry of Revolutionary days.

In the English universities, sons and grandsons of Barbadian planters and wealthy Huguenot merchants—relatively separated

and insulated from one another at home—met and developed
common respect and interests.* The planter-merchant of earliest
days had become more completely a planter, who even employed
a representative in town to handle all the worrisome problems of
supply and finance for the plantation. Meanwhile, the successful
town merchant had become more a merchant-planter as he
acquired land and produced money-making crops. However, it
was the sons, immersed in law and politics, who made up the
lawyer leadership of Revolutionary days. Public life in the law
was becoming the prime public role of an aristocratic elite.

The events of Revolutionary days found the town mechanics
and artisans in the vanguard of rebellious sentiment and activity.
Leading town merchants, mercantilists in their own right, often
were avowed Tories; while the planters were slow to favor a break
with England. But once the cries of "liberty" and "tyranny" filled
the air, it was the lawyer gentry who were called upon to lead;
and most of them were men of the plantations. "Boston is but the
first victim," they said. "The whole continent must be animated
with one great soul, and all Americans must resolve to stand by
one another, even unto death."[28]

A leading Huguenot merchant, hurrying home from Europe
because of the threatening state of affairs, wrote to his son, who
was in London at the time, that although the townsfolk had been
the first to move for rebellion, the men in the country-houses upriver were quickly seizing the initiative. "Soon," he wrote, "they
will take the reins out of the townsmen's hands; they are the
richest and most numerous, and every one thinks that he knows
enough to govern."[29] The town mechanics and artisans actually
carried the election in 1774 at which delegates were chosen
". . . to meet the Deputies of the several Colonies of North-
America, in general Congress, the *first Monday* in *September* next,
at *Philadelphia*. . . ."[30] But in selecting their delegates the townsmen chose from among the gentry. Four of the men selected—
lawyers schooled in England—became signers of the Declaration
of Independence. "The same names," a chronicler said, "occur
over and over again. The members of the General Committee are

---

* In proportion to its population, the Carolina colony sent more sons and
daughters to Europe for formal education than did any other American
colony.

also the members of the Provincial Congress, and the Provincial Congress and the General Assembly differ only in name. . . . With some few exceptions, the chief actors in the Revolution belonged to one or two closely connected groups."[31]

The unifying forces that influenced a diverse people to choose their Revolutionary representatives and leaders from among the gentry continued to strengthen the aristocratic model toward which all citizens were drawn. In later years the artisans and mechanics disappeared as a group and nothing that might correspond to a manufacturing element appeared in the community. The wealthy native-born merchants also were absorbed by the land, replaced in town by a "foreign-born element, . . . who kept to themselves, had their own clubs, and contented with the large fortunes which they accumulated, took no part in public affairs . . ."[32] After the cotton gin was introduced (1793), the lure of property ownership became stronger than ever—and possible of attainment by more people who lived on the backlands that were removed from the tides but still were worked by slaves. The community lost many of the ambitious to the up-country, while others entered the lowland aristocracy. Still others who remained continued to look approvingly, from a lower social rung, at the men of property above them.

The theme of common acceptance of the rights of property has been stressed here as the major foundation of the social order on the tidelands. Land, commerce in agrarian products, and slaves were bound up in institutions of property. These elements became closely intertwined in the activities and feelings of people who were creating a new society and, in the process, reshaping an image of themselves and of their individual dignity. The following definition of property helps to clarify its relationship to this development of "dignity":

The capability of being transferred is the quintessence of property. . . . The relation of ownership is not a relation between the man and the thing but between him and other men, whom he excludes from and to whom he gives, possession. Property is an "exclusive" right and where there are no people to exclude, the right cannot exist.[33]

A paradox in the achievement of dignity through the exclusion of others from one's possessions appeared in the institution of slavery, in which the things possessed were other humans. The exclusive possession of *things* permitted the man of property to assert his uniqueness. The Negro slave was deprived of his humanity in this institutional framework. He was an object of possession. Thus, while all others in the society pursued the ideal of personal uniqueness and self-reliance, the Negro slave was assigned to the category of a being who was somewhat less than human.

As a field hand on the large plantation the Negro was a unit of labor. He had been dislocated from ties of tribe and family in his past and usually was unable to create lasting relationships or family ties in the present, although the community which he served was one in which family name and the continuity of human relationships were greatly prized and emphasized. Consequently, if he became a more privileged household servant or trustee, the slave identified with the family he served and found the beginnings of personal identity as "Mr. James's Robert" or "Mr. Montgomery's Sam." Further, the slave was largely *mute,* completely outside the public dialogues even when those dialogues were about *him.* He served as a resonant sounding-board of feelings in the refined and emotionally restrained little worlds of the white masters.

In 1739, Negro slaves as a group found their voice briefly in the community. A slave rebellion began on one of the plantations, led by a Negro of exceptional physical qualities and inspired, it was said, by the troublesome Spanish. In this uprising, twenty-one whites were killed. One result of this incident was a slight modulation of the Slave Code, although it still permitted the slaveowner rights to use his property as he saw fit.

In the eighteenth century the attitude toward what was known even by its practitioners as "the peculiar institution" was much less defensive than it became later. In that period it was not unreasonable for the white man, comparing his own efforts to overcome nature with the efforts of others, to locate himself at the top of God's hierarchy for the races of man. Even with these natural predispositions, however, there were voices of protest from within the community. Memoirs and diaries reveal that many of the mistresses of the large plantations had a heavy conscience about the practice of slavery. One author has pointed out that prior to the movement in Boston fostered by William Lloyd Garrison, of 130 abolition parties before 1827, more than one hundred—and four-fifths of the total membership—were in the South.[34] For the most socially secure slaveowners, slaves were an economic expediency more than a symbol of prestige. Still, the Negro did remain a pawn in the white man's struggle for pre-eminence.

After the beginning of the nineteenth century, problems which had been discussed earlier in national forums again began to attract attention. In 1802, one of the lawyer-gentry discussed the peculiar institution in tones which sound strident and defensive. Slaves, he pointed out, were introduced into the state in the pursuit of agriculture and made the cultivation of the richest lands of the lower country profitable. These slaves, he said, became a vested property in their owners by the laws of the land. He feared the efforts ". . . which are not only tried individually, but collectively, to weaken this right of property; and, ultimately, to change its very nature." The spokesman painted a picture of contrasts between the Negroes' lot in a civilized society and their condition in Africa: "There," he said, "they are subject to the uncontrolled pleasure of princes; and are sometimes even slaughtered for the ceremonies of their funerals. Neither life or property is secured to them." But in the New World, by contrast, ". . . laws are passed for their security and protection. They are worked by certain tasks, which are not unreasonable; and when they are diligent in performing them, they have some hours of the day to themselves. Hence they are encouraged to plant for their own emolument . . . and are protected in the property which they thus acquire."[35] (In this social order, even the slave was protected in his exclusive possessions *relative to other beings in his same category.*)

Major irritants to the smooth functioning of the social system based on the peculiar institution persisted. In 1822, a second slave rebellion was attempted. This time the focus of discontent appeared not on a plantation but in the center of town; and this time the attempted uprising was less spontaneous and more planned. The leading organizer was a free Negro who, having purchased his freedom years before with money won in a lottery, had educated himself and continued to live in the community. Mobilization of rebellious sentiments took place in the African

Church, where many of the conspirators were class leaders.* Word was passed at prayer meetings. At the final meeting the leader read from the Bible the story of the deliverance of the children of Israel out of bondage in Egypt. But many of the slaves in town were not ready to be led out of bondage, and one of those who was approached by the conspirators reported the plot to his master. Later, after the bloodless suppression of the rebellion and seizure of the plotters, the loyal slave reported to the white man's court on the conversation in which "Mr. Paul's William" had told him of the plot:

> Do you know that something serious is about to take place? . . . Well, said he, there is, and many of us are determined to right our- selves! . . . We are determined to shake off our bondage. . . . I was so . . . astonished . . . that it was a moment or two before I could collect myself sufficiently to tell him I would have nothing to do with this business, that I was satisfied with my condition, that I was grate- ful to my master for his kindness and wished no change. . . .[36]

The chief conspirators were hanged. An official report pointed out that private property had been destroyed for the public welfare. But the muted voice of this property had been heard again, this time more coherently; for not only had the plot been planned and organized, its proponents had had their day in court. Within the community, the old Slave Code was reinstated in its strictest form, and controls over free Negroes were tightened. Free Negroes from other states or on foreign ships were forbidden to disembark at the port. (External irritants increased when the state of Massachusetts tested the legality of the Carolina code by attempting to send a free Negro citizen as an authorized agent to reside in Carolina.)

The feelings of ill-will were heightened with the slowly matur- ing belief that a revered way of life was being sold out by selfish, narrow interests in the nation. As recently as the War of 1812, the community had stood firmly for the Union and for preservation of the national honor (while New England shippers and manufac-

---

* The community report on this incident explained what was meant in this context by "classes": "Most of the black religious communities in this place, are divided into classes, over which a Leader is placed, having the confidence of the Pastor of the Church" (James Hamilton, Jr., *An Account of the Late Intended Insurrection among a Portion of the Blacks of This City* [2nd ed.; Charleston: A. E. Miller, 1822], p. 8).

turers had talked of states' rights and balked at facing the possible consequences of a naval war and blockade). But less than two decades later, sentiments had changed drastically. Cotton prices were declining, and rising tariffs boosted the cost of manufactured goods. The whole economy declined with cotton. This was not just because of high tariffs. The scramble for cheap and fertile lands had begun with the introduction of the cotton gin. Soil was used wastefully while men and families and slaves moved on for new lands in Alabama and Mississippi. One effort to recapture commerce for the tideland port was made by the community's merchants through the building of a railroad over one hundred miles into the interior from the port. But high national tariffs were the issue that brought about the test of the inherent rights of a state within the national community, dramatically revealed in the nullification controversy. Still, the small group who spoke for the people on this occasion were not unanimous toward nullification. One chronicler reported that everyone was a "State Rights" man, but some were for "Union State Rights" and were branded "submissionists." Men armed and drilled, preparing to meet the threat of enforcement by President Jackson; but an open clash was avoided by a compromise tariff bill in Congress.[37]

The events of these years of controversy and of increasing local solidarity continued the interplay of unity and separation. Following the nullification dispute, times were prosperous for the community: "Her cotton and rice were carried in ships owned at home, her importations came direct from Europe," wrote the chronicler. And the people became more committed than ever to their pattern for living: "It was a city of happy homes and cheerful intercourse. Relationships were many, friendships strong. A stranger . . . said, 'They were a high-minded, noble, generous people, confiding and confided in. . . .'"[38] But beneath the surface of this well-arranged, tidy, aristocratic society, all was not serene. A community leader had warned earlier that the winds of change were blowing sentiments of "numerous democracy" over broad reaches. In the national community, he declared, the state had no rights but what she was prepared to assert by force; thus, a people owning slaves would be mad if they did not hold their destinies in their own hands, he said. And it was not just the Yankees to the north who threatened, for this leader caught a scent that institutions based on slavery were being opposed over the entire world.[39]

Slavery *had* become a broad issue—not confined to political discussions in America over the opening of new western territories. A visitor from the West Indies was inspired to publish, in 1851, a poem about the scene of "Freedom's cutting whips . . . and chains":

> In well-adjusted lines her mansions rise,
> Where wealth and commerce meet the stranger's eyes,
> Here bland Religion fills her sober seat,
> And public buildings stand in gorgeous state.
>
> . . . .
>
> Here Liberty smiles like a new-dress'd bride,
> Equality, her handmaid, by her side!
> Their clubs of justice high in air they wield,
> Driving their human cattle to the field. . . .[40]

Under such attacks, not only did the shell of a society harden but an ideology was strung with myths and memories. Lines were being drawn: secessionists were countering with their view of the opposition. In 1850 one thundered: "The parties in this conflict are not merely abolitionists and slaveholders—they are atheists, socialists, communists, red republicans, jacobins on the one side, and the friends of order and regulated freedom on the other. In one word, the world is the battleground—Christianity and atheism the combatants; and the progress of humanity at stake."[41]

The struggle now shifted from a fight primarily for minority political rights in the nation to an effort to define a God-given mission of preserving a unique and "chosen" social order. The doctrine of purity of blood and race was invoked in the mythology which developed. The aspirants for property status searched their family trees for evidence of a noble strain. And as a representation in literature, the leading elements chose Sir Walter Scott whose gentle women and knightly men of novels like *Ivanhoe* reflected the image which the better families identified as their own.

The "providential trust" of slavery had fallen to the gentry and was not taken lightly by them. The daughter of a prosperous planter family described the responsibilities of her social position. She maintained that the Southern people had developed the poor

Negroes from a state of barbarism into a "useful, industrious, happy peasantry." And in attaining this result, she said, the heavy burden of responsibility fell on the master. This author reported her mother's reflections during the periodic trips the family took, in different seasons, attended by its servants: ". . . as she sat in the carriage . . . she could not but observe the careworn, serious faces of the gentlemen, while the coachmen and footmen were laughing and joking in careless glee with no heed for thought of the morrow." Both father and mother in her family had a strong interest in the religious training of the plantation people: "My mother had all the children brought up to her on Sunday morning and taught them the catechism, hymns, and prayers."[42]

The same author sketched a picture of the perfected arrangements of the better homes on the flat, narrow tideland peninsula— the setting which epitomized the old society: "Beautiful houses with equally beautiful furnishings and retinues of perfectly trained servants; high-bred horses and luxurious carriages; the occupants of these were usually clad in lute-string black silk dresses and shirred sun-bonnets." These fine clothes were made "with exquisite care and workmanship" by a slave member of the family, "trained from early girl hood for the post she was to fill for life and proud and happy in the perfection of her attainments."[43] On the eve of Fort Sumter, the well-bred young lady mused: "I believe that the moral emancipation of the colored race and the physical emancipation of the white race will be furthered by the present movement of the South—The South will soon be the only place for free white people and the only effectual Mission Station for the African."[44]

When war came, it concentrated the energies of the people for four years. It began with "Minutemen" wearing red flannel scarves, the grand show of a bombardment viewed from seaward piazzas, and colorful regiments forming to march away. It ended with shell-pocked houses, bushes as high as a man's head growing in the main streets, and personal sorrow in nearly every home. The community on the tidelands was center stage in the prelude of secession and the opening act of physical force. It remained active in minor scenes of blockade and bombardment during the war. And at the end it was the object of highest contempt shown by victorious Northern armies. An editorial in the *New York Times* in late 1864 said:

Sherman's soldiers are intensely anxious to be led into South Carolina. They are eager beyond measure to take a promenade through the Rattle-Snake State. We do not wonder at it. . . . South Carolina is the guiltiest . . . it was South Carolina that incited and forced other States to disunion; it was South Carolina that passed the first ordinance of secession; It was South Carolina that began the war.[45]

In his memoirs, Sherman reveals a letter from the Union Chief of Staff, General Halleck, in which the suggestion is made that it might be well if the coastal community were destroyed by accident, "and if a little salt could be sown upon its site, it may prevent the growth of future crops of nullification and secession." The field commander then advised General Halleck that he did not think salt was necessary, but assured him that the corps which he planned to place on his right wing in the drive northward would be equal to the task; for "if you have watched the history of that corps," Sherman wrote his superior "you will have remarked that they do their work pretty well."[46]

Actually, the community was spared the worst ravages inflicted by victorious troops on conquered towns and cities in the South. But the first postwar scenes revealed a setting that had been physically neglected as well as bombarded from the sea for most of four years. An eyewitness said: ". . . the whole white population was only a fraction of its usual size, while it swarmed with country negroes who had flocked in from surrounding plantations. . . ."[47] The plantations of the gentry were in disrepair and crops had not been harvested for several seasons. (Nearly one-fourth of the able-bodied white men from the state who went to war did not return.) The new freedmen heard of their emancipation and left the plantations for the city. A planter's young son later recalled: "Our servants were respectful and affectionate to the last, but they all announced that they were going. . . . the sight of the colored soldiers . . . as well as the visions of the joys of freedom held up to them, proved too strong a temptation." His genteel family found itself not only becoming destitute of property, but, for the first time "we found ourselves without servants."[48]

While the old planter gentry were seeing their "private order" shattered, their role in public affairs remained, at first, an active one. The state was required to adopt a new constitution, recognizing the Union and granting rights to the freedmen. But the state convention which met to consider these issues decided upon legislation for the control of the ignorant Negroes. A committee was appointed to prepare a code for the regulation, protection and government of the colored population. From these deliberations the "Black Code" was formulated—a natural expression of the will of people who valued order above all else, but a presumptuous slap at a national community embarking on a new experiment in equality. The code provided that persons of color were not entitled to social and political equality. But they were to have rights: to acquire, own, and dispose of property; to make contracts; to enjoy the products of their own labor; to sue and be sued; to receive protection under law in their persons and property. However, great discretion was to be permitted the courts in the disposition of colored people for the public good: an orphan colored child over age two, and colored children of paupers, vagrants and convicts, and all colored children "in danger of moral contamination," could be indentured as apprentices or servants up to age twenty-one (if male) and eighteen (if female). They would be taught the "business of husbandry or some useful trade."[49] The leading elements still hoped to hold together the fabric of their society. A planter war hero addressed himself to a group of freedmen at a public meeting in early 1867: "Last fall . . . I touched upon the duty of the whites toward the colored people, and I shall read to you what I said on that occasion. . . . 'As a slave he was faithful to us; as a freedman let us treat him as a friend. Deal with him frankly, justly, kindly, and my word for it he will reciprocate your kindness, clinging to his old home, his own country and his former master.' "[50]

National reactions to the Black Code brought on the heaviest consequences of Reconstruction. Congress and federal agents intervened. The Reconstruction Act of 1867 imposed military rule on the state. In 1868, a new constitution—modeled on that of Ohio —and a new governor were ushered in, and this time the gates to the "too numerous democracy" were opened wide. In effect, with Negro voter registration outnumbering white and with northern white opportunists flocking to the area, community leaders envisioned not merely Negro equality but Negro supremacy. Property qualifications for office-holding were abolished, representation in the legislature was reapportioned, and a system of universal public education was established. But most importantly, leaders in the rebellion were prohibited from holding office. This deprived a people who looked to the gentry for leadership of the one group among them who were schooled in the arts of politics. Not only were the gentry beset by private problems of declining fortunes, they were toppled from their public position.

Throughout the major years of Reconstruction the southern whites withdrew from legitimate participation within the framework of laws provided by the constitution of 1868. Their natural leaders had been constrained from participation. But in pride and humiliation, there was also tremendous reaction against joining affairs in an arena which had been captured from them. Only in South Carolina of all southern states did Negroes outnumber whites in the Reconstruction legislature. According to an account of 1874, of 124 men in the House of Representatives, only 23 were white—and these were "scalawags" (collaborators) and Carpetbaggers.[51] In the smaller towns, and in the hinterland, white groups formed outside the law to exert social control through terror and violence. An act of 1869 which created the state's National Guard was ignored by the whites; so the Guard became a colored force, further stigmatizing the hated controls of an imposed new order. The Negro had sinned in identifying with "outsiders."

The community of port and tideland—formerly the center of power and still symbol of tradition—seemed to be spared the most violent tempers of group and caste conflict generated in the malaise of post-Civil War circumstances. And like the gentry, its influence was abated. An observer wrote in 1874 that "the city proper is literally unrepresented in the politics of the State. Its vote is merged in that of the county. . . . The majority vote of the city is . . . extinguished in the preponderating numbers of the swamp negroes for thirty miles around, who choose the city's representatives."[52] The white population of the community retreated into its private worlds—many now forced to make a living at strange occupations—and with pride avoided the humiliations

that were everywhere at hand. But over one hundred miles away
the Reconstruction legislature held forth, while in backland towns
and rural areas the extralegal efforts of southern whites to exert
control and assert "justice" continued to mount.

The southern observer of 1874 gave this description of Reconstruction and the carpetbag legislature as seen through his eyes:
"It is a spectacle of a society suddenly turned bottomside up. . . .
In the place of the old aristocratic society stands the rude form
of the most ignorant democracy . . . mankind ever saw, invested
with the functions of government." A form of debate was carried
on in the legislative forum in which the new freedman was grop-
ing for his voice. Issues of Ku Klux Klan and free schools arose:
"Sambo can talk on these topics and those of a kindred character,
and their endless ramifications, day in and day out," wrote this
southern observer. "There is no end to his gush and babble. The
intellectual level is that of a bevy of fresh converts to a negro
camp-meeting." But even this observer sensed a certain dignity
to these proceedings, and saw an earnest purpose, "born of a conviction that their position and condition are not fully assured. . . .
The barbarous, animated jargon in which they so often indulge
is on occasion seen to be so transparently sincere and weighty in
their own minds that sympathy supplants disgust." A change must
come, he foresaw: "Is education the answer?" he asked. Yes, "but
what is education?" Will reading and writing and the alphabet
and multiplication table suffice to remedy the situation? "This is
all that compulsory education can give. . . . But here is a race
to be educated in the very elements of manhood. . . . The education they require is the formation of a race the opposite of the
existing race. . . . It is the reading and writing negroes," he concluded, "of the . . . Legislature who lead in its most infamous
venalities and corruptions."[53]

Change came in a dramatic contest for the governorship in
1876, "the memorable contest . . . resulting in the restoration to
power of the white race and the subversion of the rule of the
barbarian and the stranger."[54] Leadership in the counter-Re-
construction movement came from among the former planter-
gentry on the tidelands. The man who had pleaded ten years
earlier to both his former comrades-in-arms and his Negro
brethren for reciprocal respect and allegiance to the common soil,

organized a campaign that swept the state. He revived the white leadership that had shrunk from public affairs, put his "Red Shirt Riders" on the road in a crusade for "redemption," and urged the people to accept a contest within the laws that existed. After the election of 1876 there were two governors and two legislatures for a time, for neither Republican "outsiders" nor revived "insiders" were willing to accept a verdict of defeat. By that year, however, the nation had soured on the excesses of Reconstruction; and a Congressional board which mediated the election outcome declared, in effect, that Reconstruction was over and that government had returned to local hands.

The Black Codes did not return, but new statutes were enacted to repair the fabric of old institutions. A basic dilemma remained: torn fabric could not be restored to its former condition. Thus, a free public school system was retained, although now segregated by race, and property qualifications for voting and office holding were not reinstated. Before long some were to cry that the new governor and his Red Shirts redeemed the state from Negro misrule but not from "government by the people"—a strange doctrine brought "from regions beyond the Potomac and Ohio."[55] But whatever the change in political apparatus, the people who had participated in these traumatic events became even more attached to their pattern for a society and to dreams of how that society once had been.

The historian of the "mind of the South" wrote of the results of efforts by the Yankee to reshape this social order: ". . . far from having reconstructed the Southern mind . . . in its essential character, it was . . . [his] fate to have strengthened it almost beyond reckoning . . . to have made it . . . one of the least *reconstructible* ever developed."[56] Certainly the crowded peninsula of stately town houses with walled gardens, and the surrounding low country of avenues of live-oak with their clinging garlands of Spanish moss, held most firmly the memories of this mind.

The Finality of Names

The long history of the community on the tidelands could be carried through other chapters: economic recovery, growth of industry, the Great Depression. But let us move on to explore the statement about the "southern mind" in light of the physical, social, and cultural realities of this particular community. Let us pay particular attention to "cultural realities"—the realm of names and values which surround a people as they carry out their daily activities.

In a setting heavy with tradition and dedicated to orderliness, the *name* of something—person, family, group, even physical object—helps to locate and fix it in past, and for present and future, reference. The name tends to denote how and what something *is*—not how it may change or what it may become. When the better families began to search their family trees for noble blood they indicated that the era of "becoming" had ended on the tidelands. A society had been created, and its most privileged spokesmen justified their superior position on grounds of heredity. They had support in this from the people below them in the system. With the growing importance of cotton after 1800, those most ambitious to become men of property moved on to inland areas where land was cheap. The successful families in the coastal community became more firmly entrenched. Lesser families still did not challenge the prerogatives of their betters, and the Negro stood as a prop beneath all white men. Negroes, too, helped to harden the system as they sought an identity in the families they served. House servants made comparisons between the white families and felt superior or inferior to other slaves depending upon such things as the size of a master's home and the ornateness of his carriage.

After the Civil War there was an even stronger bond between all whites of whatever social rank. The camaraderie between leaders and followers during wartime carried over into civilian life. Reconstruction strengthened the bond, and it also gave all whites a common threat in the community: the Negro in process of "becoming." One authority points out that in this period southerners were bound more closely than ever in a "broad social sense": "public haughtiness" was receding while the "narrow private pride" of the old ruling class was enhanced.[57]

The belief in "race and blood" carried over persistently here long after other regions of the country were experiencing amalgamation of non-Anglo-Saxon ethnic strains. "In the name of our Anglo-Saxon race and blood" was a phrase often invoked by political leaders in Reconstruction days.[58] The existence of two great, visibly different groups influenced this belief. Other spokesmen echoed the faith through the years. 1874: ". . . the black is a child of vice and ignorance and superstition in South Carolina as well as in Africa. . . . Races of men exhibit the same general characteristics from age to age."[59] 1876: "The right of self-government is our heir-loom, the heir-loom of the Anglo-Saxon race in this country, and of no other race."[60] 1932: "One blessing slave emancipation brought to the white South. . . . It slowed down the tendency toward miscegenation. . . . since 1865 the mixing of pigments has greatly declined."[61] 1935: "Portugal began the slave trade . . . and imported so great a number . . . that she ruined her people. They became lazy and listless. . . . In the present day the Negro blood can be easily recognized among her people."[62]

What does this emphasis on inherent qualities mean when people identify themselves and others and react to these identifications?

One consequence is expressed in the sentence: "We Southerners are opposite to you Northerners in our feelings toward the Negroes: we love them as individuals and hate the group." The element of truth in this statement lies in the social circumstances within which people confront one another. As a "member" of a white family the Negro is loved for his particular qualities, usually identified with his personal warmth and loyalty. The group which is "hated" is that aggregate of colored people who represent a break with this pattern, and particularly those—symbolized today by formal leadership like the NAACP—who reject the Uncle Tom role. This group aspires to new identity as individuals and as representatives of all those who share their color and their history in America.

When representative people were interviewed in the community in recent years, the question of school integration was naturally vital. One society lady said: "I used to be just an American until Warren became a judge. Now I'm just a Southerner." The sensitivity to this issue made it difficult for outsiders to obtain information without triggering responses keyed to the one great issue of the day.

An Episcopal minister—a resident of some twenty-five years,

who described his church as the "Old Planter Church"— said that both whites and Negroes resented having the long-time "bond of love" between them broken by outside forces. He commented that something which could be called a "narrowing circle of exclusion" typified the community attitude to formal governmental authority. "People here defend the state to the federal government," he said, "will defend the county to the state, and would throw out the county to get local government." Apart from this proclivity, he thought that Negroes did not protest segregation as "outsiders" believed. "There are no minorities here," he said, "just two great groups. And now," he added, "each is competing to defend itself." He pointed out that the community had been a seat of tolerance of diverse groups in colonial times. But now all feelings were centered on maintaining a categorical place for those named "Negro" as a group. In the process, personal dialogues with individuals who could be "loved" had been greatly strained. "The old progress was slow," he said, "but it was on a human basis."

A director of community services pointed out that Negroes and whites had lived side-by-side on the peninsula for many generations. He said that complete segregation is maintained in the higher-income group, "except for servants." And in contrast to other perhaps more dynamic southern cities, where Negroes begin an upward climb by moving to a "low" white area, on the tideland peninsula the lowest-income groups also remained completely segregated in living arrangements. The living side-by-side occurred in the social middle. "The old people stay in the city while young couples move across the rivers to the suburbs," he said. And it was the older people of moderate means, remaining in homes owned by the family for generations, who kept their world of "names" properly arranged in the setting in which they lived.

The old homes had slave and servant quarters in the back; and now elderly widows often rented these facilities to Negroes. In their mental imagery of these situations, the elderly thought of the Negro tenants still as trusted servants. And it was true that a Negro tenant often did look out for an elderly person if she became sick, treating her with the deference due a mistress-of-the-house. A Catholic priest related this same situation to problems of caring for the aged. Medical-care plans posed a possible threat to the aged: for if public facilities were integrated, these people might find themselves being cared for in a hospital with integrated wards. In such a situation the illusion of the old relationship of mistress to servant would be shattered.

A Negro minister told how the colored population remained divided and without real leadership. He thought a part of this was a carryover from a time when house servants looked down on yard servants who, in turn, felt superior to field hands. But he agreed that both white and colored did not take readily to outside influences. "People here get to a certain point," he said; "they are on the verge of achieving something, and then there is a withdrawal." This man was not a native of the community (although native to the state) and considered himself somewhat an outsider; but he liked the community and wanted to continue his ministerial work. Ministers had the most success in leading, he said. But they had to contend with a highly divided colored population— the churches broken into many sects—and with the facts of little education and poverty. A major aspect of this educated Negro's church program was to provide guidance and tutelage to unschooled pastors in some of the small-sect churches. "If you don't know any better you go ahead and be happy," said the minister. But many Negroes who sought education and white-collar work left the community and journeyed north to crowded cities like New York.

It seemed that most of the colored people in the community had still not found a voice, except in a role carved many generations ago, only now more decorative than utilitarian. Interestingly, while Negro spokesmen complained of the divisions in the colored population which made leadership and concerted action difficult, many white leaders saw "just two great groups . . . each competing to defend itself." Some educated Negroes who were capable of dialogue were becoming voluntarily mute, fearful that things would get much worse rather than better if they expressed themselves. Partly because of this, it became apparent in interviews, leaders of both white and Negro were getting more and more distorted perceptions of what the other was thinking. Negro teachers and principals were particularly reticent to speak. They obviously had a stake in their schools as they were: but the fact

that some were interested in the NAACP indicated that they too
had visions of a different future.

A Negro lady who was president of a colored women's club
and who taught handicapped children felt called upon to defend
the NAACP. She said over and over: "It is not a Communist
organization,—the label the white community had put on the
organization. Negro teachers lost their jobs for belonging. And it
was difficult to persist in efforts to effect change—in public housing and recreation for low-income people, for example, for which
this lady had crusaded—when change was considered almost un-
American. In shoring up the old system, the community leadership
had backed away from an earlier plan to put a Negro on the
school board. At many other points of contact similar reactions
developed. The Negro clubwoman said: "In YWCA we used to
have race relations Sunday, the second Sunday in May. One year
services would be held in a white church with a colored minister;
the next year in a colored church with a white minister. That
stopped."

A tragedy of circumstances seemed to have arrested the re-
definition of names and the release of energies toward increased
dignity for all the people. But no one was crying "Race and
blood" as had been righteously intoned in the past. The tragedy
of the present was that few seemed to believe that a name can
denote only what something is and not what it may become.

The Separated and the Personalized

The physical and social conditions of the community of peninsula and lowland also serve to perpetuate the deposits left by
history. Cash has said of the South as a whole: ". . . the South
. . . was, before all else, personal . . ."; and of the Southerner:
". . . his world . . . remained always, in its basic aspect, a simple
aggregation of human units of self-contained and self-sufficient
entities. . . ."[63] From the days of the many "little worlds" of the
planter-barons to the present, the tendencies toward independence
of individuals, separation of their groupings, and the emphasis on
the personal have prevailed.

The plantation was a kind of communality which transcended

the separation between white and Negro. It was a private world where human relationships were highly personal. A part of this atmosphere is retained on old plantations that have been reclaimed and kept as show-pieces for outside visitors. A scion of a Huguenot family who returned after forty-four years to rebuild the old plantation still sensed there the climate of a separated little world. He wrote: "About a hundred Negroes, the descendants of slaves, live on the plantation with me. In their minds it is not my place; it is ours."[64]

But the outlying plantations retain functions largely as decorative museums; the city and its immediate environs are a growing center of trade and industry where over 200,000 people live, work, and carry on daily intercourse with one another. It is there that one looks for present-day ramifications of "separation" and "personal relationships."

A prominent businessman who had been active in local Community Chest matters pointed out that a Chest drive was never given a lot of support in the community. One reason seemed to be the lack of one outstanding leader such as other southern cities had where a tobacco baron or cottonmill heir led the drive for funds. Here there were only small companies. But in addition, the businessman said, people were used to giving and helping others on a personal basis. Something like Community Chest just did not reach home: did not tap basic loyalties to family, clan, and friends. Business and industry, even when staffed at higher echelons by newcomers, reflected the emphasis on the atmosphere of a "family." The old scion of a plantation provided a description of a cottonseed-oil mill where four hundred Negro men were supervised by a white superintendent. He saw informality and lack of conflict between whites and Negroes on the job, since the work setting was an extension of traditional relationship patterns. "Everywhere," he wrote in 1947, "there seems to be . . . often a human sympathy and mutual regard deepening into affection."[65]

A business executive whose company employed both white and Negro workers said that he was well satisfied with his labor force and that even the large numbers moving in from rural areas made good workers once they were trained. "They learn rapidly," he said. "The people may not have roots in the community but they are rooted in the customs of the South." One of the strongest of these customs was the persistence of paternal feelings between employer and employee.

One consequence of the maintenance of miniature, personalized communities in industry was that unions were relegated to a minor role. There were a few all-Negro unions among unskilled workers, and one company had a union that was almost all white. But since the national policies of unions were toward integration, thus far they had difficulty in creating acceptable work settings that cut across color lines. Businessmen had accomplished this by permitting human relationships in the plant to be a microcosm of traditional patterns in the larger society. An interview with the business manager of a local for skilled building trades was enlightening. (Business people were at a loss to recommend a labor leader who could explain the nature and extent of union organization in the community.) The interviewer's notes reveal her impressions. She wrote: "The building where the offices of the local were located was in disrepair. There was no directory of offices, and from downstairs the place looked unused and empty. I walked along dirty cement stairs, heavy with the smell of urine, to some shabby offices where men in work clothes waited in crowded hallways. Mr.—— was sitting in a non-airconditioned cubbyhole of a room with paint flaking off the walls." Granted that the world of the workingman's union is not that of young-lady researchers, the impressions are those of someone who had talked to union people in other communities, and found other settings. It appeared that organized labor, with its contracts, and appealing to loyalties of a type that had not yet come to represent a "family" of interests, was kept in a category of minor influence.

The question of child neglect was explored throughout this community. Many of these cases were handled privately. For example, a dependent family would be known to their minister or to friends who referred them to a minister. A Baptist minister reported that he always referred such cases to one of the Baptist institutions known to him. The Episcopal minister immediately mentioned the institution of his denomination, whose director he could call on the phone and talk to personally. And so the pattern was repeated with other informants throughout the community. The emphasis on institutions was also revealing: it indicated an effort was made to surround the child who had to leave his parental home with another "little world"—something like an extended family composed of people of similar upbringing. Thus, the emphasis in welfare programs was on the private, and on the separated and the personalized. The traditional separation of white and Negro was maintained, but there were also separate institutions for Episcopalians, Presbyterians, Methodists, Baptists, and Catholics.

The judge of the Domestic Relations Court described his functions in this community where pressures toward impersonality and specialization were strongly resisted. His functions were not always clearly spelled out by code and statute. But the judge approached his job with that touch of personal feeling that seems to defy psychological inroads of urbanism and industrialism. He would prefer to have more ready access to psychological and psychiatric services. However, when advice on these matters is pressing, he explained, "I call a friend who is a psychiatrist for an immediate diagnosis." The children and the families were not just numbers in a file of cases to the judge. Each year he visited each institution in the state to which children were committed by the court. "I try to see the children and let them know we care about them and haven't forgotten them," he said. "I'll never forget them flocking around me and clinging to my hand."

Perhaps it cannot be expected that highly personal feelings can reach across all the relationships between individuals and groups in a community grown so large. It has been pointed out that the "bond of love" between white and Negro described by many people was predicated on the drawing of familylike circles around members of both major population segments. And these circles only encompassed such bonds when each participant seemed to accept the role prescribed for him in the mythology of community life. But in industry, in churches, in schools, in most areas of civic life, the trend was in the opposite direction: toward what the Episcopal minister described as the crystallization of two great groups, each competing to defend itself.

In this situation the tendency for social perceptions to be completely confined within color lines becomes even more dominant. In the distant past, slaves evaluated their worth in comparison to other slaves on the basis of the affluence of their respective masters. A carryover of this tendency appears today in other class divisions among the Negroes. Informants among the whites pointed out that lightness of skin is a strong determinant of status among the community's colored population. An educator said that the lighter-skinned Negroes generally have the better jobs. Certain higher-toned churches, it was said, were attended only by those with lighter skin. How pervasive these standards are, and how important they remain, was not ascertained. But a significant fact stood out: the lightness-of-skin criterion did *not* hold firmly as a characteristic of present Negro leadership among the professionals in schools and churches. Education seemed to be replacing older criteria with new, which could be *achieved* by people aspiring to become something different.

Separation of groups, and their insulation from one another, was not new or very different from the self-sufficient independence stressed by families for many generations on the tidelands. But the Great Separation in this society was categorical and assumed an irrevocably divided world. When white professional people spoke of the "status" of the Negro teacher or other professional they invariably implied that this status was considered *within* the Negro group. "The Negro educator who has an income of five thousand dollars," said one, "is on an economic par with a white person making eight or nine thousand. And socially he is much higher." A Negro educator said: "We have about ten that we could call wealthy. We have two contractors, one real estate man, three doctors. Just about all that is open for one of our college graduates is the teaching profession." The terms "we" and "they" come easily in conversation with both Negro and white citizen leaders.

The extremes of the Great Separation seem most apparent in realms where personal relationships also undergo stress: in the public settings of a growing city. Where the contractual aspects of urban life threaten to make inroads, the visible symbols of "separation" are kept intact. Recently a study sponsored by the National Urban League showed that whereas Negro store- and shop-owners once had clientele among both white and colored, now their business was almost completely confined to Negro patrons, as the old order reacted to threatening change.[66] For the market place tends to be indifferent to the characteristics ascribed to the person who brings his wares to it. Thus, the urban setting may replace personal relationships with contractual ones and perhaps tend to make the individual a mere commodity, but the processes operating within it are a natural threat not only to the old human ties of an agrarian society but to assumptions of inequality.

A story told by one of the researchers who spent some months in the community illustrates how situations of daily living maintain the assumptions people have about their social world and the "others" in it. This young lady from the West gathered information for several weeks in a public social-service agency, enjoying the friendliness of new professional associates. There was a relaxed quality to human relationships in a work setting that she had not experienced elsewhere. One day a door to an adjacent office room that had always been closed was left ajar. Through the doorway she saw a room filled solely with Negro professional workers.

This open door brought home suddenly to a newcomer the fact of the Great Separation and its pervading insulations even in this friendly society.

Phantoms of Permanence and Change

A dreamlike quality pervades much of life in the tideland community. In part, this is a continuation of the romanticism that has flavored human relationships here. Local authors stress the theme of continuity: the pace of life indicates that people here are in no great rush to go anywhere because they are where they want to be; they are home. It does seem that this atmosphere captures newcomers—who are settling here in some numbers—far more than these newcomers change or reshape the community.

In the permanent there is still much that is largely decorative. In this century many Negroes have become, in a sense, decorations for the community—not just for tourists, but most significantly for the white citizens themselves. One local author described the beauty she saw in the traditional daily rounds of a simple Negro girl, whose conversations with her friends were also a delight to the ear: " 'I done bin gone and I come back. . . . I don' like it up dere. . . . I suits dis place cause it don't change none.' " To which the author commented: "Of course it had not changed!

Rebecca could . . . ring the same doorbells and sell her poor vegetables to the same families that she had known as a little barefoot girl. . . . These . . . streets were the only life she knew, and they satisfied that craving for the continuity of human experience."[67] Another local writer, Dubose Heyward, who immortalized the waterfront Negro in novel and play, said: "We have forgotten that there can be such a thing as pride of caste among the lowly; that there could exist in a man who had been born a servant and expected to die a servant, a self respect equally as great and as jealously guarded as that enjoyed by the master. . . ."[68]

Still, in 1880 the Negro population was 60 per cent of the total, while in 1950 it had diminished to 38 per cent and in 1960 was 36 per cent. Industry had come to the community but it had no place for the Negro except in menial jobs, and training facilities were lacking. While brochures from the Chamber of Commerce were inviting industry by advertising that the state's population was 99.6 per cent American-born and capable of rapid adjustment to new skills, a U.S. Employment Service survey was showing 77.8 per cent of the colored population "unskilled" and 14 per cent service workers.[69]

In 1945, a committee of colored citizens was formed to investigate community recreation facilities. After a few months, the committee prepared this statement when the members tendered their resignations: ". . . we are forced to admit that no constructive work has been or is being done. . . . In fact the facilities for Negroes have constantly receded . . . until they are now at a negative stage. . . . Because we have been forced to give vague promises for a still distant future, we now stand in bad light before our own people. . . ."[70] The following year, the white citizens took over a Negro park for the use of a circus that came to town. Signs were posted saying "WHITE ONLY" and a particular day was set aside for Negroes to attend. A report by a Negro group said: "The colored citizens displayed a cooperative spirit among themselves seldom witnessed in this city. Not one of them attended the show even after children were offered free admission in the afternoon. The show found it profitable to close down before 9:00 P.M. because of no business."[71]

Internal to the community *are* the strong attractions of feelings that this is "home." But a social system exists within larger systems which exert influence in subtle ways. A Catholic priest told an interviewer: "There are two factions here among the colored people. The oldtimers pound it into the youth to submit, to show deference to the whites and get ahead. But the younger ones are rebelling against 'yes, suh; no suh' and want to break away." Thirty-five out of forty graduates of the Catholic Negro high school the previous year had migrated to the North.

The pattern is the same in the public high school for colored children and is being compounded year by year, generation by generation. The principal said that almost 50 per cent of the high school children live with grandparents. "We ask the child, 'Why don't you pay for your books?' [the principal explained] and he says, 'Wait until my mother sends money from New York.'" And the exodus from the high school to New York continues every year. The principal said: "They have read and heard about the unlimited freedom and they want to go up and enjoy it. I meet them on trips I take, in Harlem or downtown. The majority are doing factory work. They make a lot there but aren't able to save it. They come back home here for Christmas or summers."

The problems of these restless ones are the problems endemic to the American social milieu. The uprooted join the mainstream pursuing identity and achievement. But as part of a visible segment, their problems may be accentuated in crowded, history-less settings. Accepting, in new arenas, an identification of interests with others whose problems they share, they join the groups fighting to be heard, to be permitted opportunity.

The tideland community does not see many struggles of these kinds. It modulates them. The restless energies from the colored segment of population are drained off, while the unskilled and the service workers remain to decorate, with their presence, the streets of the history-shrouded peninsula and the better homes in which they serve. A lady in one of the fine old homes near the battery spoke of her domestic help: "My Sally is seventy years old. She is supposed to come at three o'clock but now she comes at three forty-five. She does not do a lot—keeps an eye on the kids and keeps them from murdering one another. She has been with us so long she practically runs me." For both this white family and their servants there is a stability that remains insulated from change in the community.

The more "restless" white populations are congregated at the north end of town and in the suburbs. Most of the industry is in the north area. Many residents there are employed by the federal government, largely by Naval, Air Force, and Marine Services. Many are newcomers: construction workers and service personnel. Whereas in central areas of the city the proportion of Negro to white in the separated public schools is over 2 to 1, in the north area the proportions are reversed. The public school system is supported by this white population infused with newcomers. More and more of the offspring of skilled workers now attempt to go to college. And an active PTA in this north area is helping to send children to college, as are some of the business concerns by giving scholarships to the children of employees.

But in the suburbs across the rivers—where the young descendants of better community families move to build their new, picture-window homes—restless energies are rare. There is insulation from problems of the community here too, as in the walled homes near the battery. The insulation is not very different from that of suburbia anywhere in America. However, the shrines of history are close and available to help suburbanites to remember who they are. Public schools in the suburbs are poorly attended. Parents send their children into the city to private schools. And the ancestral churches on the crowded peninsula are still the churches of these suburban families—just as they were attended by many planters long ago who journeyed downriver each Sunday morning.

It seems that most significantly the central area performs a symbolic function: It cradles the institutions that have been nurtured and mellowed through time. It keeps fixed in proper arrangement—in the private worlds near the battery, in the public realm for all who participate in it—the relationships between groups and individuals that history and ideology have made sacrosanct. But behind the scenes, the undramatic changes—the reluctant exodus of better-educated Negroes, the growing importance of public schools for socially "unanchored" whites—move slowly, subtly . . . like the tides.

Property on the tidelands provided a means for the individual to achieve an identity while maintaining a stake in his community.

This concept need not be limited to communities anchored in the past. The fact that property in slaves is no longer possible has not abrogated the value of the concept of property. Nor has the diminishing availability of land dictated that now only the very few can be "men of property." What seems urgent is an extension of the concept. A nation seeking answers to problems of individual dignity in the midst of overorganization and conformity can ill-afford to give up a frame of values that has provided energies for attacking new frontiers. The investment in and for self by an individual can take many forms, some less tangible than land or merchandise. It can take the form of any talent which truly individuates the person. And when this "property"—an extension of the human personality—is not merely traded and sold as a commodity, it too gives the individual a responsible stake in his community.

On the tidelands, men of property came to make the plantation, and released energies that helped to carry a people across a continent. Their experience will be invaluable in the further explorations of the American experiment.

3

Plateau of the Conquistadores: Sante Fe

*Ascending a table ridge we spied in an extended
valley to the northwest occasional groups of trees,
skirted with verdant corn and wheat fields, with here
and there a square block-like protuberance reared
in the midst. . . . [A] friend at my elbow said, "It
is true those are heaps of unburnt bricks, nevertheless they are houses—this is the city. . . ."*
—Missouri Traders in the Spanish Southwest, 1831[1]

Golden Pathways

Once the Appalachians were crossed and new farm lands claimed
by settlers in some numbers, restless Anglo traders pressed westward. Zebulon Pike had stumbled into strange lands in the
southern Rockies in the first decade of the nineteenth century
while exploring the territory of the Louisiana Purchase. And the
news he brought coincided with the quest of those decades.

New Mexico had gold and silver from its mines to pay for
Yankee goods; and it had furs and pelts to sell—brought down out
of the mountains by a wild and mixed breed of trappers who had
entered the wilderness far ahead of the traders and the homesteaders. In 1822, at about the time the Spanish in the New World
were proclaiming independence from Old Spain, a successful sale
of a caravan-load of cheap calicoes and cottons by an Anglo
merchant excited interest at both ends of the plains. The Missouri
trader ventured west and south. The Spanish trader turned his
attention away from a long route south to Vera Cruz and toward
the shorter overland route to eastern markets—to new and strange

encounters with a people who left history behind as they journeyed west.

Several centuries of history had passed before "American culture" made an appearance at this southern base of the Rockies. By the time of these new meetings, the Spaniard of New Mexico had enclosed himself in traditions of his own.

From regions in northern Mexico, the land further north had appeared arid and limitless, yet beckoning, to the Spanish Conquerors of the sixteenth century. However, the natives were not the most reliable guides. On one journey a Spanish friar reported seeing from afar the fabled golden city of Cibola. "It appears to be a very beautiful city," he reported, "the finest that I have seen in these parts. . . . It is bigger than the City of Mexico."[2] The friar's reputation was not improved with the discovery by Coronado the following year that Cibola was only an Indian village. Still, even the great Coronado was enticed by the Indians to search for gold on a distant horizon away from the immediate world of the little adobe settlements—a trek which led him as far north as the plains of Kansas and Nebraska.

But other explorers from the south made a more lasting imprint along the trail that followed the valley of the Great River flowing down from the northern plateaus. By the beginning of the seventeenth century the Spanish had established small settlements in the valley, and the route of the Conquistadores was becoming a "Royal Road" for commerce. At the northern end of that road, in the first decade of the seventeenth century, a community was established by royal decree. Perched at the base of high mountains, on a sloping shelf rising gently eastward from the Rio Grande, the new capital of the northern provinces of Spain in the Americas was both a symbol of the order which Spanish institutions attempted to bring to primitive lands and a meeting place and terminus. Here the Spanish conquest receded from the mountains, visions of cities filled with treasures dimmed, leaving only outposts in the high Rockies beyond. Here mineral wealth of the province was collected for shipment south along the Turquoise trail through Mexico City to the port of Vera Cruz—two thousand miles and over a half year away from the isolated northern capital. Here, in the late eighteenth century, the Spanish Trail to the little mission settlements of California began. And here, finally, Anglo-America met New Spain, many years after both these European traditions had confronted the challenge of nature in the New World and had met the native inhabitants of the continent.

The commerce of the prairies that flourished for over fifty years brought contacts and, eventually, the political conquest of one tradition by the other. But it also promoted the continued division of segments of population in the community at the base of the mountains.

A Setting for Encounters

A present-day chronicler has said of the community of sun-burned adobe that even in its fourth century it remained a city of arrivals. He explained: "Many of those arriving stayed to contribute their special purposes to the . . . society . . . there. Many moved on. . . . And some . . . often went and returned. . . ."³ The paths that led to this remote community provided opportunities for people to pass through and observe, and for others to pause and participate. The commerce on these paths also supported the family life which became identified through four centuries with individual adobe dwellings. Within these dwellings the Spanish families preserved their memories and their pride in traditions passed from generation to generation. Thus, said the chronicler, ". . . the streets . . . showed in the disposition of their houses how strong was the Spaniard's desire for isolation and privacy."⁴ But outside the adobe walls were the plaza and the public settings where, through the years, groups met under circumstances that perpetuated a gulf between different traditions.

When the new capital of the northern province was established by the Spanish at the beginning of the seventeenth century, all manner of preliminary specifications for the community were set down. The dimensions of the plaza, location of church and public buildings, number and direction of the streets, distance between defense wall and nearest houses, number, rank, and powers of the governing officials, "and even the minimum number of married men allowed to form a new colony," were contained in the plans for the city.⁵ The formal arrangements of a way of life were transplanted from the Old World to the New. There was an order providing a place for everything. This order largely determined the proper public relationships between community participants.

The northern province was considered by both the king of Spain and the viceroy of Mexico primarily as a mission field. The Spanish community established in the midst of tribes of house-dwelling Pueblos and warlike Apaches was a symbol of the strength and unity of the institutions of an Old World people. The initial meetings of the Spanish with the Indian thus occurred in a setting which expressed the unity of a culture that had come to "civilize" diverse and divided tribes of primitives. An early Father Custodian described for his king the social order of the seventeenth century developing in the community. Already there was evidence (in his reference to "half-breeds") that even the most integrated of cultures was being affected by this meeting of peoples:

All the soldiers are well taught in religious matters, are humble, and for the most part are a good example to the Indian. . . . The Spaniards must have some seven hundred servants; so that between the Spaniards, the half-breeds, and the Indians, there must be a thousand souls. . . . And these folk are so promptly obedient to their governing authorities, that, to whatsoever trouble comes up, they sally forth with their weapons and horses at their own cost and do valorous deeds.

The Custodian had taken on as his primary task the building of a church and monastery. "There," he said, ". . . the Fathers teach both Spaniards and Indians to read and write, to play instruments and sing, and all civilized matters."[6]

This social order soon began to show signs of internal conflict. A controversy developed among the Spanish in mid-seventeenth century, bringing troubles which finally forced them from the province and their capital for a time. The jurisdictions of religious and secular authorities overlapped. Problems of jurisdiction could not be settled easily by outside authorities because of the isolation of the province and its relative autonomy. The Pueblo Indians found themselves with two masters who were at loggerheads. A Spanish Governor of this period openly disregarded many religious formalities and implanted disrespect for the missionaries in the hearts of the Indians. Historian Cleve Hallenbeck wrote: "He believed that the Indians should be permitted to hold their tribal dances; and to see . . . whether such were idolatrous, he had the Indians of the nearest pueblo . . . stage one of their dances on the plaza . . . while he looked on. He declared that the dance was harmless . . . and added, 'and but for the fact I am the governor, I would go out and dance with them.' "[7] After this, the Pueblo Indians staged dances in defiance of the friars, although they continued to attend Mass and believed themselves to be good Christians. The governor added more fuel to dissent by holding hearings for all Indians having grievances against the friars.

In the last decades of the seventeenth century the warlike Apaches attacked and destroyed many pueblos. A Spanish citizen reported: "The whole land is at war with the widespread heathen nations of Apache Indians, who kill all the Christian Indians they can find. . . . No road is safe; everyone travels at the risk of his life."[8] The Spanish tried to provide protection for the pueblos. But discontent rose in the pueblos too as Apache raids continued. Finally, in 1680, the Pueblo tribes organized *their* opposition to the Spanish and forced a retreat southward down the Rio Grande Valley.

As the countryside was devastated and depopulated, the symbols of the superiority of the former conquerors were destroyed by the Indians who had faced the Spanish across a separating gulf during the encounters of the first one hundred years of Spanish colonization. The Christian God was declared killed, and the Indian leader of the revolt proclaimed that "he had slain Mary and Jesus, and had erected a great wall between heaven and earth that would in the future keep out all of the white race."[9] In the funeral oration for the martyrs killed in the Indian revolt, a church father expressed clearly the division between peoples which had continued throughout the century of contact and issued in violent conflict: "If the hatred of the conspirators distinguished as to persons, they would only kill those whom they dislike; executing their intention on some and not on others. But they did not hate the individual, but only the Christian. . . . their mad action came from a hatred of the Religion."

Looking back at this violent attack on institutions transplanted to a new soil, and anticipating a return to the scene of the initial failures, the greatest wish was for a re-establishment and a more complete achievement in "cities of men" in the New World of that wholeness and integration that his religion offered to all men in its "city of God." He concluded: "Oh! that they would return to the unity of the church, so that with us they may enjoy not only that which they call theirs, but also that which is called ours, but yet is not so, because we have no ownership in anything."[10]

The basis for a more viable human community on the northern plateau was available when the Spanish returned there in a few years. This is manifest in the recorded fact that many "Mexican-Indian" servants to the Spanish of the community escaped to the south with their masters. A century in New Mexico had begun to transform the culture of Old Spain; and a century of contact had also not been without effect on the peoples who were the original squatters on the land.

The traders from Missouri who discovered the markets just beyond the prairies also encountered a strange culture there. One of them gave this early impression of the community at the end of the overland trail: "The arrival of a caravan . . . changes the aspect of the place at once. Instead of the idleness and stagnation which its streets exhibited before, one now sees everywhere the bustle, noise and activity of a lively market town."[11] Negotiations were mostly in Spanish, and these first meetings between the two cultures did not place the Spanish-speaking traders at a disadvantage or in the position of "inferior." They were meetings in a formal, business setting in which each party had a mutual interest in the conduct of negotiations. This mutual interest provided at least a partial bridge between contrasting cultures, transforming (in the eyes of the Anglo) "idleness and stagnation" into more acceptable "bustle, noise and activity." In spite of their isolation, the New Mexicans were more eager for trade than any other people in Spain's colonial empire.[12] Often neglected by the mother country and her representatives in the southern province, the northern province was thrown on its own meager resources for protection. When Mexican Independence was proclaimed in 1821 the news was welcomed in New Mexico. But recurring revolutions in Mexico City in the following decades were a source of constant tension in the province. One chronicler maintains that New Mexico "cared little who governed her provided only she could obtain protection and pay no more than her share of taxes."[13] The coming of the Anglos offered another opportunity for trade and for new contacts by a people who, actually, had never retained close ties with countrymen to the south.

The "lively market town" at the base of the mountains was the largest population center in Spain's northern province. Throughout the eighteenth century the bulk of population in the province was scattered in "loosely-compacted" clusters of from fifty to five hundred persons each.[14] Zebulon Pike brought back impressions of "quaint" living arrangements that characterized early Anglo perceptions of the Spanish Southwest. In 1807, he described the community (where he was brought under guard after blundering into Spanish territory), comparing the appearance of the dwellings seen from a distance to a fleet of flat-boats on the Ohio.[15] The more sophisticated Anglo-American encountered here another people who had performed remarkable feats of adaptation to the forces of nature. Other Anglos, viewing this unfamiliar sideshow of North American history, commented on its "strangeness." One of the first traders on the overland trail (in 1824) expressed surprise at the appearance of the New Mexicans. He said: "The alcalde . . . was a man of a swarthy complexion, having the appearance of the pride and haughtiness. . . . I had expected to find no difference between these people and our own but their language. I was never so mistaken." But once the façade of outward appearances was penetrated, the trader found human qualities he deemed admirable. He said: "Although appearing . . . poorly . . . [the women] are not destitute of hospitality; for they brought us food, and invited us into their houses to eat, as we walked through the streets."[16]

The Missouri trader who gave the most complete account of his experiences in northern Mexico expressed vivid impressions when he made inferences of social and psychological characteristics. "The New Mexicans appear to have inherited much of the cruelty and intolerance of their ancestors," he said, "and no small portion of their bigotry and fanaticism. . . . Systematically cringing and subservient while out of power, as soon as the august mantle of authority falls upon their shoulders, there are but little bounds to their arrogance and vindictiveness of spirit." Having described the whole group, the Missourian then left room for individual differences and acknowledged "that there are to be found among them numerous instances of uncompromising virtues, good faith and religious forbearance."[17] And there was a note of enchantment in descriptions of customs the Missouri trader observed; like the public observance of vespers at the close of twilight when the village bell pealed for *la oracion:* "All conversation is instantly suspended—all labor ceases—people of all classes, whether on foot or on horseback, make a sudden halt. . . . At the expiration of about two minutes the charm is suddenly broken by the clatter of livelier-toned bells; and a *'Buenas Tardes'* . . . to those present, closes the ceremony."[18]

Other social and religious customs were more alarming to men of Anglo upbringing. The trader noted that gambling and dancing were extremely popular, and it was hard for him to comprehend a people who went so easily from their churches to cock fights in the public square. "But what most oddly greets and outrages most Protestant ears," he said, "is the accompaniment of divine service with the very same instruments, and often with the same tunes" that were played for dances and other festivities.[19]

Anglo contacts increased rapidly as an impatient nation pushed its borders across a continent, sending out its "scouts" and "skirmishers" in the persons of trappers and miners, traders and homesteaders. In two decades the yearly volume of wagons making the trading haul across the plains to New Mexico increased nearly tenfold. The governor of that province began to levy a heavy tax on American wagons. The Americans believed that they, of all foreigners, suffered most from maladministration of justice because of the feelings with which this rival republic viewed "the advancement and superiority of her more industrious neighbors." It appeared to these men that even the English were preferred, and Americans were taunted about the "effeminacy of their government and its want of decision."[20] The open conflict between representatives of the two major occupants of territory in midcontinent had already boiled over in Texas. Next it came to New Mexico; and the form of its coming symbolized a pattern of social accommodation which had already begun and which continued to persist in this region.

When the American General Kearney, who had set out from Fort Leavenworth with a force composed largely of Missouri recruits, raised the American flag over the capital of the northern

contact and polarization the "organic" relationship between the divided segments (whereby each tended to accept clear obligations as well as rights *vis-à-vis* the other) was weakened and strained. Perhaps it is significant that such a society also emphasized the division between "public" affairs and "private"—an insulation which continues to the present day.

An early basis for distinguishing segments within the society was the ownership—or at least the occupation for the Crown—of land. A description of this underpinning of the social system suggests the condition that promoted feelings of mutual obligation between population segments:

A hacienda was a landed estate with definite boundaries: it was owned by its proprietor or *hacendado,* while the lands used by the ranchero (ranchman) belonged to all in common, or, perhaps more accurately, belonged to the Crown and was used by all in common. The *hacendados* and rancheros formed the landed aristocracy of the province.[32]

Thus, the Spanish developed a society in which the few were landowners. It was a society which stressed inheritance: of land and wealth and family name, and of one's station in life.

Here were conditions for a stable society, its people unified in their inequality around the symbols of the Crown and the church. A member of an old hacendado family has reflected on the mission of her family as it settled a fertile New Mexico valley: ". . . another family to help, by means of bloody battle and peaceful law, to bring civilization to wilderness—another family to help adapt the old customs of Spain to a new land, adding something to the heritage of the Spanish Conquistadores who came before them."[33] When such families kept Indian servants as slaves, it was in her view another expression of a natural relationship in "bringing civilization to wilderness."

Even apart from the ranchos and haciendas where the social segments were encompassed within a near-family relationship, village settlements were small and each community with its standard arrangement of church, plaza, and public buildings maintained the symbols of an ordered society. Free emigration to the new colony from Spain was not permitted by the Crown.

Thus, New Mexico communities were not subjected to the constant pressures of new population elements. They did not develop institutions of popular education to promote social mobility. Instead, education revolved around the church where, as the seventeenth-century Custodian described, both Spaniards and Indians were taught "to read and write, to play instruments and sing, and all civilized matters."

In the contacts with "uncivilized" aborigines, however, the gulf between population segments was extended, and the category of *pobre* and servant was pushed toward the category of slave. This occurred in those contacts where open conflict and war resulted, from which captive Indians often became slaves. Rather than providing another segment at the bottom of the system, which might give incentive and greater "dignity" to a middle-class group in-between, the institution of slavery as practiced in New Mexico tended to pull other unprivileged persons into the category of "slave." By the time the Anglo arrived on the scene the system of peonage was long established. Perhaps side-by-side with it had grown that apparent "harshness" in the public character of the man of privilege which the Anglo perceived in observing relationships of the *ricos* with *pobres* and, sometimes, with "outsiders."

The American frontiersmen who came to trade in the community continually expressed amazement at the class distinctions they encountered there. Those who left a record of their impressions always spoke of "class" and "classes of people," and they usually lumped these classes into "rich" and "poor," or "wealthy" and "lower classes"—the *ricos* and the *pobres* to which the New Mexicans often referred in their own vocabulary.

The frontiersman was sensitive to manifestations of social inequality. He reported on strange practices: ". . . the ratio of respect is generally indicated by the width of the left margin [on a letter]," one wrote. "If the letter is addressed to an equal, about one-fourth of the page is occupied for that purpose; but when extraordinary respect is intended to be shown to a superior, nearly one-half of the page is left blank." He observed: "There are other marks of civility and respect peculiar to the country, which among us would be accounted absolute servility." Among these he included the "abject idolatry" of the "worship of men in the capacity of religious rulers." He concluded that servility toward the church was only another expression of the willingness of one class of people to show obeisance to another: "The slavish obsequiousness of the lower classes toward these pampered priests is almost incredible."[34]

Of all the indications of a socially divided society the midwestern Anglo observed, the practice of peonage was most reprehensible. Where a servant had contracted a debt from his master he was required to work out this debt. Debts easily accrued to *pobres* who purchased their clothing and necessities from the master out of slim wages. Often wages were owed for a year or two in advance. Only by engaging a new master to pay his debt for him could the peon change his condition of servitude —and then he merely exchanged one master for another. Indian prisoners from wars or slave-catching raids increased the numbers of peons to the hundreds. They became so numerous that each was assigned a special task as servant to the *rico*.[35] The Anglo trader saw the condition of these "unfortunate poor" as "little better, if not worse, indeed, than that of the slaves of our South." He said, "they labor for fixed wages, it is true; but all they can earn is not sufficient to keep them in the coarsest clothing and pay their contingent expenses."

The jailing of debtors operated only upon the "unfortunate poor" and not upon the "higher classes." Thus, the administration of justice was also manifestly unequal and seemed to the Anglo to perpetuate and accentuate the intolerables of a divided society. It was common practice, the trader observed, to "soften the claws of the alcalde with a 'silver unction'"; and it was "easy to perceive . . . that the poor and the humble stand no chance in a judicial contest with the wealthy and consequential" who not only could corrupt the court but had influence enough in this society to neutralize testimony brought against them.[36]

In spite of these conditions, the trader as well as other travelers from across the prairies still noted the apparent "unfailing happiness" of the *pobres*. This remained a continuing enigma to men from the East who had never experienced unity around symbols which proclaimed inequality.

The new governor who arrived after American occupation addressed himself to the problems of poverty and inequality. In his first address to the Legislative Assembly he recommended "that the property of the poor . . . be exempted from sale under execution for all debts that may hereafter be created."[37] Well-meaning Anglos attacked the "inhumanities" of the old system which they had observed from the outside; but as participants in the new social system, they both borrowed from the older patterns and furthered the continuance of a "divided society."

From the outside, the Anglos had always felt superior to all classes of "Mexicans," sometimes referring to them as "greasers." Texans, in their contacts in the Southwest, used the term "Mexican" with insulting connotations. The Spanish-speaking inhabitants of New Mexico identified this term with the superior airs of outsiders whom they outnumbered 65 to 1 in the Territory in 1848. Whatever the inequalities accepted within their own society, the New Mexicans were unified in their pride as a Spanish-speaking people with a revered heritage in the New World. In the new dramas of politics and business which began after American annexation—now within an atmosphere that was supposed to stress equality of persons—the label "Mexican" was rejected by the Spanish-speaking. They caught the spirit of a system which proclaimed equality, and asserted to the new political leaders: "We are all Americans." But since distinctions in appearance and language were the distinguishing features of the new division of a society, they then asserted: "You are Anglo-Americans and we are Spanish-Americans."

Ambitious men from the Anglo East began to use the term "Spanish" in their public efforts to flatter the new citizens. And the distinction of "Anglo" and "Spanish" became the new polarity toward which the community gravitated as the Anglo population expanded.

Indian wars in the Southwest entailed the expenditure of large sums of money by the United States government and brought many soldiers and government officials to New Mexico. Roads were surveyed and opened; army posts were built. The stage coach and later the railroads brought opportunists and adventurers into the territory. The term "new-fledged citizens" was used often in newspaper accounts of the 1850s in reporting on activities of newcomers. These reports were carried by papers that were established and staffed by these newcomers. While

for its solitude while commuting from the local airport to businesses in oil and uranium fields. The doctor's wife was a lifetime resident in the community and was also concerned about the lack of joint community action to effect new services and other changes. She pointed out that the community did not even have a city park to serve the people's needs: "All we have is that little plaza out there," she said. For the Spanish the plaza had once been the site for all important official business and community gatherings.

A Spanish woman—a well-educated descendant of the Dons—who served as superintendent of county schools, confessed that she had very little contact with Anglo professionals offering services to the schools. The county schools were the country schools, largely; and they were still attended mostly by Spanish-Americans. This county school superintendent did not seem to have great worries in looking out for the Spanish in the outlying areas of the county. The personalized, neighborly pattern persisted there. Discipline was handled by parents, who respected the authority position in the school system occupied by one of their own. This was far different from the city, where the appointment of the Anglo superintendent of schools almost became a religious and racial issue (according to the doctor and his wife).

Estimates in the community varied, but the consensus seemed to be that the proportions of Spanish and Anglos in the city schools were about equal. No accurate count was available because these ethnic "labels" were not officially recognized on records, nor were comparisons between the groups on achievement tests made by the educational authorities. A former superintendent of the city schools said that he had had trouble with discipline problems among the Spanish. The threat of expulsion merely meant that parents would enroll the child in a Catholic parochial school. Thus, in the institutions of public education, there was no overlapping of figures of authority for certain of the community's young people; and their divided loyalties were natural to the divided pattern of the total social system.

A young Anglo girl who worked as counselor to a girls' club said that board memberships were usually held by "name" people or socialites in town—almost all Anglos—who were remote from the clientele of the organization. This was particularly true of the girls' club, which was located in a Spanish section and was attended by girls from poorer Spanish homes. The counselor experienced great frustrations in dealing with a board whose members were always asking: "Why don't you attract more nice Anglo girls to the club?" Most of the mothers of her girls were on the dependency rolls at Public Welfare, receiving aid for their children after the father had deserted; and many were periodic visitors to the Probation Department because of sexual delinquencies.

The president of a bank also looked across a wide gulf in trying to comprehend the community as a whole. A resident of the community for fifteen years, this fine old Oklahoma Baptist was interested in good works and in community service. The bank president was particularly concerned about sums of money spent on welfare in the community. It seemed to him that the Spanish just did not have a sense of how to plan or how to handle money. They lived for the day, and when they wanted something they would have it at that moment if it was at all possible of attainment. Credit buying had made many things available to more people in all walks of life. For the bank president this practice contained many evils. He tried to protect the Spanish maid who worked for him from the local loan sharks and from the practices of Anglo merchants who, he said, had a special, marked up, "Spanish price" on many goods made available on time-payment plans. He was adopting much the same attitude as the old *patron* of an earlier era—only in modern dress the practice had become largely a matter of instruction in the proper ways of business.

In recent years the influx of newcomers increased. These people sought peace and quiet at the end of the little lanes that wandered aimlessly before being lost against rocky hillsides. They could afford to choose this spot: for retirement; for cultivating an artistic temperament; for working at a modest profession without ambition to "reach the heights." But others in the community could not make such choices.

During depression years many Spanish were displaced from ranches and smaller villages by drought, and they too moved into town. There, surrounded by relatives and neighbors, they were still living in a world that expressed their outlook on life. This outlook, even in the midst of economic deprivation—for the unskilled worker found largely seasonal employment here—was a quiet one. But the prerogatives of those who could choose seemed to work against the betterment of the condition of those who had fewer choices. The tranquility of both major segments in the community left unattempted most community-wide efforts which might benefit all the people.

Signs of controversy appeared in public dialogue in the community. There was great sensitivity to issues of "race." In the 1930s, efforts of a national foundation to conduct a survey in the schools to compare attitudes of the different cultural groups on national issues brought a violent reaction. It was fashionable to be "tolerant," particularly in public; and to be tolerant was to avoid group comparisons. Thus, there was a tendency in the community for people to refuse to face up to group differences at the same time that the disparity between Anglo and Spanish influence in the conduct of community affairs grew larger.

When the first Constitutional Convention met in the Territory just after American occupation, 90 per cent of the attending members were said to be of "Spanish blood." Through the years the political parties in the state always looked to constituents in both population segments for votes, and balanced the ticket to ensure cross-sectional support. A few years ago, however, the local newspaper reported, in an article entitled "Spanish-Anglo Political Balance Shows Signs of Being Washed Out," that only two of fifteen elective officials in the statehouse had Spanish names— the lowest proportion in the history of the state.[45]

The post-Second World War newcomers had increased the Anglo population to the point where the Spanish voter wielded less influence. Since the different cultural heritages persisted and were even extolled by both sides of the community, this increasing displacement of one group by the other in the realm of public affairs could undermine the very grounds for community that most local citizens wished to preserve.

Paradise Lost, or Regained?: The Quest for Wholeness

A former social worker has captured in her writings the essence of a way of life that still persists among Spanish people of the American Southwest who have yet to be alienated from their physical environment or from one another.* The way of life she describes expresses a wholeness which the Anglo intruder often strives to achieve but cannot. The frustration for the Anglo lies in the fact that that which he seeks cannot be gained by "striving" or by "achievement." It is the product of an inheritance that in New Mexico has been passed down through centuries.

The Spanish New Mexican places the primary emphasis in life on appreciation of nature and on personal human relationships. He lives in a world in which personal, private affairs are pre-eminent, and where *El Centro* ("where you stand right now") and *hoy mismo* ("this very day") are sufficient immediate reference points for an identity anchored in an honored family name. The consequences are seen in a people who "are rich in time," who have time "for simple courtesy, for flower tending . . . for baby admiring." They are reflected in the attitude of the Spanish lady—the family matriarch—who passes over apparent tragedies in the loss of material goods due to natural calamities with a cheery, "*No importa*," but is cast into great gloom by the terrible thing the schoolteacher has said about her Carmencita: that she "makes flat when she sings." They are visible in her practice of working as a domestic for the Anglo lady for just enough days to earn the amount required to purchase the special gifts she wants for her loved ones. And they permeate the easy approach to "contract" obligations: the attitude that time schedules are not terribly significant; the preference for a friendly work atmosphere over higher wages and more labor-saving devices; the gesture of breaking off arrangements with an employer by simply failing to return for another day's work.

The rhythm of this life is blended with the rhythms of nature: the cycles of day and of season. People stop to admire a sunset, and to comment on blossoms in the spring. But they seldom anticipate nature and its moods. The Spanish father cuts only enough piñon wood each morning for the day's needs, working a little longer on mornings when the snow is falling. When the rain-

* The impressions of the values and attitudes of the poorer Spanish in the community, briefly set down in this section, are largely gleaned from the stories in Dorothy L. Pillsbury, *No High Adobe* (Albuquerque: University of New Mexico Press, 1950); and from her *Roots in Adobe* (Albuquerque: University of New Mexico Press, 1959).

fall has been plentiful for the farmer, enabling him to irrigate even fields farthest from his ditches, he immediately gathers the family and friends together for a fiesta—a celebration for sharing a good fortune that has come as a gift "this very day." People who do life's work in these rhythms fulfill the words of an old Spanish gentleman: "Work . . . should leave something with which one can decorate one's life."

Dignity in both young and old is seen in the ease with which words like *gracias* and *bonito* are spoken. Personal greetings are expected when people meet even casually, and may involve a long exchange of pleasantries about mutual friends and relatives. Like the Anglo of an earlier day who found he had to meet everybody in order to do business with any one man, the latter-day Anglo finds it difficult to "get down to business" and complete a quick transaction. First he must answer to: "How is your mother?" "Your father?" "Your sister?" "The little ones?" And if he does not wish to appear rude, he too is caught in this rhythm and requests similar information from his Spanish fellow citizen. It is little wonder that many Spanish who leave here find the world of other communities harsh and strange. One who returned to this place of assured identity said: "We don't belong out there. . . . We didn't have any friends. We were just 'dirty Mexicans.' Here people know who we are and we know who they are. We count for something. We belong here."[46]

The Anglo who came often sought integration and meaning which he had lost in his overorganized society. At first artists found here that the inspiration of landscape and more "primitive" human relationships were sufficient for their needs. But through the years even the artists began to search beyond the immediate realities for more abstract interpretations, while other Anglos began to commercialize native ways and styles.[47] A tourist trade became the major business of the community. And the private society—more correctly, *societies*—which Anglo newcomers wove around themselves took on greater importance and became a prime basis of the Anglo's stake in the community.

In the years of great Anglo invasion and of depression and war, the Spanish were not untouched by change. During the depression the older people clung to their little ranches within the county. But the younger people, who had grown accustomed to wage-work in mines and beet fields, moved to town to look for work. When they did not find it, they went on relief. A whole new pattern of expectations was conditioned into their lives. In some ways, federal relief became a new version of the *patron* system in which the *rico* looked out for the interests of his *pobres*—only this time the *patron* was a "father-government."

In spite of initial inhibitions about relief, it was natural for people to follow the course of the more certain source of security. Some critics have seen only the negative side of this picture of increased dependency on government. One Anglo-New Mexican, however, writing in the 1930s, said: "The fundamental change with the native people was that help had come to them from the outside and that the long struggle for survival was no longer merely a community or family burden. . . . For the first time they had received direct benefits as American citizens and had participated in a nationwide crisis."[48] Public health surveys, agriculture agents, adult education finally came to these people too. The projects of the '30s and '40s were a natural expression of ends held in view and proclaimed by a larger national community which could not remain content with remnants of feudalism in any part of its domain.

Following the war new motivations appeared among the Spanish. Young Spanish-Americans acquired education on the G.I. Bill and found success and new vocations in business and the professions. Those who did these things frequently moved to larger cities and away from the protective circle of mother-centered families. The former social worker has called this process a part of a game "like musical chairs" whereby: "Young Spanish Americans . . . buy modern homes equipped with every modern gadget" while Anglos ". . . are avidly buying the ancestral adobes of the Spanish people," and often turning them into "semblances of household museums unlike anything a real *paisano* ever inhabited."[49]

An heiress of the Dons views this process with trepidation, fearing that the old customs have vanished and the "quiet reserve and respect has gone. . . . The old Spanish courtesy and hospitality . . . changed, to the regret of the elders, who . . . found it hard to get accustomed to the new ways."[50]

The native Spanish-speaking New Mexicans still call themselves "Spanish"—inheritors of the traditions of sixteenth- and seventeenth-century Spain. But it was not Old World Spain that produced this particular view on life. It was Spain transformed in this part of the New World, nestling institutions amid plateaus and mountains with this physical environment to challenge the people. The community at the end of trails from South and East had encompassed many kinds of people, both as visitors and as more permanent participants. One of its continuing attractions lay in the fact that it allowed room for individuality and privacy. However, it might be a maxim for those who sought wholeness in their personal lives here to attempt to see more of the whole outside the private adobe walls.

4

A Broadened Bayou: Houston

*Volunteers are invited to our standard. Liberal boun-
ties of land will be given to all who will now join our
ranks with a good rifle and one hundred rounds of
ammunition. War in defense of our rights must be
our motto!* . . . *Let your valor proclaim to the world
that liberty is your birthright.*

—General Sam Houston, 1835[1]

Strong Men . . . and Independent People

The news that traveled eastward from the beleaguered mission
fanned winds of panic and bitterness among the colonists settled
in the valleys and along the bayous reaching inland from the
Gulf. One of the last letters dispatched by the commander was
an impassioned appeal addressed: "To the People of Texas and
All Americans in the world . . ." pleading: ". . . in the name of
Liberty, of patriotism and everything dear to the American
character, . . . come to our aid, with all dispatch."[2]

But aid was not available in sufficient strength. The impending
massacre was completed; and soon the rout of the colonists,
called the "Runaway Scrape," was truly under way. In early
March, 1836, just one day before the fall of the Alamo in San
Antonio, the largest newspaper in the bayou country reported
that the "whole Mexican army . . . are on our frontier. The inhabitants of Power's and McMullin's colonies have abandoned their
homes. . . . In ten days the people of the Colorado and Brazos

will share the same fate unless all turn out, to conquer or die."[3]

Extraordinary measures were needed to rally these independent people who had come to colonize and seek property and opportunity in a foreign land. The general commanding their volunteer army issued orders to arrest deserters, as he fell back toward the bayou lowlands, gathering together remnants of scattered militia units and new volunteers as he moved. He felt impelled to add to his order: "All persons leaving the country . . . will be required to return or their arms taken from them for the use of the army."[4] But apart from the stalwart volunteers who—more or less—followed the general, the panic continued.

At least one leader in the colony saw hope in this travail. He wrote to his sister after hearing of the tragedy in San Antonio: "I have long been convinced that some severe disaster alone could call the wretched set of men who have obtained the lead in public affairs to their sense of duty to the people, and the people to a conviction of the necessity of united and vigorous exertion." Now, he said, the people were taking on the defense of the country, setting out with their rifles to shoot every Mexican they could find.[5]

The issue was joined climactically on an April day in 1836. In a brief and bloody battle on the banks of a bayou the outnumbered Texans took vengeance on a surprised enemy, turning his defeat into rout and carnage. Years later, the Texan general mused over the victory and the army of individualists he led that day. "The achievement was in behalf of liberty," he said, "and the Anglo-Saxon race . . . redeemed themselves, and . . . showed at least that they were worthy of their sires." He elaborated on the aftermath: "After the battle, individuals thought of nothing but eating and drinking; . . . they were scattered to the four winds of heaven; eight days it took to collect them together . . . they were everywhere but where they ought to have been."[6]

Out of these experiences a new, independent republic was born on the American continent. And out of the conditions which Anglo colonizers were creating for themselves in this part of the continent, new opportunities appeared for men of property and enterprise in the lowlands near the Gulf. In August of the same year in which the great battle was fought an advertisement was placed by two New York promoters and land speculators in the region's major newspaper (with a request that it also be inserted in newspapers in Mobile, Washington, New York, and Louisville):

> The town . . . at the head of navigation, on the west bank of Buffalo Bayou, is now . . . brought to public notice because until now, the proprietors were not ready to offer it to the public, with the advantages of capital and investments.[7]

The "town" near the battleground hardly existed except in the minds of the opportunists who had selected the site for a promotion scheme. One of the promoters described the difficulties of developing this wide place on the bayou: ". . . swampy grounds had to be cleared and drained. . . . The labor of clearing the great space was done by Negro slaves and Mexicans, as no white man could have endured the insect bites and malaria, snake bites, impure water, and other hardships."[8]

Now adventurers, merchants, "soldiers" from the battle . . . frontiersmen, came to swell the town population. And around this new focus of energies a community began to form which was founded on the speculative self-interest of the participants.

A Setting for Collisions

Perhaps no Americans ever moved with more confidence to a frontier of North America than did the people who journeyed southwestward into Texas. Yet, the movement began quietly, led initially by a peaceable family man who had a contract with a foreign government binding him to be responsible for the good conduct of "honest, industrious farmers and mechanics" who joined his colony.

The national census of 1820 showed that over two million people were now west of the Appalachians. Missouri became a state in 1821, and it was there that traders from the Northeast met men of property from the Southeast. Some with ambition set their sights on trails to commerce in the western mountains and beyond. Others looked to the Southwest for cheap land and renewed independence. The hard times following the War of 1812 reached a peak throughout the trans-Appalachian West in 1820. And in that year the conditions for acquiring new land became almost impossible: the federal government abolished the credit system for disposing of land and required that the full purchase price of $1.25 per acre for tracts in eighty-acre multiples be paid in cash. The following year, a Missouri merchant-industrialist (a transplanted New Englander who had followed the frontier first to Virginia then to Missouri) received a colonization grant from Spain as he prepared to restore the personal dignity he had lost in the panic of 1819. He wrote of his plans to one of his sons:

I have made a visit to St. Antonio and obtained liberty to settle in that country—*as I am, ruined, in this,* I found nothing I could do would bring back my property again and to remain in a Country where I had enjoyed *wealth* in a state of *poverty* I could Not submit to.[9]

Before the Missourian could undertake the venture to recoup his family fortune, he died of illness contracted on the return trip from "St. Antonio." Now another son took up the contract and prepared to found a colony under the terms granted. "The objects of this settlement," the son announced, "are entirely agricultural. The richness of the soil, healthfulness of the climate, contiguity to the sea, and other natural advantages, promising a reward to our labors, which few spots on the globe could furnish to an equal extent."[10] The caravan that crossed the Red River into the Mexican Frontier was swelled by people from Mississippi, Missouri, Arkansas, and Kentucky, many of whom had made written requests to join the colony after word of it spread through those areas. Settlers were to pay 12½ cents an acre for land, with over one thousand acres offered to each family. The caravan moved west along the Old San Antonio Road from Natchitoches, Louisiana. And in the wooded bottomlands of the Colorado and Brazos rivers the three hundred families of the first colony made their homes and began to cultivate crops of corn, cotton, and sugar cane.

The ample spaces of Texas encouraged these agriculturalists to spread out. Most families lived on farms thirty or forty miles apart. Their leader wished them to learn the Spanish language. He took an active part in the political life of the province which was just feeling repercussions of an upheaval that replaced Spanish rule in Mexico City with an independent government.*

* A stipulation was included that all who immigrated must be Catholics

And "independence" was a key attraction to this Anglo colony. "I think that your removal to Texas" (the founder wrote his brother-in-law) "will make your children independent, which they would never have been in Missouri."[11]

A census of 1825 showed 1,400 people in the colony and 443 slaves. This population was distributed in a spacious province that counted a mere "2,516 souls" in its only two "Latin" settlements in 1822, when the Mexican governor of the province had reported: "The population of this province is very backward and it is absolutely necessary for the nation [Mexico] to make some effort to people it. Admitting foreigners would be the easiest, least costly, and most expeditious method of enlarging the population."[12] A new constitution in 1824 forbade further introduction of slaves into any part of the Mexican Republic. But the Anglo leader, with support from Latin friends in the province, was able to circumvent the constitution on this point.* A Mexican statesman in San Antonio assured him: "I agree with you that the great development of your colony . . . depends among other things, upon permitting . . . slavery; that by such action many men of property will come; and that without it only the wretched will come who cannot advance the province."[13]

The peaceable family man quietly pursued his plans—with the backing of many Latin officials—for populating this remote area of the Mexican Republic. "Yes, we will be happy," he wrote his wife before she joined him. "We will arrange our cottage—rural—comfortable—and splendid. Gardens and rosy bowers, and ever verdant groves, and music, and books, and intellectual amusements can all be ours."[14] The people of his colony went about the business of working the soil, defending themselves on the frontier,

---

or agree to become such. This requirement was never met by most colonists, although it did defer the establishment of Protestant churches in Texas. (See Samuel Harman Lowrie, *Culture Conflict in Texas 1821–1835* [New York: Columbia University Press, 1932], p. 52.)

* A Mexican law of 1828 assured that contracts made by immigrants to the state with the servants and hirelings they introduced were guaranteed. Thus, the American slaveowner stopped on his way to Texas and made a contract before a notary with his slaves. In 1829, a petition to exempt Texas from a new antislavery decree was granted. In 1832, the term of the labor contracts was limited to ten years (but by 1842 the issue had been resolved by force of arms). (See Eugene C. Barker, *Mexico and Texas, 1825–1835* [Dallas: P. L. Turner Company, 1928], pp. 74–80.)

and pursuing a homely social life apparently with little thought of the distant Mexican authorities. Open spaces and family independence seemed to mitigate the development of conflicts.

But conditions for collisions were close at hand.

The movement of population into Texas had become a subject of heated debate in national forums in the United States. Discussion of this movement, and of the motives of the majority of immigrants who were slaveholders, caused verbal clashes between political factions long before physical conflict came about.[15] But even in 1827 Henry Clay envisioned open conflict as he attempted to persuade Mexico to sell Texas:

> These emigrants will carry with them our principles of law, liberty, and religion; and however much it might be hoped they might be disposed to amalgamate with the ancient inhabitants of Mexico, so far as political freedom is concerned, it would be almost too much to expect that all collisions would be avoided on other subjects. . . .[16]

From the opposite side of the cultural cleft similar fears were voiced. A Mexican general on an inspection trip through Texas reported to his president in 1828:

> It would cause you . . . chagrin . . . to see the opinion that is held of our nation by these foreign colonists, since . . . they know no other Mexicans than the inhabitants about here. . . . Thus, I tell myself that it could not be otherwise than that from such a state of affairs should arise an antagonism between the Mexicans and the foreigners.[17]

The weakness of local Mexican troop garrisons meant that settlers took care of their own defense against marauding Indian tribes. It also meant that indifference and contempt increased toward Mexican laws and Mexican ways. In the original "Terms of Settlement" a clause stated that "No frontiersman who has no other occupation than that of a hunter will be received."[18] But the ratio of single men to married men steadily increased in the colony following the first census; and along the Texas-Louisiana border pressures were building from "a motley crowd" of people, who were unrestrained by negotiated contracts: "The speculator, the merchant, the surveyor, the planter and stockman, with the sprinkling of black-legs and criminals . . . every man a sovereign in his own conception . . . [wrote one historian] . . . these

from North Carolina wrote to his friends and relatives: "I am laying the foundation of a large fortune. . . . My expenses here are enormous, for I live in the best style, but I make clear over and above all expenses more in one year, than I can in Carolina in half a dozen. . . . Besides my position in Society is the most desirable."[25]

The forces holding a community together were manifested most clearly when an external challenge to local pride and feelings of superiority was posed. The old enemy Santa Anna retaliated against Texan overtures toward expansion into New Mexico by dispatching forces to occupy San Antonio in 1842. Popular outcry was so vehement that the great warrior-president of the Republic had to veto a declaration of war against Mexico to avoid conflicts that would sap the strength of a young nation. When an army was gathered to repel the invaders, the bayou community led in volunteers. A local newspaper endorsed an invasion of Mexico to avenge the men of a local volunteer company captured on the Texan expedition into New Mexico. And as in the battles of 1836, in this campaign of 1842 individual commanders refused to be constrained by orders they did not like. One force proceeded against orders to cross the Mexican border, whereupon it was cut off and surrounded—again subjecting Texans to indignities from men over whom they felt an intrinsic superiority.

On the eve of Texas annexation to the United States, the community on the bayou had come upon hard times. An editorial in a newspaper declared that low prices, scanty crops, sickness, buildings going to decay ". . . might well discourage the timid." But the elements of prosperity were firmly implanted in the Republic, the editorialist said. Resolutions at a countywide meeting approved the move to join the American Union.[26] The population of the town stood at 2,073.* Frock coats, elevated sidewalks (an accommodation to the mud), and two-wheeled, horsedrawn carts, driven from the wharves on the bayou by Negroes to the hotels where travelers stayed, left a lasting impression on the visitor. The numerous saloons—"really magnificent" and "always well filled"—also impressed the traveler.[27]

---

* The first census after annexation (1850) showed the town population to be 2,396, while the county population was 4,668, including 912 (or about 20 per cent) colored.

The chance to vent local antagonisms toward Mexico, which followed quickly on annexation, brought enthusiastic local response. The newspaper noted that over one hundred prominent men in the community were among the volunteers: "[The] County now, as heretofore, furnishes her full quota . . . to meet the call of the commander in chief . . . ; such has been the enthusiasm here, that several daring spirits . . . dashed off to the seat of war long before the Governor's Proclamation arrived."[28] The county actually sent four regiments to the war with Mexico, meeting the entire quota asked of the state by the Governor.

After Texas entered the American Union the tide of home-seekers and landseekers into the state increased steadily. Some maintain that the lure of its cheap land in 1849 was second only to that of gold in California.[29] The bayou lands were accessible both by overland routes and from the Gulf. Immigrants came in a steady stream. The newspaper in a town on the northeastern border of Texas recorded the overland movement throughout the 1850s: (December, 1851)—"Whenever we step to the doors or south windows of our office . . . we see trains of wagons halted. . . ." (November, 1854)—"The town is almost daily filled with wagons of immigrants from Tennessee, Kentucky and Alabama." (December, 1858)—"Immigration exceeds everything we have ever seen. At least fifty wagons per day pass through. . . ."[30]

In the bayou community, population more than doubled between 1850 and 1860. In 1860, the town population was some 4,800; the county, over 9,000 (including 2,062 colored).[31] German families were predominant among foreign immigrants.

Newcomers soon were assimilated as Anglo participants. Just as elsewhere in the South, when foreign immigrants became men of property on large plantation lands they usually acquired slaves and became committed to this institution, conditioned to aggressive assertion of personal and property rights. The extension of slavery had been the major issue in national forums where the question of Texas annexation was debated. On returning from imprisonment in 1835, the father of the Anglo colony (who claimed to be "the owner of one slave only") had adopted a stronger stand in advocating slavery for Texas: "*Texas must be a slave country,*" he wrote. "*It is no longer a matter of doubt. The interest of Louisiana requires that it should be, a population of* fanatical abolitionists in Texas would have a very pernicious and dangerous influence on the overgrown slave population of that state [Louisiana]."[32] The constitution for the Texas Republic had legalized slave ownership, encouraging many southern gentlemen of property to choose Texas as the place for a new agricultural enterprise.

Texas entered the Union as a slave state. But by 1860 it was not the defense of slavery that animated the people of the bayou community so much as the defiant posture of *secession* as this theme was caught up by an independent people. The song "Dixie" was sweeping the city that year. The scene at the news of Lincoln's election was described by a newspaper reporter as positively thrilling. Business was suspended. A Lone Star flag forty feet long was raised on a new one-hundred-foot liberty pole in Courthouse Square; and everyone wore the symbol of secession on his hat— "a blue rosetta with a silver star in the center."[33]

Not all were elated at the imminent break with the Union. The old warrior of 1836 (now governor) spoke out at a public meeting: "I tell you that, while I believe with you in the doctrine of State rights, the North is determined to preserve this Union. They are not a fiery, impulsive people as you are . . . ; but when they begin to move in a given direction, where great interests are involved . . . they move with the steady momentum and perseverance of a mighty avalanche. . . ."[34] When the vote on secession had been counted, however, the local newspaper bannered: ". . . Secession Triumphant . . . Heaviest Vote Ever Polled in the County . . . The People Aroused." West Texas towns and counties—more removed from a plantation economy— returned Union majorities. Particularly the German colonists in those areas were noticeably cool toward the Confederate cause. But the bayou community left no doubt of its majority sentiments. The statewide figures showed secession favored in a proportion of 3 to 1.[35]

Soon military units were formed and marched off to the major arenas of war. Once more, local enthusiasm for battle was high. The town became a major military center. Outfits like Terry's Rangers, armed with double-barreled shotguns and long two-edged knives called "Texas toothpicks," performed trick-riding feats on their half-broken cowponies for the edification of the local populace. But the thrill of combatting an immediate, tangible enemy was missing—except for minor skirmishes on the state's borders and with Yankee forces engaged in blockading Gulf ports. The victory which brought independence from Mexico had been won in a bloody fifteen-minute battle in the heart of the colony. The new struggle for independence dragged on interminably, the enemy soon objectified only in the impersonal effects of a strangling blockade.

Descriptions of the war years leave the impression that the community adapted readily to the war. The dazzling uniform became an entree to society in a young community that had remained relatively open to new symbols through which members of a growing population strove to "be somebody." One account recalls, however, that possession of a minimum of fifteen slaves entitled a man to exemption from the draft which was resorted to as the war dragged on. Another story has been passed down of a dashing young man who was conspicuous at social affairs in his officer's uniform, but who was found later to be hiding from the draft by living anonymously in town. Only the wealthiest could obtain wheat flour for bread or "the genuine coffee bean." And while it was rare for a civilian to be seen in new tailor-made clothes, throughout the war ". . . the officers in their grey uniforms and military headwear created a dazzling sight."[36]

In April and even into May of 1865, the newspapers reported meetings to revive lagging spirits. But soldiers now were expressing their hatred toward the cotton speculators they blamed for the failure of the war. The garrison at the port on the Gulf, facing the blockading Yankee forces, was decimated by desertions. And when the troops began to evacuate these Gulf positions under orders, the ranks swiftly melted away as men swarmed northward into the community on the bayou.

The disintegration of this army at the close of hostilities was not out of tune with the social atmosphere of the community. "Nor did public opinion often condemn them" (one historian wrote of the soldiers) in expressing bitterness toward speculators who stayed at home. These were not the orderly Southerners following the lead of gentlemen officers, returning in dignified resignation with horse and side-arm to rebuild a ravaged home and farm. These Texans were in a hurry to put the immediate past behind, to grab a personal stake, and to get on with the future. They used the community—the focal point of speculation and wartime society—much as others before them had used it. Two thousand former soldiers gathered at the doors of the Ordnance Building. They sacked the military storehouses, took the personal property a man would need as an immediate grubstake, and headed home. There was no consuming climax to the Insurrection for them; but likewise there was no lingering whimper.[37] And at least some of their frustration and bitterness was directed at those within their own society.

At the close of the Civil War, federal military authorities appeared and emancipation was proclaimed. Freedmen were advised to remain at home and work for wages and were told not to collect at army posts, for they would not be supported in idleness. Local sentiments favored the maintenance of "kind and protective care" over former slaves. One Texas newspaper published the opinion that even though slavery was abolished in name, there would be a return to a character of compulsory labor which would make the Negro useful to society and subordinate to the white race. A paper in the bayou community said that paid compulsory labor would replace unpaid. The feeling was strong that three-fourths of the states of the Union would not adopt the amendment abolishing slavery. But when the officials of the Freedmen's Bureau began to arrive, the atmosphere changed. As the first postwar summer wore on, complaints increased of Negro vagrancy, theft, vice, and insolence. In July, a newspaper said: "We cannot help but pity the poor freedmen and women that have left comfortable and happy homes in the country and come to this city in search of what they call freedom. Nearly all the old buildings are not fit for stables."[38] In addition to this concentration of uprooted Negroes in town, other Negroes were appearing in a new, conspicuous, and highly visible role: Negro regiments were brought in in late summer and fall to replace volunteer regiments being discharged from the Union Army.

The conditions for collisions once again were accentuated, but rather than the affirmation of individual dignity in contests between equals within a community, internal collisions now took on a negative aspect. Conflict between unequal groups threatened the older code controlling conflict between persons.

But conditions under Reconstruction did not merely unleash destructive violence by whites against Negroes and Union men. Widespread disorder and lawlessness gave free sway to many "turbulent characters."[39] By the census of 1870, the proportion of colored population had increased to almost 40 per cent of the total in both city and county (a threefold increase over 1860). A Negro riot occurred in 1866 over the arrest of a Negro. Murders and depredations were reported in surrounding towns. The appearance of a Reconstruction regime had disastrous repercussions in a community that had always relied heavily on informal controls and on elbow-room to absorb the effects of internal collisions. New informal standards now tended to approve violence against the "enemy" groups within: Negroes and the scalawags who manipulated them. But these new standards and practices also tended to eat away at the older personal code of conduct between equals.

These years brought intensified hostility between the segments of a society. And where elements of the Negro segment were clearly identified with an intruding authority, the reaction was violent. The Reconstruction governor had organized a state guard —all Negroes. The guard was unruly and lawless. According to a Reconstruction chronicler, eventually all met a violent death: "None of them was ever arrested for anything he had done, because when they were found they were wiped out. They were placed in the same class with snakes, wolves and other undesirable things and the average white man thought no more of killing one of them than he could have thought of killing a snake."[40]

The Ku Klux Klan appeared in 1868. By then other activities were beginning to occupy the people. That year a newspaper report said: "Two months ago . . . you might plod your way home through the dark and mud to the great danger of being knocked down or being garroted at every corner . . . but now the streets are illuminated with gas. . . . Two of the principal streets . . . are traversed with street railroad cars. . . ."[41] Early in 1870 (the year in which Texas was readmitted to the Union), a white man's party was organized with the expressed aim of preventing Negroes from holding office and to oppose political and social equality of the races. A political meeting was held in the city in 1874 to

a place of cotton-crested fields, choked with malaria, an abiding place for only 'hot-blooded Southerners and swarthy Africans,' and a hiding spot for the scum and scab of other States." Now the invitation was sent to outsiders of all trades and skills. "For sectionalism, like slavery," said the guide book, "is dead, and over the grave the capital of the North is being wooed and won to wed the rich resources of the South. . . ."[47]

The old and the new existed here side by side, each paying homage to the other. A consequence was that people retained firm models from the past around which to pattern new strivings.

In the first year of the twentieth century a newspaper announced that automobiles had come to the community. Another sign of a new era appeared in the news that labor organization had expanded among tradesmen in the city, who had even been emboldened to strike for higher wages. Prosperity in the "Golden Nineties" had centered largely on agricultural developments and the lumber industry. But the importance of the lumber industry carried into many new areas of activity. For example, it was unionists in the burgeoning building trades who played the most prominent role in the labor unrest of 1900. It is noteworthy, too, that the strike was settled without the development of strong class antagonisms. Contract relationships were changing but not obliterating the older personalized patterns of the social system.

The great momentum of this society enabled its participants to fashion new roles around old models. This momentum was reinforced by the continued emergence of new challenges from the physical environment. When surface land for crops and grazing became less lucrative for speculation, the wealth in minerals beneath the land was exploited. The discovery of extensive oil deposits in fields along the Gulf Coast started a boom in building trades and the lumber industry in the community. It also provided new outlets for the interests of the successful men who were making the city the center of their business activities.

In the early years of the twentieth century there were many signs to indicate that older challenges had disappeared and that a rural people were about to experience industrialization. However, local literature of that period belied the more urbane tone of the pronouncements of commercial and business people. Education emphasized the transmission of a vivid heritage. A book of *Texas*

Hero Stories was published in 1908 for use in the elementary school system. In colorful, often bloody, descriptions of rough-hewn, self-made empire builders, the author revived images of past heroes. For example, the Bear Hunter (David Crockett) whose "wisdom was not learned from books"; the leader at the "15 minutes of destiny" in the battle on the bayou, when the slashing, cutting, clubbing Texans with their rifles and bowie knives routed a demoralized foe; the Texas Rangers, "nature's noblemen" whose rank was one of "personal courage, pluck and patriotism." The author concluded that faith, courage, energy, and self-reliance sustained men such as these who were drawn to Texas.[48]

By 1910, the population of the city had grown to nearly 79,000 and the city area expanded from nine to sixteen square miles. By 1950 the city population would have increased steadily, decade by decade, nearly fifteenfold over 1900; while area encompassed by the city would expand steadily to 155 square miles. Thus, the urban experience of living in close proximity to many others would be extended constantly to greater numbers of people, but the density of city population, over-all, would remain relatively the same.

New land subdivisions typified community growth: electric railway lines extended the reaches of the city, particularly south toward the Gulf and along the axis of the deepened bayou ship channel. A technical university, endowed by a cotton millionaire, opened in 1912, with a faculty staffed by men of academic distinction from as far away as Harvard and the University of Tokyo. During the First World War, an army camp in the county was utilized as a National Guard mobilization center, and a flying field nearby became a major training site for airmen. After the war a local newspaper said: "Officials of Washington have recognized the natural advantages . . . [the community] offers as a flying center."[49] New plants provided new jobs for a growing population during the 1920s. A motor-assembling plant was built on the site of an old school, formerly a landmark as the building that had housed Confederate Military Headquarters in the Civil War. An account noted that utilitarian factory walls replaced graceful white columns "to make a landmark of progress."[50] The first skyscrapers appeared on the skyline in the years before the Great Depression.

A footnote to this juxtaposition of past and present: In 1921, a year when big buildings were going up throughout the business district, 2,051 persons were inducted into the Ku Klux Klan in a single ceremony on a prairie just south of town.[51]

Through the depression years and after, spokesmen would boast of their town as the place the Great Depression forgot. By 1936, local businessmen were proclaiming: ". . . the nation's cotton and oil capital, the greatest port in the South, and the business capital of the Great Southwest, celebrates its *Centennial of Progress!* This will be a year . . . of industry surging upward in its new era of prosperity."[52] And certainly the figures on population growth do not contradict the contention that, in certain respects, a boom continued through the '30s and '40s. A report stated that in one month in 1938, twenty-eight oil companies in the nation removed their offices to this city on the bayou. Private capital flowed in from outside; and rural population continued to leave the Texas countryside in the hard years to congregate in the community. There were still jobs for an expanding population: such jobs as the building of low-cost homes to house the new-comers who were the source of the demand for homes.

As fortunes were made by proportionately fewer, the gap between "haves" and "have-nots" was accentuated. But the people who worked the industries did not sink to a mere subsistence level. As in the past, the community used any available resource to sustain local self-reliance and perpetuate expansion. And those who came helped to continue this type of community life. Thus even during the 1930s and 1940s, and with renewed vigor in the 1950s, at least those in the Anglo segment of the population were able to sustain dreams of individual opportunity.

Texas was an extreme example of a pattern of population concentration manifested country-wide in the United States. And the explosive metropolis on the bayou was a major focus of a rapid shift in population throughout Texas. In 1900 the population of Texas was 82 per cent rural: no city of more than 60,000 existed within the borders of the state. Even in 1940 the state was still more than 50 per cent rural. The small town dominated by agriculture typified the context in which most Texans lived. By 1950, however, the ratio of urban to rural population stood at 5 to 3. In that decade, when the population of Texas was growing by over 1¼ million, more than half of the state's counties were losing people: the great gains were registered in cities of more than 100,000.[53]

Part of this dramatic shift-in-a-decade took into account realities that earlier censuses had ignored: suburban districts were re-defined as "urban" rather than "rural." Still, while the character of major work activities continued to draw more people away from pursuits close to nature, the influence in this rural-to-urban interchange was not all in one direction. Cities expanded to en-compass more of the space in formerly rural counties, allowing in private living arrangements for a semblance of the less crowded way of life. The "wide area to fill" helped to perpetuate the influ-ence of the country ways cherished by these people.

Along the bayou, city continued to reach out into country. And if that which was "city" gained greatly in importance in the com-munity it was largely in contexts for work: the skills and the human relationships newly circumscribed by factories and multi-storied office buildings. But those who continued in great numbers to choose this place as the center for their life were preponderantly a people recently removed from the small towns of Texas and Louisiana. They were still steeped in the tradition that in struggles to tame a physical environment a man must demonstrate his indi-vidual prowess.

New Contests . . . New Conflicts

A public-health nurse who dealt with many newcomers in the community on the bayou remarked: "This place is comprised of a rural population that has come to the city to make more money." In effect, the story of the community has been about these kinds of populations moved by these kinds of aspirations. What have been the consequences? First of all, "these kinds of populations" represent people conditioned to assert their individuality in per-sonal struggles with their environment. They represent, too, peo-ple who tend to resist urban social forces that would fractionize their lives and alienate them from their friends. At the same time, the aspirations these people have contribute to energies toward achievement and new beginnings. The result is an atmosphere replete with individual and group competition—and ripe for con-flict. For the fast-paced city promotes contacts and collisions as it fosters physical movement and change. And when similar goals of achievement reach the consciousness of all segments of the society, the potentials for conflict are enhanced.

History has laid down a base for present contests which has not been erased by the swift pace of contemporary events. For the majority there is a heritage that identifies them with a strain of superior humans that approached a climax in historical destiny in the New World as its representatives explored the Texas prairies. An old chronicler of the community's formative years speaks for the pride of this majority: ". . . it is the racial instinct of the Anglo-Saxon breed ever to trudge westward to find new lands and to see where the sun spends the night."[54] The general who led the Anglos in the decisive battles and through the first years of independence spoke of the kinds of implements which were an extension of the personalities of these people as they struggled with their environment. The tyrant who trifled with these artifacts of a culture posed a direct threat to the dignity of the participants: "Santa Anna . . . demanded of them not only the public arms, . . . one or two pieces of ordnance . . . , but their private arms, their rifles. . . . They refused to surrender their private arms; they were their friends—their safety. They were their protectors . . . ; they were necessary to their existence, and they procured the meat upon which their little ones subsisted."[55]

The transformation and assimilation of newcomers has proceeded through the years, as people acquire identifications with modern counterparts of these old artifacts. (Comparatively few in the community are foreign born: the largest migrations from overseas occurred between 1836 and 1860.) Now the image of the future Texan was beginning to look much like a space scientist or an astronaut. Or perhaps the astronaut, like the airman of the Second World War, was beginning to resemble the local definition of a Texan. A school administrator said: "Our school system has gone all-out for the space-age subjects."

In recent years the community had the nation's highest murder rate per capita. Modern conditions of freeways and spatial crowding of newcomers in central neighborhoods, coupled with a tradition of self-assertiveness, increased the potentials for collisions. A judge of the Domestic Relations Court decried to interviewers the present-day emphasis on violence and its transmission through the mass media. They sympathized with his viewpoint. One of them ventured that a tightening of laws relative to firearms might help matters. Whereupon the judge quickly rejoined: "Oh I think we must guard the right of a man to keep and bear arms. It is one guarantee of his freedom that a Texan refuses to surrender." (The judge doubtless would have approved of the method through which one big oilman of the 1930s reminded the community of individual vigilance: flying a pirates' skull-and-crossbones flag atop the oil company building "as a warning . . . that liberty is a right and not a privilege.")[56]

The contests inspiring the Anglo to great effort in the present are of much the same order as contests of the past. Ten years ago "the city's most spectacular citizen" was said to be a rags-to-riches (service-station-to-wildcat-well) oil millionaire, who built his own superhotel on the outskirts of town after (reportedly) being told to tone down the parties he threw while a guest in a downtown hotel. For increasing numbers of arrivals from the rural hinterlands the possibilities of emulating this model become more remote. Pressures and tensions continue to mount for them. Just the city itself, with its tantalizing yet often unrequited promises, requires adjustments that many fail to make. School counselors say that their most pressing guidance problems reflect the tensions induced by ambitious parents among the children in the central schools where newly arriving rural whites are concentrated.

If the problems of many Anglos are great in the contests of the city, those of population segments that must play by somewhat modified rules are much greater. Traditionally, the Latin American must fight the longest odds if he aspires to define new roles for himself and his group in the total community. The Anglo leader at the Alamo wrote in the last letter sent from that besieged outpost: "The citizens of this municipality [San Antonio] are all our enemies except those who have joined us heretofore; we have but three Mexicans now in the fort; those who have not joined us in this extremity should be declared public enemies. . . ."[57] Subsequent generations of Latin Americans have lived with such stigmas, ascribed to them in events etched most vividly in the memories of Texas culture.

Recent estimates indicate that less than 5 per cent of the total population of the bayou community is Latin American. Social forces have tended to narrow the circle of relationships of this small segment, almost eliminating broader public participations and keeping private associations largely within the bounds of the Spanish language. The great bulk of this segment, entering Texas after 1900, came from Mexico's illiterate peasant population. They entered West Texas rural areas as farm laborers and eventually congregated in some numbers in urban communities. In 1936, the Texas centennial year, a Latin American wrote a book in which he tried to enhance the place of the Mexican in Texas history ". . . in order that the word 'Mexican' shall no longer be misconstrued as 'savage'. . . ." and that "patriots whether Mexican-Texan or American-Texan, [might] share equally the glory of a resplendent ancestry."[58] But the "resplendent ancestry" could not be revised to implant new cultural memories around old events. It remained for *new events* to provide an opening for new social definitions.

In recent years a compelling passion simply to be accepted more completely as *Americans* colors the thinking of Latin Americans who have taken the lead for their group. A successful restaurant-owner in the community expressed his views to an interviewer. Like other Latins who have caught a new vision of themselves in Texas communities, he mentioned, with great pride, the six Congressional Medals of Honor won during the Second World War by Texas boys of Latin American descent. This man had come to the community at the age of twelve from the Rio Grande Valley where his father had been a farm laborer. The son had supported the family by moving them to the city after his father's death. Now a man in his fifties, the restaurant-owner still kept a workbook for English-language lessons on his desk.

He explained the core of the program undertaken by the Latin organization—the LULACS*—in which he had served as national director. "At first," he said, "we were thought to be troublemakers. But this is a very patriotic organization. The Latin American is very much concerned about being a good American." The problem faced was how to break a circle of low economic status, poor schooling, little or no knowledge of English, early marriage that worked together to maintain barriers to achievement and fuller

* League of United Latin American Citizens.

participation in the larger social system. "I traveled all over," he said, "and I found things were worse here than anywhere; worse than in New Mexico or California. And I—we—decided that the language and the schooling problems were where to begin."

A study in 1942–43 first documented the crisis-point in education. A statewide study of Latin American school population from the first through the twelfth grades showed a swift recession in student numbers at each grade. But the crucial period was between the first and second grades: 37,000 recorded for Grade One dropped to one-half that number for Grade Two. Numbers then dropped steadily until enrollment in the twelfth grade was less than 8 per cent of the total for the first grade.[59] "We have set up preschools to teach the little children just four hundred basic words of English before they start public school." And with this humble beginning—utilizing as teachers Latin American girls with an eighth grade education*—a revolution was begun by the LULACS. The immediate goal was to ensure 6½ years of schooling for each child. Many innovations were needed to break the old pattern. English-language broadcasts were introduced on Spanish-language stations of the Southwest to get the language of the schools into the homes. A broad selling campaign on the importance of education was undertaken.

Progress depended upon new self-perceptions in the generation that had undergone new experiences during wartime. Some men had done remarkable things: boys with only five years of schooling still tried to use their veterans' educational benefits. A crisis was at hand now, however, in higher education with the expiration of the G.I. Bill. But a revolution was already under way. New incentives and new opportunities were being capitalized upon by elements of a population who, like the sincere spokesman with the English-language workbook on his desk, were saying: "We only want to be better Americans."

The Negro population—represented by 1 in 5 of all residents— encountered diverse social forces in this setting. The strength of historical definitions of "place" and "proper role" in a separated society were manifest here. But the local pace of change and

---

* The interview is several years old and the situation an extremely dynamic one. More recent information indicates that the LULACS now find and utilize as teachers Latin girls with a twelfth-grade education.

movement was infectious—and it thrived on the expansive outlook which viewed physical space as broadening and opening rather than as confining and constraining. Thus, the Negro found room here to begin to shake off the past and to aspire to achieve. As yet, however, achievement still left him evaluated largely within his ethnic segment.

Through the years since emancipation a concerted effort was made by Negroes to enter the local contests. They began early to find a voice. In socio-economic terms, they stood well ahead of their Latin contemporaries and they faced no language barrier to educational achievement. But both the static and the changing were apparent in the situations of the Negro population.

Even in 1866 there were obvious disparities in individual attainments among Negroes. A newspaper story that year mentioned the hovels built of planking and waste timber and occupied, sometimes, by twenty or thirty Negroes. But the account added: "There are, however, a few Negroes who have bought lots and erected thereon some very nice cottages."[60] In 1915 a community "Red Book" of the colored population reflected the orientation of Negro leadership in that day. The term "Afro-American race" and a strong emphasis on religion appeared persistently in the Red Book. One spokesman wrote: "Each race, and especially the Afro-American, has found that greater advancement is to be made along rational, racial lines. . . . A worthy man in his race . . . loses that worthiness when he attempts to obliterate social and racial barriers imposed by a beneficent Jehovah. He must stay in his own to prove the worthiness of his life." Recognition was given to the shift to industrial occupations; to the growth of Negro wealth and of home and property ownership; to the reaching toward commercial independence as a group; to the lessening of illiteracy. "A more cordial relation between the races has followed in the wake of educational progress," wrote one leader. Another advocated emulation of the "really fundamental qualities" of the white race: ". . . the stern qualities of thrift, character, economy, willpower and self-mastery." But perhaps more startling to present-day eyes are such statements as this: "We owe a debt to the organized Christianity of this nation . . . [that has] . . . exerted an inestimable influence . . . in lightening that historic burden which the white man bears in all lands and zones of the globe."

Or the statement that slavery was a blessing in disguise: "It brought them to that land which is today, to them, a land of freedom and opportunity, to which the jungles of their native land and the barbarians now inhabiting them can in no wise be compared."[61]

The "Afro-American" identified in that day spoke of himself as a certain type of American. He was careful to distinguish himself from African ancestors but still accommodated to his "superiors" in the majority race. His energies were directed by his leaders toward contests among his own, "to prove the worthiness of his life." Forty years later, circumstances, and attitudes, had changed considerably.

Shortly after the close of the Second World War, a Negro college was opened in the community, supported by tax funds. Ten years later a Negro sociologist who was a dean at this university was commissioned by local business interests to prepare a study of the Negro as "a consumer." His report began: "This report is designed to supply advertisers with a factual and theoretical basis upon which a Negro consumer market can best be understood and exploited. It is a simple description of how the economy of the South's largest city expanded to incorporate a large number of Negroes into its orbit. . . ."[62] The descriptions which followed pointed up significant things about the Negro population as they achieved greater affluence: the members continued to maintain ethnic ties through close neighborhood association; however, the possibilities of broader participation in the urban market place began to introduce them to relationships that were more socially "liberating" (for as the professor said: "Apparently a man is a man when he's a consumer").

Today's urban, "consumer" Negro was still insulated within a segment of population. His aspirations, although confined largely within that segment, sprang increasingly from the larger cultural milieu (the disseminations of radio, television, and other mass media); and the tone of his statements about himself underwent marked changes. While three Negro magazines were rated most popular with Negroes in the study, *Life* and *Look* ranked next among periodicals and were taken by almost all of the highest-income group. When housewives were asked: "What is the most attractive feature of newspaper advertisement?" 81.9 per cent replied: "Ads that do not seem to be stereotyped and earmarked for Negroes." The upper- and middle-income groups defined by the study also expressed disaffection with rhythm-and-blues music of so-called "Negro" radio stations. Youth groups among them had banned this type of music from their social affairs.[63]

The professor dedicated his report to "An *American** mother who reared and educated three children on a wage usually thought to be inadequate for one." He told an interviewer that in the new Negro households people were investing more in the personal, individual value of their children. As among the white middle class, there were now more dancing schools and swimming schools among educated Negroes. And such things were contagious. One clear-cut finding of the study was that since *all* income levels were still congregated together in Negro neighborhoods in the community, consumer practices and preferences showed little variation within the segment. The report said: "This residential pattern sets in motion a wave of imitative consumption that often makes buying a matter of 'keeping up with the Joneses.' "[64] Thus, different income classes retained similarities—particularly the visible similarities—as they lived in close propinquity. Differences in privately stated preferences—least obvious to the casual observer—differentiated income classes, the interviewers on the study discovered.

Negroes still lived in a series of adjoining subcommunities, each having its main street and its round of service institutions. But economic affluence was widening the social setting for the Negro as a consumer. The report explained this widening circle of relationships: More than four-fifths of families sought personal services at institutions in their local neighborhoods; some three-fourths used food stores near at hand; nearly two-thirds dealt at gasoline service stations near their homes. "On the other hand," the report stated, "larger purchases like automobiles, furnishings, appliances, and apparel are usually made at institutions located in or near the downtown district of the city."[65] In the contests of the city, personal ties were still important for Negroes in their neighborhoods. But in the midst of surroundings where change and movement predominated, it was no longer wealth or family background or church affiliation that determined one's position

---

* Italics mine.

vis-à-vis his fellows. The professor maintained that *overconsump-
tion* was the new criterion of class: it was one's visible prosperity
that counted. A corollary to this was the discovery that the least
privileged income class was often the most extravagant in conspicuous buying habits, and the most deeply in debt. At the same
time, in the quest for achieved identity, new contract relationships
were fostered in the larger market place. As a place where
Negroes came as consumers among other consumers, this setting
had useful, but limited, possibilities for furthering perceptions of
equal human worth and dignity. Only as these new evaluations
were echoed in other—occupational, professional—areas of participation would the energies released in the market place re-
inforce new social definitions in the total social system.

Tensions between Past and Future

In the first decade of the present century a prominent socialite
wrote: "[The community] . . . has grown so big in the last eight
years that it has lost much of the sweetness and homelikeness that
once so characterized it. Where there was once one social circle
within its borders, there are now many." Size and pace of community growth were intensifying the problems of maintaining old
forms of human relationship. However, local residents wished to
preserve these forms. The socialite stated that oldtimers were
saying: " 'There are so many new people that I can't keep up with
them. And such nice people, too. It seems a pity not to know them
all.' "[66] The impersonality of an urban setting where most people
must be strangers to each other was already—fifty years ago—
being experienced. Yet, a nurse from the Midwest who lived and
worked in the community in the 1950s commented recently: "It
was such a charming place of truly unsophisticated people. I rode
the bus to work every morning. And many mornings before we
reached my stop there would be a conversation going on that had
involved just about everyone on board. They just didn't like to
sit and stare at one another like strangers."

Others have noted that this growing metropolis has characteristics combining "openness" with the tendency to draw circles of
friendly, personalized association around separated groups of
people. A crucial clue to the style of life is the fact that *new*

circles do develop, and now often do not touch each other, while
the kinds of human relationships they perpetuate are anchored in
the past. And the open acceptance is a heritage from a day when
the visitor to the infant community commented that it was "everybody's wish to be somebody in the general company." Specialization is resisted in this quest to be somebody: it is the whole man
who competes with his peers; it is well-defined groups, their
values and standards, with which the whole man identifies.

Representatives of the local churches advised interviewers that
pastors in the most numerous denominations were not too eager
for cooperation outside their well-defined circles. Membership on
the Council of Churches was by local churches and not by denominations. Almost all the Presbyterian churches were represented. The Methodists, in addition to Council representation, had
their own interchurch association within their denomination. Of
the Baptists—the most numerous Protestant group in the community—the Council director said: "They are always afraid of
losing their autonomy. Even the director of their own denominational association says he has trouble getting individual Baptist
congregations to cooperate with one another."[67]

However, some Baptist congregations with young ministers
were moving in the direction of greater sophistication and toward
cooperation outside the narrowed intimate circle of trusted
friends. A young Baptist minister who had served as a medical
corpsman in the Marines in the Second World War now acted as
religious coordinator to the domestic relations court. He explained
some new accommodations to old practices: "When a congregation is planning a revival, the trend now is to bring in someone
who has a congregation of his own rather than calling on a full-
time, professional evangelist. I've also found that a minister can
control the degree of emotionalism at a revival in his church if he
reserves the right to choose the songs for the services." But even
the young ex-Marine felt that interchurch cooperation had to be
tempered by guarding the deep emotional ties people had to
particular congregations and denominations. Newcomers from
rural areas often were not happy in urban Baptist churches. Not
only were they out of tune with a less emotional brand of Christianity but, as the director of the Council saw it, they did not feel
at home where they no longer enjoyed the prerogatives which

active participation in important positions in churches in their home town had formerly given them. Thus, Pentecostal and Holiness sects acquired many new adherents from among newcomers to the city. New circles were constantly appearing to surround the whole man with persons he could know and trust and to help insulate him from the din of the city and its alienating, disenchanting sirens. This tendency was not confined to poorer newcomers. Some of the newly wealthy people in the community exercised their individualism by precipitating, and sponsoring, the formation of new church congregations.

Representatives of the Catholic hierarchy appeared more aware of change in the growing city than did their Protestant counterparts who sensed more the persistence of rural forces. Perhaps this indicated that the Catholic population was gaining most in numbers from migrants from larger cities outside the state. Many Catholics settled here longest were of the more static and traditional Latin American elements. Now, however, the fastest-growing parishes were in the suburbs. Parochial schools were expanding to keep up with an expanding child population.

A priest expressed alarm at some local developments. In a sense, the Catholic in his suburban context for living was in danger of becoming less distinctively a Catholic. At least, he was not modeled after the American Catholic of older ethnic neighborhoods in eastern cities. There were no real ethnic parishes, except for some Mexican parishes. The priest reported that in an expanding suburban parish in which he had served, the majority of marriages he performed were interfaith marriages. But ties within the Catholic subcommunity were still strong, and the value-system of that subcommunity remained resistant to specialization. For example, clinical considerations were secondary at the Catholic social agency in evaluating a home: the major criterion, as explained by the monsignor, was whether a family was "an emotionally mature, practicing Catholic family." This judgment was made in the agency by those considered by the church to be emotionally mature, practicing Catholics.

The community pattern did not reflect dissociation from religious affiliations. A Jewish spokesman said that there was much more affiliation with synagogues and temples here than in cities in the North and East. Old institutions changed to meet new physical and social conditions; but they resisted being washed away or "washed out." Most of them also retained a semblance of being *private* affairs: the realm in which the whole man could be identified more clearly. For the clear distinction between the individual's public role and a private one was resisted in spite of increased urban complexity.

In education, a strong force toward emulation of the "better" by the "lesser" operated. This institution reflected a class-conscious society, but one in which aspirations were promoted.

A private Episcopal school was considered the elite grade school in the community. The director of a Jewish social agency indicated that many Jewish families, like others aspiring to the best for their children, tried to get their children into this school. Similarly, one public high school stood out because some 95 per cent of its graduates went to college. It became the model for the high school in a new suburban development adjacent to this elite area. The major university in the community was privately endowed and took many of the graduates of these top-rated schools. Entrance standards were the highest in the state, and competition for entrance keen. While most universities in the state surrounded their students culturally with a religious frame of values, the local technical university drew its circle around an academic elite. Its graduates achieved many positions of prestige in professional circles and were particularly influential in the public school system.

Constant change was occurring in more centrally located public schools. City areas that once were referred to as "high middle class" were now said to contain "low middle class" populations from the country—the beginners on the ladder of achievement— and even "low class" elements were designated in central schools. The latter were usually Latin Americans. Latins who had begun to break through the insulation of large Spanish-speaking families dominated by the older generation were appearing in more central city schools over a wider physical area. The junior high school was a good step above the average attainments of this ethnic group as a whole.

One Negro high school also had stood out traditionally as "the best," sending some 45 per cent of its graduates to college. However, a guidance counselor maintained that a newer Negro high school was beginning to surpass the older pace-setter. What were Negro pupils' ambitions now? "As a person from vocational guidance, I am just another speaker when I speak at a white high school," the counselor said. "But when I speak at a Negro high school I receive rapt attention, because vocational opportunities are uppermost in the minds of these young people." The counselor said that Negroes aspiring to college formerly had great ambitions to attend one of the large, nonsegregated midwestern universities, or a high-ranking Negro university like Howard in Washington, D.C. But the local Negro university was becoming more attractive and helped to meet growing demands. There were also indications that more would be admitted to the University of Texas in years ahead. "Most Negro commencement speakers," the counselor said, "stress one major theme: 'You must be *more than* qualified to compete for opportunities.'" The counselor repeated a story told to a high school student body on a vocational guidance day by a Negro architect. He had described a situation where a group of Negroes planned to construct a church and wished to give the contract to a Negro architect and a Negro construction firm. But these professionals were not able to do the job on a competitive basis with other firms in the community, and lost their opportunity.

There was a continuing pressure here to assert a pride in group reference. There was also a predisposition to draw upon historical memories in making these assertions of pride. But a distinctive feature of this tendency was the implication that the future would not be a replica of the past.

Even the more advantaged who aspired to greater dignity sometimes appeared as hybrid products of the blending of old and new. A psychologist represented this type. He identified himself as a relative of a famous millionaire and the bearer of a famous Texas name. Raised a Baptist in an old eastern Texas town, he now attended the Episcopal church and lived in one of the more fashionable new suburbs. The role of professional psychologist seemed secondary to this man's major identification of who he was. In fact, he was somewhat at odds with many in the field of social services where he worked, because he believed they did not make enough attempt to upgrade their profession. Concurrent with his chief employment, he conducted personnel testing for firms housed in impressive downtown skyscrapers—work that came his way as a result of personal contacts among well-to-do businessmen.

For the less advantaged, ethnic identifications remained clear. A Negro social worker, who worked for an old, private agency that in recent years had established a separate facility to accommodate Negroes, saw herself primarily as a public relations person for the agency in "my community." Her commitment in this community was clearly to reaching toward new goals by her people. This meant overcoming older habits that could inhibit new achievements. An example of her attitudes appeared in her approach to problems of the Negro unwed mother. From her perspective, education for all her people, both male and female, was of crucial importance. And the older pattern which saw the unwed mother keep her child and remain with her family was a definite deterrent to the personal plans of a young Negro girl to obtain education. "One of my most frustrating disappointments," she said, "is to see a girl influenced by parents and relatives to keep her child after a plan for adoption has been worked out. It means the end of vocational plans and ambitions."

There were aspects of the social system in the bayou community that could deter achievement for some. Transitions to new roles were not always easy for the individual. Perhaps the forces described made the definition of new social roles more difficult for the underdog. For these conditions required that larger parts of those things providing identity for the person in the community be changed at one time. A new identity could not be pieced together so readily through the development of specialized talents and the acquisition of a profession as it may be in a setting where identity is less assured for all.

There was some security from urban anonymity here in attachments to segments of a society. These segments held people together on more permanent grounds than those of short-run, expedient interests. There was a further anchor in the persistence of the personal touch in spite of the increased importance of contract dealings. Perhaps most significant of all for this story: "Property" was not solely in land, passed from generation to generation. Property had taken on new forms for providing a basis for individual dignity. On the bayou, men in search of new beginnings continued to affirm—as in the early days—that, in a community of free men, "Only talent, or . . . its useful application, is taken into account."

The basic problem was how to provide a context in which people could face one another in competitive contests in a manner that continued to affirm the value of the "other" as well as of the self. Only then could destructive conflicts without rules be avoided.

PART II. *Movement Toward Homogeneous Societies*

Communities were formed at different times, by different people, and under different conditions in the varied settings offered by the American continent. Many in these settings came to feel they had created arrangements of human relationships which could see them and their offspring through all foreseeable generations. They ascribed a degree of sanctity to social forms grounded in their historical experiences. While this persistence of the old and revered played an important part in America, it was not the main current of revolution. For at each point where there were those who seemed to have found the "good" society and to be content with the preservation of an established order, new "discontents" appeared.

The westward movement brought men face to face with new challenges of nature; and it brought them face to face with one another under new conditions and in new situations. There were different answers to problems of community life. And along this road there were no final solutions and there could be no final contentment with a "perfect union."

5

The Fertile Prairie: Bremer County

I would have my countrymen still *remember that the*
Valley of the Mississippi presents as happy a com-
bination of every requisite calculated to conduce to
man's happiness, as is presented in any other region
on the face of the earth.
　　　　　　　　　　—*A Glimpse of Iowa in 1846*[1]

The Prairie, the Forest, and the Stream

Midway across the country, on sloping prairie drained by the
Mississippi and its tributaries, the richest farmland the American
heartland had to offer awaited settlers. But in the rush of a
people to their "manifest destiny," tides of migration bypassed
this area for a time. The trails which led to Oregon and down to
old Santa Fe had carried adventurers to the ends of the continent
before men stopped here on the northern prairies of Iowa with
their families. Then, in the late 1840s, at about the time Mormon
caravans were moving on to the Utah deserts, settlers came to
till this soil.

　Forests of cedar, oak and ash, that skirted the prairies, were
cleared. Cabins were erected. Crops were planted.

　Along one of the streams that flow southeastward across this
land to the Mississippi, a German immigrant came to a site which
pleased him. There, in a stand of heavy timber, he built a cabin
for himself and his wife. In a short time he was joined by a
brother with a family. Within a year, two more settlers came—

this time, "Americans" from New England. They shared the cabin with the German immigrants through the first winter. Then, when the wives in this little community complained that they could not see the sun in the daytime because of the trees, the men cleared the forest back from the cabin and down to the river. In this clearing, which continued to expand as new families arrived— from Indiana, Ohio, and Illinois—began the town which later became the first in size in a county which ranked with the wealthiest in the state of Iowa.

In 1845, the population of this rural county in the American Midwest consisted of four people. By 1850 these numbers had increased to twenty-five. Then came the decades of greatest expansion, during which the population increased to almost 5,000 by 1860, to over 12,500 by 1870, and to more than 14,000 by 1880.[2]

Perhaps the newcomers were attracted by the glowing accounts of the independence and opportunity that awaited the prospective farmer in this region. Men who had seen it, publicized the northern valley of the Mississippi:

Thus you will perceive that *within* the sum of $400, you can be comfortably settled upon *your own* eighty acre tract . . . furnished with a comfortable log house, a good yoke of oxen, a horse, cow, twelve sheep, poultry, pigs etc.; likewise farm wagon, plough and farming utensils generally, with thirty weeks' provisions laid in, until a small crop is raised for subsistence. Here, then, you are not a 'tenant at will,' but reposing, as it were, beneath your 'own vine and fig tree,' with none to molest or make you afraid.[3]

Whatever the attractions, the settlers came. They were a sedentary lot primarily. At times a farmer had moved on from a previous frontier that he or his forebears had pioneered. But once on the fertile prairies, the midwestern frontiersman made his home. In fact, the publicizers of the region were advocates of domesticity. They noted that "married persons are generally more comfortable, and succeed better, in a frontier country, than single men," and that "a wife and family, so far from being a burden to a western farmer, may always prove a source of pecuniary advantage in the domestic economy of his household, independently of heightening the enjoyments of domestic happiness."[4]

From the beginning of migration to this rich hinterland, a change in the character of the pioneers was noted. These were not subsistence farmers or adventure seekers. Aside from those who came from the Old World, the midwestern pioneers came from the Ohio valley, the mid-Atlantic states and New England. They, as well as the immigrants who came here from the Old World, crossed the major lines of commerce and communication which had been developed in America by the 1840s and 1850s. There were established facilities for westward emigration. Even in 1840 a commentator wrote that immigrants carried with them all the necessities and most of the conveniences of life, were secure from danger, and formed settlements which were dense in population and close together.[5] In overwhelming proportions, the population was native-born American. Those who were foreign born were mostly German, Irish, British, or Scandinavian, and found little trouble in gaining acceptance in the thriving, industrious communities of the midwestern prairies.

In the community begun by the German immigrant in the clearing by the river, the German-born population continued to be a significant proportion while the community grew. As the years passed, it was not only the seekers after eighty-acre tracts and one's own "vine and fig tree" who found vocation in the county and its largest town. For as population increased and congregated in the county, services and local industries developed. One of the men who had shared the foreign immigrant's cabin through that first winter continued to clear land and, with the intention of establishing a town, had this land surveyed into lots by a judge from a neighboring county. The survey was completed in 1854 and filed in 1856. During the summer of 1854, as settlers continued to arrive, the trails from clearing to clearing began to be replaced by roads. A main street was partially cleared. A hotel was opened. A courthouse was erected.[6] New services, occupations, and institutions continued to develop.

The brother of the first settler established a brick and manufacturing business, which his wife and sons continued after his death.

The first store was opened in 1853, the year in which the town became the county seat.

A saw mill was built in 1853, and another in 1858, taking advantage of the county's abundant timber resources.

The Baptists built the first church in town in 1856. The first newspaper was begun that same year, as was the first school, although a brick school building was not erected until 1861. In this construction, again, local resources were used. Two more school buildings were erected, one in 1868 and the other in 1870.

The railroad reached the community in 1865, connecting it with major markets in the big cities just east of the Mississippi. During that last year of the Civil War the town shipped 500,000 bushels of grain transported in 1,250 railroad cars.

A public library was founded in 1867. A German Lutheran college, originally founded in Michigan by German settlers, was transplanted to the community in 1879. In 1880 there were nine churches in the community, including one Roman Catholic, and by this year the county population had stabilized at some 14,000. (It did not surpass 19,000 in 1950.)

Perhaps half of the population in 1880 were German-born or of German descent. It was said that these German inhabitants, who emigrated almost exclusively from the northern—Protestant—part of Germany, came "poor, bought land at low rates on long time, making small payments and by industry and frugality" became thrifty and substantial farmers.[7] Few of the German-Americans became tradesmen or mercantilists. These enterprises were reserved for the Yankees from New England, and other industrious native Americans, who had crossed the Mississippi in search of a new start. They were the "townbuilders" who created a thriving center of rural commerce, one of the many settlements—"dense in population"—which provided vocation and human contacts for people as they confronted nature on the prairies, invested in its resources, and tamed them to their purposes.

The community grew steadily and naturally. The initial differences among the settlers were tempered by the common circumstances confronting all. There was a diversity—of ethnic backgrounds, of religious sects, of languages and opinions—but all came to form one society. There was independence in individual hopes and aspirations, but there was also an acceptance of mutual interdependence from the day when the founders, each with his own ambition to pursue, shared a cabin against the rigors of the first winter. An early writer noted the phenomenon of new amalgamation and mutual dependence in communities on the prairie frontier:

> Men must cleave to their kind, and must be dependent upon each other. Pride and jealousy give way to the natural yearnings of the human heart for society. They begin to rub off the neutral prejudices; one takes a step and then the other; they meet half way and embrace; and the society thus newly organized and constituted, is more liberal, enlarged, unprejudiced, and, of course, more affectionate, than a society of people of like birth and character, who bring all their early prejudices as a common stock, to be transmitted as an inheritance to posterity.[8]

View from the Prairie

The world outside did not intrude greatly on the prairie community in its formative years. When it did, the people felt they had as much influence on external events as the events had on them. It took more than ten years to build the railroads from the Mississippi to the Missouri after the land grants were made in 1856. And then the process was accelerated because of the need of a country at war for grain from its heartland. Before that war, hardly a dozen daily papers were published in the state. Most of these were only of local interest. The lead editorial in the first issue (1856) of the *Republican*, the first newspaper published in the prosperous county on the prairie, said: "To local matters we intend to allot a large space, and ask the public to make this office the connecting point of local intelligence, that we may be able to disseminate the same through the ramifications of the post-office, to the end of the earth."[9]

Local discussion on "almost every subject that may arise" was considered beneficial by the *Republican*. But these discussions would be carried on in the proper spirit, and where this spirit was maintained, the community need not fear fanatics who "many times damage the cause they espouse." The local newspaper thus was to be an instrument of the public dialogues. It desired to be "positive" but not "dogmatic." It would "weigh carefully and give due consideration to the opinions of everyone, and ask only the same from others in regard to our own."

But the world outside from which these settlers had come was not shut out completely. True, the people did not consciously think of their movements to new homes beyond the Mississippi as helping to fulfill a nation's destiny. They probably did not reflect on the development of their granaries, which within ten years permitted the shipping of a half million bushels to outside markets, as a factor in the growing strength of a national community. For the most part, they lived apart from the issue of slavery—it was not vivid in their daily experience. Still, the issues that dominated the national forums *were* issues which made a difference on the prairies and called for the formation of opinions.

In 1854, eight years after admission of the territory as a state in the Union, the two Senators from Iowa voted for the Kansas-Nebraska act with its clause permitting self-determination on slavery for new states. In the national forum Horace Greeley said: "What gain had freedom in the admission of Iowa into the Union?" And men in the state did not let the votes of their Senators stand unchallenged. A new governor was elected in 1854 on a platform which insisted on the inviolability of the Missouri Compromise, which had settled on the abolition of slavery for new states in the West. (In fact, Iowa had been the first free state born of that Missouri Compromise). In 1856 the *Republican* was saying:

This is the great political question of the day. Is this continent to be overrun with slavery, or is the fundamental principle of the Declaration of Independence to be carried out in good faith, as was intended by the illustrious penman of that important document. . . . If the powers that be thrust slavery into Kansas, or in any other organized Territory, and organize it into slavery States, then our position must change and we shall insist upon its being expelled from such territory. We shall not hold ourselves accountable for the consequences, if the slave power compel us to change from the defensive position we now occupy to the aggressive one—of thrusting back slavery from territory thus invaded.[10]

An attitude toward human dignity was being refined by the experiences of men in the community. It was not at first a coherent doctrine of faith, to be championed and defended aggressively. And neither was the sense of a national community—embodied politically in the Federal Union—a coherent faith for most men of this region. They were developing a sense of local and regional pride and strong identifications with the shared experiences of community-building on the prairie. But the sanctity of the national Union and the right of equal citizenship and freedom for all races in America—these were doctrines which required personal experiences to become articles of faith in a way of life.

These experiences came for many with the Civil War. Several local companies were recruited, and although they were attached to different regiments in the Union armies, great local pride was expressed by those who served. But a sense of commitment to a national community was also reflected, as in the fervor of the local schoolmaster who enlisted in 1861 "to sustain the flag of my country." As active participants in the great national drama of the 1860s these men campaigned largely in the West—with Grant, and later with Sherman, along the Mississippi and across the South.

At first the men from the western prairies had no deep moral qualms about slavery. They did not identify themselves with a brand of fiery Abolition which still brought hoots and catcalls and even stronger reactions to its advocates back home. The Army policy at first was not to accept fugitive Negroes into the lines. But with the hard war that set in after the terrible carnage of Shiloh, this policy changed. And while the western soldier still had not appreciably changed his sentiments toward the Negro as a man, he began to experience this being in a different way as he helped to carry out the new policy of the Army of receiving the fugitive Negro into his lines, putting him to work and providing him subsistence. It was rebel "property" that was being destroyed or appropriated by the policies of total war; and the Negro, as property, was one of the props which had to be taken out from under the Rebellion.

The longer the war went on and the deeper into the South he penetrated, the closer the prairie soldier came to a commitment to destroy the institution of slavery as a human wrong. The local schoolmaster participated in the Union raid on Meridian, Mississippi, after which the armies were followed by "about ten miles of Negroes," to use Sherman's words. The weary, hungry, but cheerful columns of blacks bore witness that the Negro slave was not "satisfied with his lot" but would follow the dream symbolized by the army in blue even when it turned him away from all the certainties he knew. By the time he had marched with Sherman to the sea and had turned north toward Richmond, the soldier from the West had seen much of the colored man who had been so remote from his experience in the community of equals back home. Increasingly, experiences with a formless, homeless rubble changed to particular experiences of friendship. Stories were told of slaves who risked their lives to furnish the men with food, shelter, and clothing, and to lead escaped prisoners to the Union lines. Marching through South Carolina, Sherman's "collection of western pioneers on the march," as one historian has called them, had become an army of abolitionists. At the end of the fight for Union, the man from the prairie sensed that it was not solely an issue of property rights or of states' rights that was being decided, but an issue of human rights.[11]

The county lost eighty-four during the course of Civil War campaigning. The experience cemented the community's commitment to a national community and to what the local newspaper had called the "fundamental principles of the Declaration of Independence."

In more strictly local experiences, too, a style of life had developed on the prairie. The physical realities which surrounded the people were land, crops, small mercantile establishments—the tools and elements of farming, of agricultural industry, and of farm services. Wheat, corn, and oats, along with other grains, were the staple crops. Vegetables and fruit orchards were also cultivated. From the first, community farms were self-sustaining. At first wheat was the principal crop marketed. Later, the raising of stock became paramount; and still later, the community concentrated on dairy exports. A native Iowan has described the elements of this life which was bound so closely to the work that men performed on their physical environment: "There were no labor unions, no Social Security, no minimum wage and quite often a days work was from 'can see, to can't see.' But few watches were in use and quite often the old clock on the kitchen wall was out of repair. . . . . Usually a day's work was what a team could stand, and sometimes the driver's idea on this matter differed from that of the horse, which resulted quite often in injury to the animal."[12]

In such a community, self-reliance was a prime virtue and an important doctrine of faith. Industrious people had always been able to bend nature to their will or to develop enterprises to serve the needs of others. There were always things to be done, daily challenges to be accepted. Man could meet nature, persevere, and prevail. And men could come together without suspicion where they could meet face-to-face, confident in the other's stake in the community.

Sounds of the Present

Today, as one moves along the main street of the town which is the county[13] seat of this area, there are no sharp contrasts to break the impression of a neat, clean, prosperous community.* In the central business area the small stores are uniform, two-story buildings. The earlier blacksmith shop, wagon shop, and harness-maker have been replaced by automotive establishments. But the Sears, Roebuck sign has beckoned to the seeker of general merchandise for many years. And the local shoe store, furniture store, paint store, and bank stand as the contemporary counterparts of merchants of an earlier era.

The town traffic situation is handled adequately by a few traffic lights and six police officers with two patrol cars. The community has not found it necessary to make its streets one-way. Illumination has been improved with the installation of mercury vapor lighting. Work in town on new curb and gutter improvements has kept pace with new work on rural roads. A recent issue of the local weekly newspaper—now the *Democrat,* not the *Republican*—praised both the five-year program for improving the town's streets and the planned paving of two rural roads which would give the county "a good system of farm-to-market pavement."

New residential areas have grown on the outskirts of town, and

* The community description in this chapter combines impressions of a rural county and of its largest town.

some of these homes have gone beyond the normal, moderate range to more expensive brackets. But the contrasts in housing are not nearly as vivid as the uniformities. The community replaces and improves, but it does not dramatize differences and new styles. Even the contrast between "town" and "country" is not great.

Tree-lined streets and lawns gradually give way to well-kept pastures, dotted with neat barns and silos, along the highway leading out of town. And in the county, with its slightly less than 21,000 inhabitants, there are numerous small towns, each with considerably less population than the 6,000-plus that now reside in the county seat. Between these other population clusters, the pastures and farmhouses form an unbroken panorama of rural life, linked by roads and the flow of farm products to the major trade center astride the river. The whole is a community, economically and psychologically, with its cultural and commercial heart in the county seat. Within the whole, the significant events of daily life tend to evoke similar sentiments among people who have grown up, like their ancestors, in this area.

A local woman described the homogeneity of the community in several dimensions. First of all she noted: "Here one is either Lutheran or German or both." It is a fact that most residents are of German stock, although by far the majority now are native-born Americans. After one hundred years of settlement, only 1 in 35 of the county residents is foreign born, and these few are mostly from Germany and Denmark. The local woman also pointed out that even changes in farm life have contributed to community homogeneity. She lived in one of the newer residential areas in town. Some farm people, she said, had even nicer homes than she had. A sister and brother both lived on farms. Their way of life was little different from her own. "My nephew is in the local 4-H club and is raising a steer as his project. But if he didn't have that steer to raise his life would be no different from that of boys living in town."

The Catholic priest in town provided a similar picture of homogeneity as he described the small religious minority which he served. "My parishioners are mostly German by descent and by far the largest number of them are dairy farmers. We don't stand out conspicuously as Catholics in a Lutheran community because we have been here a long time too, and we are far more like the rest of the people in the community than we are different from them." (There were only two Catholic churches in this county which had forty-one churches and thirty-one ministers.) A Lutheran minister spoke of the community's people as "middle class." He identified two small "lower-class" religious sects in the community, but said that only a few families were aware of the existence of these sects until quite recently. Most ministers in the community agreed that there were very few "religious defectors": most young people married within their own denomination.

There are some "class" distinctions in the community stemming from the size of one's home and the nature of one's work. And as moneyed income becomes more important with the development of home-grown industry, social and economic disparities will increase. But where practically all occupations serve a common rural base, and where the line between respectable town and prosperous country is a hazy one, distinctions of social difference become less important. Add to this the fact that few families can boast of a longer history in the community than that of other families, and hereditary distinctions of social class are also blurred.

In an American community the high school reflects the social structure of the whole community. The local principal was hard-pressed to think of any significant problems among his young people. The minor ones he did mention related to persons from outside who had transferred to the school in the past two or three years. In the high school there was pride in the uniformly high quality of academic work—the students had ranked recently in the top 3 per cent on national standards. A former superintendent of these schools said: "Our schools enjoy a wonderful teacher–parent relationship because of the high type of family here. There are no slum areas or low-type persons to deal with. We have very few transients. We have no industry that brings in people from outside." A local canning company once imported Mexican labor for a few weeks at a time, but the company had provided housing for these outsiders. "The community didn't even know they were here," the superintendent explained, "because the families were not moved in and the children were never in school."

A large proportion of the students in the schools went on to the local Lutheran college. (The college was now enrolling some 50 per cent of the graduating class at the high school.) This lengthening of formal education experiences within the community was also furthering the inbred homogeneity of the population. In addition, the gap between generations was narrowed in several ways, as is usually true where occupation and/or land can pass on from father to son in a community. But in the operation of the public schools there were other ways in which the gap between generations was narrowed. The young people participated in total community life as they took part in affairs at school. An editorial in the *Democrat* concerned one aspect of this communitywide participation, applauding the plan to publish the school newspaper as a part of the county newspaper. The editorial stated: "The distribution of the news in a newspaper with 5,000 subscribers not only gives a wider publication of the student's efforts but also lets more adults get a chance to see what is going on in school."

People in the community were interested in themselves, in their children, and in other people like themselves. The *Democrat* concentrated on local news and on local people. The front page of one issue presented subjects such as: "Local School Registration"; "School Board Posts to be Filled"; "C of C Has Moved into New Office"; "Hospital Committee Plans Meeting with Civic Groups"; "Supervisors Want Corn Cut Back" (to give motorists at rural intersections a better view of approaching cars); "Local Police Get Letter from Man Helped Here." The story accompanying the last-named article told of a man from Minnesota who had deserted his wife and finally ended up in this community. Local police and the Salvation Army had helped him and talked him into returning to his responsibilities at home.

In their commitment to the growth of a prosperous rural community in the past one hundred years, the people were firm in a sense of individual responsibility, and they were very much aware of the fact when someone was an outsider. Interestingly, the local newspaper published on page 2, under a section titled "Court House News Briefs," the names, charges, and fines of traffic violators, along with the names of contestants in civil and criminal cases. These were matters of community interest and public information. One who was "in and of" the community must share foibles, when apprehended, along with honors and awards. There was no escape to anonymity in remaining in good standing locally, for the community was a personal matter. And because of this, as the county attorney explained, people were often reluctant to testify in local cases. As for attaining the status of an "insider," this, too, was a personal matter. The same housewife who said that "here one is either Lutheran or German or both" also added "or an outsider." One could be an outsider even while living in the community by the very fact of being too visibly different. In the earliest days of settlement in this region there was little tolerance for the deviant or the nondomesticated. In 1840 a commentator said:

> It is truly to be regretted, that the virgin soil of Iowa has ever been defiled by the tracks of a *polite mobite,* a *popular murderer* or a *legalized thief,* but it is quite gratifying that neither the soil nor climate agrees with such gentry. They have, therefore, found it convenient to make but a short stay in the country; and, after visiting us, they . . . generally take up their march to the south, perhaps to Texas.[14]

The visibly different person was *still* at a disadvantage in the community. One person who was interviewed recently told of visiting in California during the summer. He had enjoyed his visit, but was quick to add that he wouldn't want to live there. There seemed to be so many foreign people in the town in northern California he had visited. He said: "We're Americans here. Out there I saw nothing but Italians and Portuguese and people like that."

Of course, "difference" in a community need not be a matter of color or ethnic background. A local Home cared for dependent children who came for psychological treatment from all over the state. But in the high school which some of these children attended it was more difficult for them to be accepted into normal patterns of activities. Where a child had behavior problems before coming to the community, his local experiences of exclusion might push him toward more openly expressed antisocial behavior. One teenager in the high school said that some of the boys from the Children's Home were becoming delinquent and adopting the uniform of rebellious youth—the black leather jacket and the long haircut. He declared: "Actually the kids in the Home are real nice when you get to know them. The recent arrivals seem harder to get acquainted with. Some of them are proud of looking different and acting funny." He added: "The ones that get into activities are O.K., and are accepted like anyone else."

In a sense, the community had not learned to accommodate to outsiders such as these.

The Broadening Rural World

The tone of statements made about the community's way of life changed subtly in recent years. The immense pride was still there. The confidence in the future was unshaken. But a shift in emphasis could be noted. Brochures from a revitalized Chamber of Commerce emphasized: "Industry . . . working partner in a successful community"; and "There's room for more industry. . . ." The town now was advertised as a center of "industrial opportunity," "civic progress," and "graceful living," in that order.

The change began following the Second World War. A local company which had been turning out a line of earth-moving equipment was incorporated in 1946. From its first, hand-built model, produced in 1941, this company had grown by 1960 to an $8,000,000-a-year business, with some three hundred employees and an annual payroll of over $2,000,000. Its manufactures were shipped to nearly every country in the free world.

There were other signs of change. A Lutheran life insurance company located its national headquarters in the community and operated a large field force, selling to members of Lutheran denominations in twenty-three states and the District of Columbia. A new million-dollar building was completed by the company in 1958, and by then over 140 local people were employed on a payroll of some $500,000.

The Carnation Company had converted an evaporated-milk plant to an enlarged powdered-milk plant in the community. In 1960, 130 local citizens were employed in this branch of the company's instant products division. Thus, while creameries and dairies were an old and honored part of local commerce, the community was keeping pace with new processes in this industry too, extending the reach of local products into broader and more distant markets.

These were the three major local industries in 1960. But the Chamber of Commerce was quick to state: "Even though these industries contribute greatly to the community there is room for more industry in this community that has so much to offer." The community was not seeking new people; it sought new vocational outlets for its own people. It considered industrious people to be one of its major resources. A brochure said:

The labor supply for . . . industries is drawn from the city and from an area within a 20 mile radius of the city. The estimated population of the area is more than 25,000. Coming from a state which has the lowest rate of illiteracy in the nation, our . . . workers are unusually well qualified. Many . . . come from rural areas where they have acquired a high degree of mechanical aptitude through working with machinery and equipment. . . .

The pattern of population growth and movement reflected these economic changes: The town population grew from 5,124 in 1950 to 6,336 in 1960. The total population in the county grew from 18,884 in 1950 to 20,968 in 1960. Thus, although the whole county was still growing gradually, the town was gaining population at a rapid rate. And over 1 person in 5 working in town was now employed in manufacturing.

What was the significance of these changes? It should be noted first that the major industries in the community were still "home grown" or at least anchored to the people by common ties of interest and sentiment.

The farm and earth-moving equipment producer was an enterprising hometowner, who personified the community's pride in initiative and industriousness. He had built his first piece of equipment by hand, modifying implements he and many others had used for years in their farming. Now his good fortune was shared as the good fortune of the whole community. Improved equipment required less men to work the farms; and these men were coming into town to participate in a million-dollar industry that *exported* to many countries.

The insurance company which had located its home office in the community was a *Lutheran* life insurance company. Perhaps its directors considered this location to be the heart of American Lutheranism. At any rate, this business too represented an export. This time the link was with other American Lutherans, across "23 states and the District of Columbia."

The milk-processing plant was also a natural expression of a vital part of life in the community. Now the products of the dairy herds, reaching distant markets for many years, were being carried even further, and in new forms.

All these developments represented transformations rather than radical dislocations in the community's way of life. The energies of this small but dynamic center of American life and culture were being felt in new ways. Farms were consolidating, less stable small businesses were closing down, and even the smaller villages in the county were disappearing. More people were being employed in local agricultural industry. But just as in the past, the common ties and the common economic base of the community modulated divisive forces present. The Great Depression was softened largely through the strength, durability, and independence of the farm way of life. The county never experienced a complete farm failure. Many people in town during the depression had worked in the WPA program, and there was less cash being circulated in those years. But as informants explained: "On the farm at least you eat." And this rich land had continued to feed and sustain the people through a hard period.

Today, it is estimated that only one-fourth of the young people in the county are in 4-H clubs. Yet the rural influence remains strong: the young people in 4-H were reported to be from the "families of leaders." A major reason for the maintenance of a high standard of living was rich soil. Industry also depended upon this land and upon the people who had grown up on it. True, industry saw changes and the introduction of new patterns of human relationship. For example, the truck drivers at the Carnation plant were now members of the Teamsters Union. And the UAW finally was voted into the farm and earth-moving equipment plant (by one vote), after a layoff of personnel occurred a few years ago. But on the occasion of the cutback, the managers of the plant had found a job for each man laid off.

Figures available for 1958 showed that of 230 eligible employees, only 26 belonged to the union.

In spite of changes evidence seemed to point toward the continuance of the same social and cultural tendencies carried forward from the past. The founders of the farm-equipment plant had actually financed their business as a community enterprise through local subscriptions. And their young executives were also home-grown products. A doctor who had observed changes through the years and had seen the community accommodate to crisis, still saw the mold of homogeneity as the strongest determinant of the attitudes of the people. Even as disparities developed in a setting where money had become more important, he noted: "Some people who have practically nothing mix with some who have quite a lot."

Internally, the community remained viable and was actually growing—holding increasing numbers of the young both for higher education* and for vocations. Leaders sensed, however, that in order to hold the human resources in the midst of technological changes, new industries had to be attracted. Although natural, comfortable, home-developed industries were preferred, these could not be relied upon to answer the problem completely. The approach to outside entrepreneurs seemed to be (and it rang true to the community's spirit since before the Civil War): "Come and join us in our rewarding, industrious, meaningful way of life." It seemed to imply too: "We will shape you to our pattern."

The community on the prairie had persisted for one hundred years. It had been relatively closed to all but like persons. It had not been the scene of dramatic meetings of people, where cross-currents of cultures collide. Even the railroads had been late in coming to the area; and when they did come, they provided largely a link through which the local people could market their resources in the world outside. Since the early explorations of Zebulon Pike, this region had been bypassed except by those who went in and stayed. Thus, the social and economic life of the settlers was held largely within a range of common experiences as they developed their style of living, close to the soil.

Within the community people were conditioned to be inde-

---

* The enrollment at the local Lutheran college increased from 175 students in 1945 to 1,051 in 1960.

pendent, proud, and enterprising. They continued to see themselves in this way and to hold up these values for others. In their close associations there were few problems of personal identity. As long as an individual was encompassed by that circle the community drew around the "we," he shared the sense of a meaningful past, of personal worth in the present, and of purposeful direction for his future. The great challenge came in attempting to project an identification with these values into larger human circles in a shrinking world.

6

A Basin Beyond the Mountains: Boise

*I love the mountains, the mountain streams, the
western atmosphere, and the hospitable people with
their western ways . . . ; and even the frequent
solitude has its fascination.*

—Young Western Pioneer, 1875[1]

Along the Trail

The traveler who crosses the Rockies and continues on toward
the Pacific finds the stretches between habitations wearisome and
long. In mid-nineteenth-century America the pioneer crossed a
hostile wilderness of mountains and deserts. American civilization
had scarcely penetrated beyond the Rocky mountains. There
were outposts, to be sure, along the Pacific coast—expanding
rapidly following the first discoveries of gold. But the basin
regions offered no lures for permanent settlement. This arid backland was still the domain of the Indian and the wild-animal herds
which sustained him. By 1850 only Mormon colonists, oppressed
in traditional social settings of civilized America, had chosen the
Basin West as a home suitable for Anglo-Americans.

In the decades from 1840 into the 1870s the Old Oregon Trail
carried the heaviest wagon transportation the country ever knew.
Some emigrants continued on to Oregon to join the settlements
in the Northwest which Marcus Whitman and other missionaries
had pioneered. Many turned south beyond the mountains and

167

headed for the gold fields of California. Along the Old Oregon Trail—through sage and sand and lava beds, between the high mountains and the coast—were a few way-stations. Trading posts and forts had been established by British and American trappers in the years before the nation's population began spilling into the West. One such fort was built by the Hudson's Bay Company on a major tributary of the Columbia River. It declined as a trading post after Oregon Territory came to the United States in 1846. But as the waves of settlers moved west, this fort became a goal and a temporary haven for their caravans. An early pioneer's diary noted that the fort was an asylum for the sick and needy and that its master always fulfilled the part of the Good Samaritan.

Thus, a way-station off the track of flowing currents of American culture early gained a reputation for tranquility and hospitality.

There *was* something that could draw men back into the basin regions and against the mountains. It had already attracted many from the East to the far-western slopes of the Sierras in California. Now new gold discoveries brought tides of seekers into the northern basin area. Most of them doubled back from gold fields in California, or retraced a route traveled earlier along the Columbia River from the northern coast.

In the spring of 1863 gold was discovered in the basin near the fort on the tributary of the Columbia River. That same year, a new army post was established some miles downriver from the old Hudson's Bay fort as a supply point and outpost for protecting the northern trails to the West. And in the months that followed—while Gettysburg and Vicksburg and the Emancipation Proclamation were being etched in the nation's memory in other regions—it was estimated that 20,000 men traveled in "on foot, on horseback, and on the backs of burros." The coastal area was filled with miners and prospectors. A new strike was an irresistible lure. One who was there recalled the rush: "There were saddle trains for passenger transportation, pack trains for freight. All supplies at this time came from the west, mostly by boat up the Columbia River to Umatilla Landing. Trails were built connecting the Old Oregon Trail, and later these were converted into roads, and wagon transportation to the mines began."[2]

According to early accounts, the miners who came to the basin preferred law and order to the mob rule and violence which often obtained in such camps. Perhaps many of the miners—part of the back wave from the coast—had been mellowed by previous experiences in other camps. Whatever the reasons, the mining camps in the basin soon established a basis for organized justice. Law and order was regulated by miners' meetings or a miners' court. And while considerable latitude was given, it was also recorded "that the miner's court could deal swift justice."[3] Where conditions of lawlessness existed, vigilantes were formed and soon cleaned things up. In a short space of time the atmosphere was so cleared that "crime became unknown"; "men could travel unmolested; miners rarely locked their cabin doors. . . . So perfectly had the work been done that often miners left their gold dust . . . on the outside of the cabin door."[4]

However, not all gold-seekers came from the camps and settlements of the West coast. By 1864 there were still movements of population occurring from the East. Wounded and discharged soldiers drifted west from both the Union and the Confederacy. Midwesterners who had seen families dislocated and lives disrupted by war sought a different life away from the farm. Others came to escape the disturbing issues of a people warring against themselves. A young man who had been to the new gold fields had advice for those who wished to follow him: "Have a good reason for breaking the old moorings before looking for better ones, and when you start on a trip of this kind, do not cherish the idea that it is to be but a holiday excursion, soon to be over, when you will tumble into some rich gulch, only to come forth laden with stores of gold."[5]

But many oldtimers in the West must have felt that the newcomers did, indeed, underrate the profession of mining. One said: "Plenty of new men came, but they were not miners. They did the best they could. But, O what a time we had making miners out of corn-and-hog-raisers from Iowa, and pumpkin pilers from Missouri."[6]

With a war to fight in the East, the army had been weakened in the West, and the Indians on the plains took advantage of this situation by attempting to prevent emigration at this time.

This meant that emigrant trains had to be highly organized and consolidated so that a minimum of military escort could provide a maximum of protection against attack. Thus it was not just individual adventurers who arrived from the East in the gold camps but *groups* of people who had moved together and shared deprivations since breaking their previous associations in their former communities. A settler described this "bright side to the emigrants' travel. . . . They were compelled to move in organized companies of considerable size for protection; they were mostly from those middle or southern states whose people were noted for their social disposition; and usually the train's organization included programs of social features. Horseshoe pitching was the favorite game for the middle-aged men; card games were indulged in by all; while music, singing, and dancing were the supreme amusements. . . . A visit to a well-organized emigrant train furnished diversion for the settlers, and the visitor was usually made to believe that every emigrant was on the reception committee."[7]

The associations formed on the road persisted in the communities at the end of the trail. A local newspaper published the following notice in 1863: "The pioneers, known as More's Party, who came into this Basin a year ago, will give their first annual ball this evening at the Magnolia Hall. This will doubtless be the grandest affair of the kind that ever took place in the territory."[8]

Later that same year the newspaper published another notice, prophetic of things to come in the town which had developed around the new army post by the river:

In view of the long winter evenings . . . between now and spring, parties in town are about to resolve themselves into a literary society. We . . . now call attention to it . . . in order that those who prefer spending their time in that way rather than in drinking saloons—the only places of public resort at present—may think of it, and . . . resolve . . . to join an association of this kind that has for its object their advancement rather than to pursue a course that can only result in their debasement. . . .[9]

The amalgamation of old and new, veteran and greenhorn, speculator and homeseeker from both ends of a continent, developed into a distinctive pattern of life in the remote northern basin against the mountains. It was a white man's world—insulated from hostile Indians and at first excluding Chinese and Negroes from working in the mines. But it was not solely a man's world, although the female population was a small minority. It was reported that women had a prominent position and received much attention. In 1864, a local newspaper quoted a letter expressing the opinions of one young man in town: "It is better for you to pass an evening once or twice in a lady's drawing-room, even though the long conversation is slow . . . than in a club, tavern, or the pit of a theater. . . . All men who avoid female society have dull perceptions, and are stupid or have gross tastes, and revolt against what is pure."[10] Later, it was reported that the proportion of children to adults in the basin was much larger than usual in mining camps two years old.[11]

The swift and sudden influx of population to a backland area involved great problems of supply. While the pack trains and supply wagons continued to ply the trails, some newcomers took steps to promote the self-sufficiency of the burgeoning population. Their enterprise began to shape the enduring character of this community in the northern basin region west of the Rockies.

Domestication of a Boom

Perhaps too many of the newcomers were really *not* suited to the rigors of mining, as some old sourdoughs suggested. Or it might have been that the valley and rich bottomland near the basin where gold was mined presented inviting opportunities to ex-farmers. At any rate, many miners did turn to farming. And as claims were panned out, the switch to farming increased. The rule of those days was to sell an exhausted claim to the Chinese, who came into the region in large numbers in 1867 and after. But even in 1864 knowledge of the large market for farm products around the gold camps attracted people who sought permanent homes and plots of tillable land in the valleys. Vegetables and other farm produce were on sale in the stores of the community which serviced the mining camps. In 1865 the local newspaper urged farmers "to plant and sow as extensively as means will permit," suggesting that if they had raised five acres of potatoes in 1864, ten acres should be the goal for 1865. In 1866 the governor of the territory noted that speculation was giving way to a well-regulated economy. By this time hundreds of acres in the valley at the foot of the basin were under cultivation.

These developments indicated a change of pace in activities in the gold basin and the agricultural valley. And the valley, with its growing community, increasingly drew population from the camps and settlements in the basin. The newspapers of the day described a condition far different than might be expected for a young community, adjacent to mining camps, on the western frontier. An account in mid-1864 reports an agreement among the town merchants and businessmen to close "our houses and places of business on Sabbath days," stating further that "we hereby truly and firmly bound ourselves to adhere to the above agreement."[12] The following week the same newspaper noted with pride that the community "on Sabbath last presented all the appearance of a quiet, staid old New England village."[13]

At Christmastime, 1864, the newspaper reported that shooting matches, horse races, dog fights and man fights, ". . . with fearful consumption of bad whiskey," were the usual popular sports throughout Oregon and California on Christmas. But instead of this, in the basin community, ". . . numerous family gatherings and social parties were had all over the city, which while they set no bad example nor confirmed any bad habit, do make people better acquainted with each other and strengthen the tie of friendship in the community."[14]

The new conditions encountered by people who were deciding to start over in the West seemed to intensify the multiplication of new social associations. Settlers brought their traditions and past habits with them, but even more they sought a new identity in a different locale.

Most of the traditional churches were soon represented in the community; and all appeared to thrive with the continued influx of new families. Both Catholics and Protestants had established ministries in the first year of settlement in the community.

While the traditional institutions provided an initial basis for domestication and order—a tie to the heritage from the past—it was the parties and the balls, the lectures and special schools, the meetings of secret societies and fraternal orders that received most attention in the local press. "Balls, parties and glee singing are the amusements of the hour," said the local paper in the fall of 1864. And when the new hotel, the Overland House, was thrown open to the public that same season, the event was called "the grandest affair that ever came off in the territory."[15] Other announcements advertised such community activities as "Lectures in Phrenology," "Professor Newell's Singing School," a local raffle, and meetings of the many fraternal orders and lodges that had been organized.

By 1870, with mining camps declining and population generally receding from the northern basin region, the permanent settlers in the valley had established a forward-looking community. Farms were flourishing, businesses still prospered; but most important, people's lives had become intermingled in the web of social institutions they had created for themselves. They now had a stake in one another.

The phrase used most often in local circles to describe the community's history following the early mining days was: "No boom and no bust." It never became a major focus of heightened activity or development; still, it passed with relative tranquility through periods when other regions were feeling strongly the effects of economic and social dislocations. It became more self-reliant as a community, and perhaps the people became more dependent upon one another. As irrigation increased, the meadows and farms and orchards of the valley intensified the man-induced contrasts to the sagebrush plains. The townspeople extended these contrasts by planting trees of all kinds along the residential avenues and streets. Together with the indigenous cottonwoods which bordered the river and its tributary streams and the man-made canals in the bottomland, the trees planted by the community became the landmark of an oasis cradled against the mountains.

Through these years the community was apart from, and somewhat out of touch with, major developments on the national stage. Indirectly, however, happenings in the region and the community were felt in a broader arena. For example, the flow of gold from the mines in the basin in 1863 had a very real impact on the nation's destiny—helping at a crucial time to swing the financial balance during the Civil War in favor of the North.

Much later, the struggles over individual, corporate, or public development of irrigation and power in the valley also had wider repercussions, influencing national legislation and the development of reclamation programs. But the citizens of the community seldom envisoned their problems in such a broad perspective, and although they sought to improve their community and to give it better chances for growth, they rejected encroachments from outside. Their own reluctance to become more linked to the larger world was enforced by the physical remoteness of their community.

The Pony Express, inaugurated in 1860 to carry mail cross-country from St. Joseph to Sacramento, was discontinued within a year because of the establishment of transcontinental telegraph service. However, in this western Territory it continued service until 1864, when a stage line was brought into the community. The telegraph did not reach the community until 1875. In the Territory, the community remained the hub of stage lines radiating to smaller outlying towns and mining camps. But it did not become an important terminus of communication lines connecting other major population centers.

The transcontinental railroads had tied the ends of the country together in 1867, and by 1880 several lines had been completed across the West. But the community in the northern valley west of the Rockies had been completely bypassed. Finally, the Union Pacific undertook to build a line from Utah into Oregon. When the decisions were made on locating the right-of-way, this Oregon Short Line passed fourteen miles south of the community. Locally, the rebuff was considered a deliberate effort by representatives of the railroad to foster "paper towns" which they owned in the Territory and to destroy the community. But a few years after completion of the Short Line in 1884 the local newspaper boasted of the community's refusal to die. Instead, a new schoolhouse was erected at a cost of $80,000 and "the county sustained the city by building a court house at a cost of $75,000." Finally, the legislature for the Territory authorized the erection of the Territorial Capitol in the community. Thus, the community "from its own inherent energy, courage and intelligence . . . held sway," said the local editor, adding, "and now railway companies are spending their thousands to reach the streets of the indomitable little city."[16] However, although a branch line was constructed as a link to the Short Line, it was not until 1925 that the main line came to the community.

Under these early conditions of isolation, population growth was gradual in city and county. In 1900 the city census showed some 6,000 inhabitants, a growth from little more than 2,000 who lived there before the railroad began to serve the community. Then, with irrigation and reclamation programs undertaken in the following decade, population almost doubled. In 1920 numbers reached 21,000 in the city and grew to 26,000 by 1940. In 1950 and 1960 the city was stabilized at around 34,000; but the county reported some 70,000 in 1950 and 93,000 in 1960, reflecting the suburban growth.

Thus the community continued to grow steadily as an agricultural, service, and government center, drawing people from surrounding smalltown and farm areas. Stability—with no real "boom"—permitted assimilation of this population while a community renewed confidence in its ability to meet problems and crises as it had met them in the past "from its own inherent energy, courage and intelligence." And those who stayed—as most did—and those who sought vocations there, chose the way of life of the quiet little valley over the lures of bigger population centers.

The Balanced Forces

When a community grows to include 90,000 people in its extended area and comes to serve a market area of several hundred thousand, it begins to develop characteristics which distinguish it from the "typical" small town. More specialized services and occupations are developed and participants cannot easily identify the other persons they meet in the community in their daily intercourse as complete, specific individuals. However, when the growth is gradual the new builds more easily on the old. Thus, the smalltown atmosphere may persist. This is particularly true when a community is relatively isolated and independent of larger centers and when a history of self-sufficiency is prized by the people.

In the present day, one is struck by the unanimity in attitudes toward significant community issues echoed from many different vantage points in the social system. Private differences in beliefs and views and practices are cherished, but they must be kept private. In the public arena, the softening of issues and the moderation of controversy are the rule.

Even during the Civil War the community's people did not split violently over the issues or enter into controversial debates, although they came from both Union and Confederate regions. Early newspaper accounts reported political contests between Republicans and Democrats in which sentiments split along the lines of Union vs. Rebel. But this in no way impeded the fast assimilation of newcomers into the rounds of social activities and into membership in the local clubs and fraternal orders. One account of the early years said that the "union-threatening democracy of the southwestern states was in the majority" in the town's society. Still, the town had actually developed around a Union army post, and early social functions took place on the post and were indicative of a cordial relationship between the military and local society. Whatever the actual sentiments of the largest numbers were toward the great national issues of that day, the newspapers of the time stressed that all parties in town joined in mourning the death of Lincoln. The day this news arrived was reported to have been one of the darkest days in the history of the community.

Later, at the time when the Territory was about to become a state and residents were voting on the new constitution for the state, the issue of the position of the Mormon population was faced. Many Mormon families had entered the Territory, particularly concentrating in rural areas where they had developed prosperous farms. The great fear of that day was that this group of people, standing together *as an identifiable group,* could hold the balance of political and social power, "acting only at the dictation of their priesthood." The answer decided upon at that time was "exclusion" from the rights of full citizenship. A clause in the constitution disfranchised anyone who would not take an oath when registering to vote that he did not belong to an organization, order, or association which encouraged or taught polygamy. Another clause stated ". . . nor shall Chinese nor persons of Mongolian descent not born in the United States, nor Indians not taxed who have severed their tribal relations and adopted the habits of civilization, either vote, serve as jurors or hold any civil office."

The newspaper reported on the problem of the hour in 1890:

So it may be seen by the whole country that the people . . . , without division of party, have taken care of this Mormon problem. . . . The people . . . will not permit their government to pass into the hands of men who acknowledge, even make it a matter of religious faith, to yield a higher political as well as religious allegiance to a power outside of the constitution and the laws of the Territory. The people . . . would outlaw no man for his religious faith. No people are more tolerant of differences of belief. But they will demand that every man having a hand in its political government, in all secular matters shall yield his allegiance to that government. There is no other way in which a government by the people can be maintained.[17]

Subsequently, of course, the Mormon church made its peace with civil authorities over the issue of polygamy so that the deepest fears of the formative years in the Territory were allayed. In the community the Mormon was no longer excluded as a public participant; and he no longer was feared so greatly because he too shared as farmer and merchant in the peaceful valley many of the perceptions and experiences which others shared and cherished. Once it appeared that the Mormon's religious beliefs could be held as private views and that his public attitudes need not be dictated by his private membership in his church, the community could accommodate to him both as man and as spokesman of his religion.

Through the years, the community continued to emphasize that one must at least pay lip service to a firm belief in the way of life all shared. And today, there is abhorrence of the possibility that group might be set against group to stir up conflict damaging to the quiet equilibrium of balanced social forces.

The editor of the local newspaper stressed that people here did not often get excited over very many things. The paper emphasized a "Letters to the Editors" column as a method for promoting public discussion. But even on major national issues, he said, no one is throwing bricks. "And," he added, "we want to keep things that way." The discussion in the newspaper over the one-way streets and over the new ordinance requiring the leashing of dogs in the city represented controversy at about the pitch which could be coped with comfortably.

A local Catholic priest told of the one time when he really got into trouble in the community. There is a large Catholic population here, and its history in the valley is as old as that of any other religious group. Catholics represent a cross-section of the community, some families dating back to rich Irish miners of the gold-rush days. The priest said that with a relative balance in numbers among the major denominations—Catholic, Mormon, Protestant—there is a lot of cooperation on community problems. However, on one occasion the priest had taken public issue in a speech with the program and approach of a Fundamentalist Protestant group that was helping out in a recreational program for boys. He said: "On that occasion I was almost tarred and feathered for being so outspoken." The newspaper and other local leaders had taken the Father to task for taking a stand in public as a representative of one group talking about another segment of the population *as a group*. He had committed the greatest sin: provoking group controversy in public.

A leader in the Mormon church expressed similar views. He said that basically there were no extremes in the community. The members of the Mormon church were also fairly cross-sectional in occupation and socio-economic standing. Most Mormon children went to public schools—there were no Mormon parochial schools at the secondary level. He felt that the Mormons had been persecuted as a minority in the earlier days but had overcome this situation. Their current adjustment seemed to emphasize church-related activities and less participation than other groups in communitywide civic affairs. However, Mormon children and their parents were quite active in public school matters. The church leader believed that troubles developed for young people when they dissociated themselves from "their own kind." "But this community," he said, "is not a breeding ground for delinquency, and our people are quite concerned and active in civic affairs relative to their own vocations." As family men, Mormon fathers relied heavily on their church for private friendships, but this did not isolate them or their families from broader community dialogues.

The minister at the Methodist church—the largest Protestant

church—described his "middle-class" congregation. He indicated that this was a community in which there was much support of programs a church might sponsor. The relative isolation of the community had something to do with this. He too felt that the answer to the problems of young people was in channeling their energies into activities: "Give them recognition and you make them feel that they are a part of something important," he said. One way in which his church had done this was in establishing outlets for all age groups in church organizations. In its multiple choir program, for example, which included ten choirs, the church had even established a nonsinging choir for boys whose voices were changing.

The superintendent of public schools occupied a position giving him a broad perspective on the community. The "balanced forces" that he saw were, he felt, a blessing to the institution of public education. The greatest fear he voiced was that one group—specifically the Mormons—might some day predominate and be a source of conflict. The superintendent[18] had formerly served the school system of a town in the southwestern United States.* He much preferred the cooperative atmosphere of this northern valley to the extreme conflict between highly visible groups which typified the divided Anglo–Spanish culture of his earlier experiences in school administration. He enjoyed his present assignment in this community of few extremes. Public support of schools, and of school activities, was no problem. Parental interest and participation was high. In contrast to his former assignment, here the adult sponsors and board members on service and youth clubs and organizations usually were from the same types of families as those of the children and adults being served. Parents backed the schools, wanted their children to remain in school, and worked with school authorities on discipline problems. Thus, young people's acceptance of models of authority radiated outward from the intimate private circle of the family to broader public roles in the community. This fact helped to account for a low delinquency rate and for the lack of organized, antisocial gang delinquency.[19]

A balance of numbers and of influence among groups in the community had perpetuated a cooperative system, with a mini-

* The community of Chapter 3.

mum of public conflict tolerated. Practically all the people were
of Anglo origin—usually several generations removed from Old
World ties—whose immediate forebears came to this area from
the midwestern and southern regions of the United States. Occupations represented some variety, but tended to be "clean"
and respectable, anchored in farming, government services, and
merchandising. Even the organization of public welfare services
—coming to the county first in the Great Depression—had earned
acceptance by becoming respectable. The director of county welfare had formerly been a small businessman. His strongest friendships were still among businessmen and members of the Chamber
of Commerce. As administrator of welfare, he now patterned his
department after the model of a well-run business, striving to
raise the prestige of his workers and to gain acceptance for their
functions in the community. It had not always been easy, even
in this region that claimed to have weathered the Depression
"without a breadline." The director said: "You know back in the
thirties I was a relief administrator, and I used to be *called* to
come over to the State House to explain and justify a policy.
But now I am *requested* to appear, and I'm treated as an equal
and not as an inferior by the people in the Capitol."

There was no "lunch bucket crowd" or heavy industry in this
northern basin and valley, and the community did not want
them. Newcomers still won acceptance, as they had since the
days when lawlessness was first tamed in the mines, by their
readiness to cooperate. The people in the quiet valley did not
wish to disturb the apparent calm of this way of life.

Private Respectability and Public Tranquility

The community of the Basin West was now too large for the
shared intimacies of a small town. It was a small city rooted in
a smalltown heritage. It had grown to a size where a clear distinction could be made between that which was *public* and that
which was *private;* however, the participant found that he could
not separate his life into compartments and find acceptance in
playing one role in private and another in public. For a man
was known as much by his private associations as by the professional position he held.

The importance of social affairs and private clubs carried over from earliest times. One woman in the local Junior League said that there were more parties per day per capita here than one would find anywhere else in the country. She also gave a clue to the relationship between what might be called "private respectability" and "public tranquility." She explained that so much depended on keeping social affairs on a friendly basis that people would tolerate someone in a professional or business sense during the day simply because they invited him to parties and wouldn't want to break up private friendship patterns—a reversal of the big city pattern where organization "contacts" are all important and often dictate socially important "friendships." The Junior League member mentioned a situation where a local car dealer was considered a little too aggressive by most of the other businessmen in town. But they would not attack him in public because then their wives would not be able to continue to include this man and his family on invitations to parties.

The president of the local community council had a similar impression of how one must operate in order to get things done in this community. He said that people were pretty close to one another and that "we don't publicly criticize our friends." He explained that he might tell a man to his face, over coffee or a cocktail, that he didn't think much of the way he was performing a job, but he would never think of denouncing the man publicly. And in matters relating to the community council, the council too would be loath to propose a resolution that would stir up controversy, particularly if personalities were involved.

A doctor who had formerly headed the county health department told how he gained professional acceptance and initiated his health programs. First of all he had to sell himself as an individual to the commissioners before he could take the freedom of proposing health programs. He could only be accepted professionally after he had sold himself as an individual on a personal basis —accepted for his commitment to the community and its way of life. This doctor *was* committed to the community pattern for the "good life." He preferred to live "with the undeveloped wilderness at my back door" than to practice in a larger city where his training would bring greater monetary rewards. The pattern of "go slow" and "don't meddle too much" was his approach too, as it had become the approach of all those who, if not born into the pattern, gained acceptance in the community by adopting it as their own.

The doctor's public-health nurses were another case illustrating the point. Many of them had come to the community not too many years earlier when a polio epidemic caused local health authorities to seek outside help. Some 150 nurses had been sent to help meet a serious emergency here in the Far West. But when the danger had passed and some of the nurses stayed on and settled in the peaceful valley, they found themselves practicing public-health nursing in a far different manner than before. Here, theirs was an educative job. They counseled and provided information on health matters, but they were not expected to move aggressively into poorer areas to condemn health practices and sanitation methods of local families. They served *all* the people. Families were allowed to be different in their private health and hygiene habits. Yet, the nurses had access to even the finest homes—for consultation in obstetrics, for example. They performed a respectable service for the whole community. After some years on the scene, a nurse from the East commented: "That's the way we do things here."

Not every participant learned to adjust to local ways. Some did not care to. One woman who was a relative newcomer to the community and was active in the League of Women Voters said that the League was considered to be composed of "radicals" who stirred up controversy and, thus, trouble. This group seemed to be a social outlet for women who were fairly new to the community and did not enter into many other social affairs. This woman said that she did not play bridge and that her husband, a doctor, did not belong to the Elks, Lions, Kiwanis, Masons, or any other such organizations. Her interests were in attempts, through the League, to promote programs fostering dialogues on significant issues—local, national, and international—which did not attract a lot of community interest. The League of Women Voters had been able to play an active part in local politics by adopting the more subtle techniques of telephone campaigning and thus foregoing much of their public electioneering. They had been successful in this way in helping to elect the new juvenile judge.

The case mentioned most often, however, of a professional who never legitimized his position was that of a doctor who came to the community to head a new mental-health program. He also penetrated the community at a time of "crisis" when a homosexual scandal involving public figures had rocked the town. But the doctor and his wife always remained aloof socially. Although born a Mormon, and a native of the state, the doctor had taken his professional training in the East and in Europe, and somewhere along the line he and his wife had turned Unitarian in religious affiliation. Not only did they avoid local social affairs, but it was felt that the doctor wore his professional mantle too heavily and put too much faith in his high-toned professional education. When he began to take hold of his public duties aggressively, pushing for mental-health facilities in the schools and making public speeches, he came under attack in the local newspaper. Within a few years of taking up his mental-health position in the quiet community in the peaceful valley, the doctor left for other parts. This was his fate not for being different, but for being different in the wrong way.

A part of the American dream was transformed in this tranquil site beyond the mountains. A little that was raucous and opportunistic, tamed by a great deal that was enterprising and sober, shaped a community that was self-sufficient, proud, and dependent on its own inner resources. Growth through the years had drawn people largely from quiet rural areas, in which they had become surplus hands on efficient, mechanized farms and on newly consolidated sheep and cattle ranches. Some young people in this region were like a young man whose mother wrote: "He loves these wooded valleys and the mountains crowding in upon us, but he has seen his parents become content to let these hills be their permanent horizon, and he thinks he wants something more."[20] But the people who stayed found rewarding vocations here and the means and atmosphere for easy communication with their fellows. In spite of relative isolation, most residents agreed with the brochure of the local Chamber of Commerce, proclaiming: ". . . There's Always Something to Do."

The society woman who spoke of the community's penchant for partying said she made it a practice to get away at least once a year to the East or West coast in the same way that the prosperous local businessmen kept in touch with outside happenings. But, she said, it was always good to get back once more—away from the immediacy of problems of cold and hot war. Of course, not all on the local scene could get away periodically, or even wanted to. But the community was kept informed of the world outside.

Two television stations carried local and network programing, although most network programs were displayed locally via video tape and were scheduled a week behind the nationwide schedule. The newspaper carried far more news of the larger world than did the paper in the rural community on the prairie. Several pages were devoted to national and international news. Articles were subdued in tone, and brief. There were no banner headlines to startle and jolt the reader into buying; yet, the newspaper held its own in circulation with the big city dailies from Portland and Salt Lake which also served the community. Perhaps a clue to the approach this major news medium took to international problems can be seen in a cartoon that appeared in a recent issue. The picture was of a chastened Castro in a woodshed scene with a strong-armed Uncle Sam. The caption read: "Old Fashioned Remedy Still the Best."

Here in the quiet valley, where there was "Always Something to Do," the problem now was to find things to do relevant to broader commitments in the people's lives and worthy of a heritage of pioneer settlers. The original settlers accepted the challenge of nature and geographic isolation. Their descendants might find it difficult to ignore the problems and the people of a larger world.

7

Midland Crossroad: Racine

The fusion of the European with the Yankee takes
place but slowly, even on the new soil of the west;
for the Yankee is not a man of promiscuous society;
he believes that Adam's oldest son was a Yankee.

—A Foreign Commentator, Boston, 1839[1]

The Yankee Moves to the Midlands

Along the southwestern shore of Lake Michigan there were oak-
openings* and prairies which contrasted with heavily forested
areas just to the north. On an exploratory trip, a Massachusetts
entrepreneur found this stretch of land, ready to be tilled without
much labor of clearing, and chose as a site for a settlement a
place where the river passing through emptied into the lake. In
1834 he returned with two other men on horseback, and with
the help of an Indian guide supplied by an old French-Canadian
trapper he found the mouth of the river chosen earlier as a site.
The other two men built a cabin to shelter them through the
first winter. The resourceful Yankee from Massachusetts staked

---

* "Oak-openings" refers to lands where timber consists largely of discon-
tinuous and sparse stands of oak. Such lands were ready for the plow with
a minimum of clearing required, in contrast to more heavily forested areas.
Historically, the Yankee seemed to prefer the oak-openings, while the
German who soon followed him was satisfied with smaller acreage and took
on the job of clearing the forest. The Yankee usually had capital and
acquired, initially, a much larger farm.

out a plat of 160 acres along the lake shore. Then he set off for Chicago to get backing for his investment.

As is often true in American history, the restlessness of a people had not been contained by the constraints of treaties and formal legal arrangements. The Black Hawk Indian War of 1832 had occupied the attention of much of the nation. Companies of volunteers joined with Army regulars on the frontiers of the Old Northwest Territory to put down the disorder and force the Indians to retire farther west. A treaty was signed in 1833 ceding one-third of the area of what would later become the state of Wisconsin to the United States government. The rights of the Indians to occupancy were reserved until 1836, while the federal government obtained the right to survey the land during this period. But settlers could not wait.

The Indian War had been reported fully by correspondents from newspapers in the East. Stories of the fertile lands being opened spread through communities in New York and New England where enterprising Yankees saw a chance to apply their talents and resourcefulness in new areas. A writer of this period said:

> Loading a wagon with a plough, a bed, a barrel of salt meat, the indispensable supply of tea and molasses, a Bible and a wife, and with his axe on his shoulder, the Yankee sets out for the West, without a servant, without an assistant, often without a companion. . . . He is incomparable as a pioneer, unequalled as a settler of the wilderness.[2]

Evidence shows, however, that the Yankee seldom came to the midland areas "without a companion." Nor was his trip without planning. There was little movement into this new Territory in 1834, except for exploring parties sent to report back to interested groups in eastern communities. But during the winter of 1834–35, in the towns and rural villages of the East, preparations were made—among groups of people who had formed societies and emigrating companies—for moving to the newly opened Territory.

Most of the pioneers into the Wisconsin Territory west of Lake Michigan came by northern water routes across the Great Lakes. Thus they opened avenues soon to be used by people from Europe who would join them in building communities near the crossroads of a nation. True, a few came overland, on foot or horseback, through the Cumberland Gap from Virginia and the Carolinas. But the greatest numbers—Yankees and upstate New Yorkers—pioneered the river, canal, and lake avenues that soon made the heartland of a country the center of human energies transplanted in part directly from the Old World.

A historian described one of the paths that led families to the new lands of the Old Northwest Territory. Whitehall, New York, he said, was for some time the canal port for Vermont families, who arrived there by stage or farm wagon. Here they took the boat on the Northern Canal to Troy, where other families from northern New England and New York also congregated. From Troy the emigrants followed the Erie Canal to Buffalo, then took a steamboat on the lake to Detroit. At Detroit there were alternatives: sailing craft and steamers were available for the long water route around the northern tip of the Michigan peninsula; or wagons and prairie schooners could be used for crossing the 180 miles of the peninsula to St. Joseph, where ships again took aboard the families and their possessions and transported them to the Wisconsin shore.[3]

Throughout the year 1835 settlers came, mostly by sail and steamboat, to stake out claims along the lakeshore lands. Trails could be broken easily here—only the swamps had to be avoided —for heavy stands of timber were no obstacle along the extreme southwest shore. The land had not yet been surveyed, but the government did not make a serious attempt to safeguard the Indian occupancy, and few Indians were still on the tract in 1835. Those that remained were docile. Plats of land amid the oak-openings were quickly shaped into a white man's world. In fact, the transformation from wilderness to civilization was so rapid that within a few years after first settlement a newcomer found not nature but transplanted institutions, which now needed to be revised, providing the greatest challenge to his ingenuity.

"Enterprise" was the catchword of this place and this time. A local historian extolled the virtues of these citizens who possessed the "vital spark of Enterprise" in building their community. But in those early years there was also a strong bent toward specu-lation. The land boom in the new territories of the West was on in earnest in 1836. Real estate appeared to be the means not only to self-reliance and freedom but to quick wealth, and speculation in town-sites and mill-sites abounded everywhere in the new West. Chicago was the focal point of this speculation. In Chicago were two large auction rooms whose walls were covered with plats of real or imagined villages. It was said that as many or more "paper towns" as actual towns were disposed of, at premium prices, lot by lot.

Undoubtedly some speculators were routed to the community on the lake shore by the enterprisers in Chicago. But the greatest influx continued to be of people coming directly from New England and New York, often following relatives and friends. Five or six frame houses were built during the first year. One of these was a two-story hotel. Most who came were farmers, although many were mechanics and village storekeepers. But it was still the land that was the great attraction, and the rural areas outside town grew faster than the village itself. The great Panic of 1837, coming hard on the excesses in land speculation of 1836, was weathered, and the local historian could report that within a decade the village rested firmly upon a basis of "honest pay for honest labor."

The local newspaper described the community in 1838:

We have a jail, two fine public houses . . . a number of stores, dwelling houses, mechanics' shops, etc. . . . . While many places, that, during the rage of speculation for the last two years, have outstripped us, now retrograde, . . . our march, not having been in advance of the surrounding country, which is now rapidly settling, will continue onward.[4]

The community also attracted a fair share of professional men "and men of affairs . . . young and ambitious, who had flocked to the new territory from the East, seeking fame or wealth or both."[5] A description of one of the earliest of these settlers tells a great deal about the institutions developed here. This early citizen was from New England by way of New York, had a background of "inheritance," professional training (in the law), an interest in "enterprise" (whether business or politics, private or public). Upon settling in the new community in 1836 he opened a law practice and also operated a general store. One writer reported on this complete "man and citizen" of the founding era: "In the social and civic organization and activities of the settlement, the village, and the city that was his home, he took the part of a man and a citizen . . . and in every . . . possible way identified himself with the work, responsibilities, and other common interests of the community."⁶

Once the Territory was finally surveyed, the settling of land claims soon provided an outlet for legal talents. Settlers had made informal agreements among themselves that the lines which each had laid down on his 160-acre tract would be the bounds of his possessions even if the government survey should subsequently establish different lines. Adjustments were to be made informally, on the basis of verbal agreements, by deeding, one to another, any odds and ends necessary after plats had been surveyed and purchased. But following the final government surveys, not all settlers felt obligated to be true to their word. So in June, 1837, an organization of the settlers throughout this southeastern Wisconsin region was formed for the mutual protection of settlers' claims and for fixing boundaries between claims, for all these settlers were trespassers in the eyes of the national government. "It required wise counsel," said the historian, "as well as firm purpose and concerted action, to enforce fair dealing by those who were otherwise disposed."⁷ The founder of the community on the lake was made president of this organization, and the community's first lawyer became a legal referee of a judicial committee which functioned as a people's court. In this newly settled region people built their institutions for resolving grievances almost as soon as they built their homes. The court of the people heard all cases and finally settled all disputes arising over land claims. It was reported that this government by the people, without the sanction of written law, had the force "of a practically unanimous public opinion."⁸

In many ways the opportunities for the individual, who had brought "civilization" with him, were tied to his mutual dependence on others and his acceptance of rules formed by the many for the good of all. Households were self-dependent for material things; but in the rural areas away from the lake it was common for groups of people to get together to assist on the farms with work that might be impossible for one family to complete alone. At these industrial bees, men, women, and children would gather from miles around, not just as an occasion for work, but to fellowship as well. An account of these rural community affairs is provided in a Wisconsin history:

> These gatherings . . . were occasions of much boisterous jollity, and through the familiar meeting of young folk the source also of much frontier romance. The humors of the day were often uncouth. There was a great deal of horseplay, hard drinking, and profanity, and occasionally a personal encounter during the heat of discussion; but an undercurrent of good-nature was generally observable.[9]

In the town, too, there was great interest in activities that concerned and benefited everyone. When the new hotel was erected, the project was described as an "old-fashioned raising." Many different individuals in the community had contracted for various parts of the construction job. It was a business affair, but the whole community had a stake in the outcome. When the job was completed the townspeople joined together in festive mood: ". . . from the close of day until early morn a happy crowd danced away the night under the inspiration of music, furnished by a hod-carrier, on a three-stringed fiddle!"[10]

By 1844, 1,100 settlers were recorded for the town, and by this time 10,000 were reported to be in the county. A large farming area was being cultivated in support of a young city that was already beginning to make its first strides in manufacturing. Seventy-five per cent of the settlers of this first decade were reported to be from New England and New York. In the census of 1840 the family names in the community were predominantly those of English-speaking peoples; but a first sprinkling of immigrants who soon would bring a new flood of population—Irish, German, Scotch, and Scandinavian—could be noted.

Wheat shipments in 1844 reached 1,500 bushels a day, surpassed only by the grain trade of Chicago. One entrepreneur had developed an extensive packing business. Another was building schooners to carry the community's farm products across the lakes to eastern markets. Still others were preparing to produce new products that would help to revolutionize the economy and society of a whole nation.

Challenges that Transform

People who move to a new setting bring at least a bit of the past with them. They do not start completely anew; still, the way they shape their institutions is influenced by the new challenges of the time and the place in which they find themselves.

Churches and schools were among the first institutions transplanted to this new ground. But religion was less formal and ritualistic and regularity less strictly enforced than had been the case in New England. There was an openness on this frontier which led to experimentation with institutional forms. If ministers were less learned and less formally educated, and their ordinances less exacting, they closely reflected characteristics of the populations they served. Far less distance developed, socially, between the minister and his parishioners, and the position of pastor was not as formal as it had been in New England communities.

In such an atmosphere, public education also found fertile ground. It had flourished for almost two hundred years in the older New England states by the time of the Wisconsin settlements. Now there was a sense of urgency on this frontier to bring popular education to the people. In an editorial printed in 1843 in his newspaper, the citizen from New England (described as the town's first lawyer) advocated a community tax fund for the support of free public schools:

> The advantages of such a fund . . . are far beyond all human calculation. Its influence will not be confined to the youths alone, but it will affect the minds and character of all ages and classes. . . . Indeed, aside from this fund, I believe [this community] will raise more money in proportion to its size for the purpose of education than any other place because this fund will create a taste for education. . . .[11]

The community soon became a model for the rest of the state with its coeducational schools. In 1853 a new school building (described as "magnificent") was completed, and in 1857 the first high school class in the state was graduated from this school.

At this same time, population groups from Europe were adding to the dialogues out of which institutions were being formed.

By 1850 the German and Irish populations in the state and the community had increased greatly. The German population was strongly represented at the state constitutional convention of 1846. In this convention a prominent German doctor led a movement to secure a provision which would enfranchise immigrants without compelling them first to complete the process of naturalization. He said: "Political equality and good schools will make the people of Wisconsin an enlightened and happy people. They will make them one people."[12] The constitution adopted for the state did provide that all who were *bona fide* residents and had declared their intention to become citizens should have the right to vote at any election if they had resided in the state for one year preceding such election. This first bow to equality among participants promoted the amalgamation of the following decades.

The Territory needed people for its land and its new manufactures. It was a choice setting for the evaluation of a man "as a man"—or in terms of his talents and his capacities for enterprise. But at the first state constitutional convention where the people accepted "white foreigners" as soon-to-be equals, they did not go on record similarly for their Negro countrymen. Although the lawyer-editor from the lake community led the fight for recognition of full civil and political rights for the free Negro in the state, he found little support from any political party. The opposition, particularly the Democrats, felt that it would be poor policy for a territory aspiring for statehood to give the South reason to suspect that Wisconsin was on the side of abolition.

However, not long after statehood was achieved in 1848, a more dramatic crystallization of views regarding the Negro was occasioned. The federal Fugitive Slave Law of 1850, requiring the return by court order of runaway slaves, was not popular in the community. This extreme southeastern region of Wisconsin was known as the "Yankeeland Strip," stronger in its "Northern" views than other areas in the state where foreign-born population groups were already in the ascendancy. Moreover, the community harbored a few runaway slaves and also numbered some freedmen in its population. By 1854 the community was being called a "hotbed of abolitionism." One evening during the spring of that year a Negro runaway, who was employed in a saw mill just

north of town, was forcefully apprehended by two federal mar-
shals and their deputies. He was taken off to jail in Milwaukee
to await deportation. But a newspaper editor in Milwaukee got
word of the affair and aroused people there to a mass meeting in
the courthouse square. The news had also reached the smaller
lakeshore community to the south; and there another mass meeting was held at which it was resolved: "We, as citizens of Wisconsin are justified in declaring and do hereby declare the slave-
catching law of 1850 disgraceful and also repealed."[13] Soon after
a contingent of one hundred from this meeting arrived in Milwaukee to join the group in the courthouse square, the jail door
was battered down and the fugitive released and handed over to
the underground railroad.

A local newspaper reported on the happenings in the courthouse square in Milwaukee after the arrival of the "delegation":

At 6 o'clock, the friends of law and order came to the conclusion
that it would be unsafe . . . for a human being to be locked up in
jail over the Sabbath, against whom no crime had been alleged. Ac-
cordingly, a courier was dispatched for a team, and as the Court House
bell rang the tocsin of liberty, the writ of open sesame was enforced,
while the sun sank smilingly in the west, as he shed his last rays on
the spires of Milwaukee for the 11th of May, 1854—a glorious prelude
to the coming day of rest."[14]

The citizens went on record as favoring nullification of a federal law if it conflicted with their sense of right and fair play. It
became customary at antislavery meetings throughout the country
the next few years to adopt a resolution endorsing the action in
Wisconsin. But this somewhat incongruous antislavery and pro-
nullification position was soon adjusted as public discussion
brought about the alignment of parties and the final hardening
of the national issues around the concepts of "union" versus
"secession." Thus antisecession sentiments solidified, and in 1860
the governor of the state, in an address to the state legislature,
could say: "The right of a state to secede from the Union can
never be admitted. . . . Wisconsin is true, and her people stead-
fast. She will not destroy the Union, nor consent that it shall be
done."[15]

The political campaign of 1860 was intense in the lake com-

munity. The Republicans were called the "Wide Awakes," and
the local history reports that nearly "every man and boy in the
town belonged to some marching or other political club. . . ." A
typical rally was described as an all-day affair, complete with
"Wide Awake" marching clubs, bands and drum corps, and the
"Lincoln Rangers" on horseback. When parades passed through
the Fourth Ward of the city, where most of the German and
Irish immigrants lived, there was likely to be disorder. (On one
occasion, it was reported, a parader was hit on the head by a
brick and nearly killed). Parades ended with speeches by dig-
nitaries in the public square. In the election that followed, the
community as a whole went heavily for Lincoln. Shortly after the
election people began to gather in public meetings to discuss the
meaning of the national events then unfolding. Many shades of
opinion were represented in resolutions that were offered for
adoption. These ranged from efforts of extremists to "brand the
traitors," to statements of belief that government was, after all,
formed for the benefit of the white race. The local historian reported that "everybody had a chance to say his say, and out of it
all did finally come the correct solution of the problems."[16] The
stronger resolutions against slavery and secession were adopted.
On April 17, 1861, five days after the firing on Fort Sumter, the
local newspaper carried a message to the young men to answer
the President's call and to unite in the formation of an independent rifle company. This call rang out in the press: "Our Country
is in peril. Young men, are you ready—have you any love of justice—any sense of right—any fire of patriotism burning in your
breasts? . . . The President has called for one regiment from
Wisconsin; are you willing to show yourselves good citizens,
devoted patriots and living men?"[17]

Neutrality could not be tolerated. The newspaper called for
citizens to "mark the traitors" who talked "damnable treason."
Flag raisings became an everyday event. A report of the committee on resolutions was read to a "monster war meeting" held
in the public hall and "attended by all classes of citizens, men
and women." It was resolved that ". . . the citizens . . . will
stand by the constitution and the Union, and aid in the enforcement of the laws to the best of our ability."[18]

Soon, even opposition from the Fourth Ward was silenced. The

Irish, politically schooled in the Democratic Party, moved to back President Lincoln and the Union. The Germans, more reluctant and less politically sophisticated as a group, also were recruited into the colorful "nationality" regiments which represented the state throughout the major campaigns of the war. Although much of the German press in the state was anti-Civil War, and although great reluctance toward the war was apparent among rural Germans particularly, the community never required troops on hand to ensure a peaceful draft. The people gave Lincoln a majority of four hundred in 1864, while heavily German-populated Milwaukee was voting 2 to 1 for McClellan that year.

Companies from the county were engaged in battles from Bull Run to the last siege of Richmond and Sherman's march across the South. Reporting on casualties at Bull Run, the local newspaper said: "No one who has not seen the anxiety depicted on nearly every face since the moment news arrived of our regiment being in the late bloody battle, can form any idea of it."[19] At the Battle of Chickamauga in 1863 many men from a local regiment were captured. (The roster of men from the community taken as prisoners at some time during the war contained 360 names.)

The young men participated in this growing identity of a national community, and their relatives shared this experience with them. In one sense the war was as important to the changing character of the local community as it was to the clearer definition of national union in America. It gave a strong impetus to the amalgamation of peoples of many different origins who called the crossroads on the lake their home. Throughout the state it was estimated that 50 per cent of the 91,000 men who served were foreign born. At first, the Germans and the Irish preferred to serve in their own nationality regiments. But later a change occurred. One Wisconsin writer reported on this change: "[A] large number of foreigners served, first and last, in mixed organizations; they touched elbows with Yankee or Southwesterner in camp, on parade; exchanged deepest confidences . . . ; and it was often a comrade representing another race who was entrusted with messages to loved ones at home and with the dying soldier's effects . . . after the war this comradeship . . . was an important new impulse fostering the amalgamation of the race elements."[20]

And after the war older concepts of "race" were also subjected to change. Something new—called "American"—was fashioned in the society of the midlands.

The Pot Simmers

Immigration in the nineteenth century reached its peak in the United States at the very time Wisconsin was among the favored lands. The routes followed across the northern waterways by New England Yankees were also natural routes for Europeans, displaced by famine and revolution in the Old World. The greatest waves came in the decade or so between Wisconsin statehood and the Civil War. The population in the community on the lake had already grown rapidly before this greatest influx hit the state. In 1840 the community population numbered about 3,500; by 1850 it had grown to 15,000. When the tides of German immigration reached the western lake shore, a broad English-speaking base of population already existed. In 1855 the community population stood at about 20,500 and grew only to around 23,000 by 1865.

These stabilized years were also years of war, controversy, and political dialogue in which many forces contributed to the shaping of a common pool of interests among the people. After the first amalgamation experience, the community grew to about 26,-500 in 1870, with arrivals now coming more from Scandinavian countries as German immigration waned during and immediately following the Civil War.

Generally, the pattern for the community was that the Irish followed the Yankees and were followed by the Germans. People from England and Wales—and Bohemians, in lesser numbers—came concurrently with both Irish and Germans. Scandinavians arrived later and replaced the Irish as second to the Germans in numbers in the foreign-born groups. The pattern also showed initial settlement in the rural parts of the county and later movement into the city where ethnic groups congregated in their own neighborhoods. Then intermarriage between the groups became prevalent and, finally, further amalgamation came through the experiences of public education and new occupations that developed in a city where new industries were being created.

The census of 1870 showed that 40 per cent of the community's population was foreign born, while slightly more than this percentage had by then been born in the state of Wisconsin. Among the foreign born, Germans accounted for 35 per cent, Scandinavians for 20 per cent, English and Welsh for 17 per cent, and Irish for about 10 per cent.

Who were these people of diverse ethnic backgrounds? According to accounts, farmers and young craftsmen made up the greatest number. Economic problems among rural families in Europe apparently were a major contributor to the movement. The farmer and the village craftsman of a European town often joined forces, together with neighboring families, to go to America. The revolution of 1848 in Europe also contributed educated German professionals to the stream. The German immigrant usually continued westward immediately from his port of entry to the United States, having decided on his settlement location before leaving his homeland. The Irish often spent a few years in eastern cities before going on to frontier communities. A Wisconsin newspaper in 1848 cited a letter in the *New York Tribune:*

> You are now indicating to Irish immigrants that course, which alone can conduct them to honorable independence and comfort. Too long have Irishmen remained crowded together in cities and along our seaboard, over-competing with each other in laborious and ill-recompensed occupations. Let them now seek the free air of the West. . . .[21]

Wisconsin was presented in the emigrants' handbook as a "haven to the middle working classes." Ads for farm hands, mechanics, and day laborers in Wisconsin appeared daily in eastern newspapers. Irish leaders in Wisconsin promoted emigrant aid and colonization societies. Their ads boasted that "Fifty years' labor in New England or twenty years' toil in Ohio are not equal in their results to five industrious years in Wisconsin."[22]

The Irish in the community on the lake did not appear to form rural colonies as the Germans did. They preceded the Germans. They came early to the city and were soon active participants in public affairs. Many then moved on to other frontiers—perhaps building and following the railroads westward—as the

German flood increased. For all groups, and particularly the non-English-speaking ones, events and conditions continued to break down their insulation from one another.

The shared experience of the Civil War was one such event. But the issues surrounding the war, and other more local issues, also contributed to the discussions upon which democratic process thrives. The non-English-speaking groups depended heavily at first on the leadership and views of their own newspapers. For example, the Bohemians in the community voted the sentiments of the editor of the Bohemian newspaper; and the rural Germans followed the lead of their own newspapers. But the German Democratic Press was strongly anti-Civil War. It expressed the views of a class of Germans—usually settling in rural neighborhoods in Wisconsin with countrymen from their own province—that had never known a unified country in the Old World. It was the role of the "forty-eighters," the German intellectuals who had sought unification of a country in Germany in the revolution of 1848, to interpret the issues of the Civil War and to make "Yankees" out of the greater number of German-Americans during the course of the war.

Moreover, as has been noted, the city on the lake shore had given early support to a public school system. For a number of years foreign-born elements, except for the Irish, were not numerous in the city, while the public school gained great prestige among the population during those years. The pattern of movement from farm to city was particularly noticeable following the Civil War. Even those among the foreign newcomers to the city who helped financially to support parochial schools were apt to send their children to these schools for only a few weeks and otherwise to keep them in the public schools. The result was that the language and social habits and customs of the American-born Germans in the town could hardly be distinguished from those of the Yankees. The community seemed to be the right size for the kinds of encounters and communication between individuals and groups that readily permitted assimilation of diverse peoples.

Germans who settled farther north in Wisconsin, and those settling in larger cities like Milwaukee where ethnic urban neighborhoods were maintained, frequently remained German to the third American generation; while the Germans in the smaller community along the southeastern lake shore became Yankees in the second generation.[23] And from this generation, too, the Congregational, Methodist, and Presbyterian churches gained large numbers of young communicants whose parents were members of the Lutheran, Evangelical, or Dutch Reformed churches. The process continued, with variations, through subsequent generations and among other ethnic groups.

Amalgamation and "Americanization" were proceeding at such a pace that opposition voices were heard, attempting to reassert grounds for traditional group identity. The storm arose over a compulsory, statewide education bill passed in 1889. The law stated that every child between ages seven and fourteen must attend school in the city, town, or district in which he resided for a period of at least twelve weeks in each year. Furthermore, no school was to be regarded as a school unless it taught reading, writing, arithmetic, and United States history in the English language.

Over this issue the Irish and the Germans tended to take opposing sides. The German parishes—both Catholic and Lutheran—generally had built most parochial schools. Many of the Irish had not only been educated in the public school system but also had become teachers and administrators in the system. Most of them felt a loyalty to the public institution. However, many Germans stood behind the State Democratic Party platform of 1890, designed specifically for the "hyphenated-Americans" from whom the party drew its support. The platform stated:

> To mask this tyrannical invasion of individual and constitutional rights, the shallow plea of defense of the English language is advanced. The history of this state, largely peopled by foreign-born citizens, demonstrates the fact that natural causes and necessities of the situation are advancing the growth of the English language to the greatest possible extent.[24]

The Irish view was reflected in a letter printed in a Wisconsin newspaper that same year. The writer declared himself of "Irish birth" and belonging "to the Catholic Church," but reared from infancy in America and educated in the public schools. ". . . I do not now see any reason why I should slap my Alma Mater," he wrote, "but on the contrary I believe that it is manifestly my duty to do what I can to expose that fallacious doctrine enunciated by the democracy in their platform."[25]

The process of amalgamation proceeded. The state developed one of the most comprehensive public school systems in the country. This system continued to bring young people in the community together in shared participations which shaded into both public and private realms of their lives. Available statistics on the rural areas in the county in 1905 showed: one-third of the Irish who were wed that year married into another ethnic group; one-fourth of the Norwegians and Swedes married non-Scandinavian Americans; English, Scotch, and Canadians seldom followed traditional ethnic patterns in their marriages; only the Germans continued to resist intermarriage, with less than one-tenth marrying outside of their group. Figures for the city would doubtless have shown an even more dramatic pattern of amalgamation.[26]

In the city, new occupations had developed around home-grown industry. An urban mode of life was providing new "names" for the culture and new labels by which men identified themselves and were identified by others. Traditional groups were having to make more accommodations to one another. For example, the churchgoing Puritan had long been irritated by the disposition of the German to make Sunday a day for "jollity and beer." But opportunities for enforcing the blue laws diminished, and the Germans were permitted to have their beer gardens, music, and dancing, so long as no flagrant disorders occurred. It was reported that large classes of "tradesmen"—apparently of varied national origins—began to support the more joyous Sunday as a desirable means of preventing unfair competition. And the laboring classes were generally in favor on the ground that employers should be compelled to grant "one day's rest in seven."

The wagon and farm-implement plants that now made this a major manufacturing center were initiating the final social transformations of the melting pot. One local company employed Danish craftsmen almost exclusively and was the chief agent for bringing these later immigrants from Europe to the community. But the more common pattern was for industry, with its new occupations and its opportunities for the appropriation of middle-class wealth, to complete the process of obliterating—at least in the public realm of social participation—the symbols of traditional ethnic identity. Men with pride in skilled craftsmanship became "craftsmen" first, and German- or Bohemian- or Norwegian-Americans second. And as young people met in the public schools and married across ethnic lines, the older bases of group identity became blurred even in the intimate, private, newly formed family circles.

The lives of the most enterprising builders of this community on the lake shore tell much of its story. The businesses which native Americans founded were passed on to second and third generations, so that in the space of one hundred years certain family names attained prominence. Interestingly, however, just as the initial success of the grandfather was *achieved* in this new setting, so a business empire seemed always to be recreated through the vision and enterprise of the offspring. The man who broke with his past and began anew on the midland frontier achieved a new basis for his identity and for his self-evaluation as a successful person. His sons also achieved their success through enterprise and education, although the initial risk and sacrifice of starting a business was usually not experienced so dramatically by the offspring. But sons often began businesses of their own, or at least transformed completely the old company by pioneering new products or instituting new processes. And some descendants of the Yankee or other English-speaking pioneers went into other professions. The number of men from these family lines who served as mayor or in other public office, and the number who were prominent in local philanthropies, indicates that the early pattern of broad participation as "man and citizen" was perpetuated through the years.

This frame of experiences was the model emulated in varying degrees—and perhaps around different kinds of enterprise—by members of the European ethnic groups who also achieved new identity in the community. The skills of craftsmanship among many Germans of the early immigration established a kind of initial rank among them in America and also provided a mark of distinction for them in this community which valued such skills. However, these valued qualities identifying the "fine old artisan" as of superior German stock could not be transmitted easily to subsequent generations. Thus, the social advantages of such distinctions tended to be personal ones and could not be handed on. But children of "lesser" German families could strive to achieve their own basis for personal distinction in the community. A frequent part of this striving involved participation in the public school; and here the change of family name by this generation often occurred: from "Weiss" to "White," or from "Schwarz" to "Black," for example. Thus a new personal identity was a beginning for a new, "Americanized," family identity in subsequent generations.

In these non-Yankee groups too, the leading figures were "whole" men who distinguished themselves as man and citizen. The interest of the German intellectuals in schools and other public issues early involved them in the major controversies of the day. It has been pointed out by one Wisconsin historian[27] that the German intellectual had been concerned in the Old World with broad political and social issues. For example, he had contributed to the development of statewide school systems in German provinces. The Yankee, on the other hand, had had long experience in local initiative and local action as a citizen and he brought to the midlands a tradition of community-supported local schools. These German and Yankee traditions complemented each other in the development of the comprehensive school system in the state and its local communities and influenced the broad concern for public issues which characterized the thinking of leaders of the community.

In recent years the belief in whole participation was reaffirmed by ethnic groups. Thus, a Danish Folk School Farm stated its goals in these terms (1944): "We believe that an individual is not a farmer one day and a citizen the next. Therefore, we are trying to observe unifying educational principles which will help these young men to think of all the phases of society, to consider their own lives as a whole, and to regard their citizenship as an everyday affair."[28]

A family of community-builders represents the basic story enacted on this stage where enterprising men-and-citizens explored new facets of the American experiment. The brief biographies set down in the *Wisconsin Dictionary of Biographies* tell a story of change built around a common core: of new challenges accepted by succeeding generations that continued to maintain a stake in their community. Three generations appear in one family contribution:[29]

Home Products Manufacturer (1833–1919): Born near Elyria, Ohio. Moved to Wisconsin with his family in 1841. Began his business career as an office boy with a Wisconsin railroad company and later established a book and stationery business in partnership with another man in a town near the community. In 1882 he moved to the community and became a parquet-flooring salesman for the local hardware manufacturing company. In 1886 he purchased the flooring business from the company. A few years later he established his own factory for manufacturing floor waxes and wood finishes.

A son became a partner in the business in 1906. The son became president of the firm when his father died, and served as president until his own death in 1928. "He was largely responsible for the international expansion of the company, and had widespread business affiliations in [the community] and in other cities."[30]

A grandson of the founder of this concern continues as president of the firm. The company is one of the major businesses in the community today. The grandson grew up in this community to which his grandfather once gave a public park. He attended the public schools and now serves on the executive board of the Boy Scouts. His grandfather pioneered the community chest. His father served on both the community chest and the park board for many years. Today, the grandson can still call many of the workers on the shop floor in his company by their first names. There is no union in his plant. The business has been a family affair, and a community affair, for three generations. Its president still personifies the "whole man and citizen" of the earliest leadership in the community.

A Community Approaches Homogeneity

It would be a gross simplification to say that the community on the lake had achieved homogeneity so that traditional nationality groups no longer could be identified. True, census figures show that the percentages of foreign-born people decrease every year now that major migration from the Old World has ceased. But the community still thinks of its "melting pot" tag as an indication of continued heterogeneity. When interviewers talked to the mayor, this former small businessman stressed the diversity of "nationalities" in the community, but he emphasized the unity which typifies the cooperative efforts of the people when they address themselves to civic problems. A community brochure said: "The . . . method of getting things done is through voluntary public cooperation and effort." Occupation rather than ethnic background is more apt to provoke controversy now.

The airing of public issues; the toleration of private differences; and a lessened distinctiveness of traditional groupings in both public and private: this was the process unfolded through the years on the lake shore. These have been the kinds of experiences emphasizing the interdependence of the participants in the community's dramas. Satisfactory answers were found through cooperation in settling land disputes among Yankees in the frontier days; and similar methods were applied later by a more heterogeneous population to answer problems of schooling the young, building industry, meeting a depression, and generally developing a shared pride in the institutions which a whole community created. Through these experiences differences decreased as nationality groups came to be molded by the new institutions they were creating with their fellow citizens.

Throughout the years when local institutions developed, the dialogues between groups and individuals went on. Somehow a community consensus was always reached. However, when issues were extremely emotional, a majority consensus might abruptly shut off further dialogue. This occurred at the time of the Civil War when the local newspaper advised citizen-patriots that men in their midst were talking "damnable treason" and to "mark the traitors." But for the most part the people developed a shared pride in what the whole community had achieved. Thus one did not find a highly competitive struggle going on *within* the community. There were outlets for men's talents in the industry of the community; and a good life and decent income could be enjoyed by all.* These achievements of the postagricultural revolution—the development of industries which required craftsmanship of workers—enabled *new* pride to build upon the older pride in nationality, initiative, and enterprise.

A recent Chamber of Commerce brochure reported:

> Throughout its history, [this community] has been blessed with a plentiful supply of skilled, productive labor and this supply has continued to grow with the city. Together the industrialists and the workers built [the community's] international reputation for craftsmanship. Together, they have built and are still building a community in which the man who runs the shop and the man who runs the machine work together off the job as well as on. They serve on the same boards and committees. They respect each other's opinions. They share in the pride of community achievement. . . .[31]

Early industry was developed by local men of vision and enterprise. Later, much industry moved in. Some of it came from the Chicago area. As the brochure stated with pride: industry sought the community because of the local labor force.

Today, this is the home of several world-renowned industries, including the largest producer of automotive radiators in the world and the largest producer of jacks and mufflers. Before the 1930s when automobile manufacturing solidified into a few major producers, a number of automobiles were designed and produced in local machine shops and garages. As early as 1871 a local doctor designed and operated the first self-propelled steam highway vehicle in the United States. In 1895 the first auto with pneumatic tires was manufactured by the local Hardware Manufacturing Company. The development of talents important to such industries furthered the amalgamation of a heterogeneous population.

The major religious denominations in the community are Catholic and Lutheran—the former having more adherents and the latter the most congregations. In talking to religious spokesmen, one finds little clear-cut evidence of distinctive characteristics separating the churches, or at least separating the members of the

* According to the 1960 census, the median income was higher here than in any other community except one in this book. The "very high" and the "very low" were not prevalent. (See Appendix I.)

different churches. There are doctrinal differences between the major religious groups, of course. But these differences are not manifested in observable social practices and behavior. Both major denominations were initially strong with the German population and both were the strongest advocates of parochial schools at one time. So, historically, Catholic and Lutheran have often been on the same side of public issues.

A Catholic priest and a Lutheran minister both described their parishioners in much the same terms: ordinary wage-earners and craftsmen in local industries. "Originally this parish was a German parish," the priest said. "Now it serves about twenty nationalities; but I preach to them in English. We once had a Lithuanian, a Bohemian, and a Slovak service. But these nationality-group lines are pretty well blurred now. Two of our parishes are considered Italian parishes. But the priests that serve them don't even speak Italian themselves." Another priest—a Slovak who had received many honors for community service—explained: "The German services went out with World War Two. The Poles have married the Italians, the Irish have married the Slovaks, and even the Danes are not separated much any more. At odd hours here at the church I'll hold a service in Slovak, just for the oldtimers." A Lutheran minister noted distinctions between people in the Protestant churches, but he reported these distinctions as more "social" than based on older nationality ties. He described the Lutheran churches as largely "middle class" while the Episcopal, Presbyterian, Methodist, and Congregational churches were a shade above this broad middle ground. A Methodist minister reported that his church services had once been conducted in Norwegian as well as in English. But since 1943 this was no longer true, although the church was still considered predominantly Norwegian-Danish.

In a sense, the shared problems of immigrants had cast the members of all denominations in the same mold. Their religion was seen as relevant to the present: it emphasized the moral values of good family life, self-reliance and industry, and concern for the other fellow. One woman pointed out: "There is no real 'society' here. I suppose you might say the Plymouth Congregational Church represents some of the more substantial families. But most families have been here for many years and this cuts down class distinctions. Our people keep well informed and are not easily stirred up." She spoke of social acceptance: "Living here, people are comfortable and they are among friends. New people in the plants are not left out of things: they are invited to the social gatherings." She noted that wages are high, and said this raised the "status quo of the whole community." This condition also seemed to lessen struggles for status and soften conflicts between groups within the community.

The mayor and other representative persons spoke constantly of "our people" and of "our children"—referring to all those in this "interdependent we" in the community. Distinctions were seldom made of different groups within this "we" who were more or less deserving. One public-health supervisor made a few such distinctions, but when she spoke of "problem cases" she referred mostly to transients and a few poorer truck farmers of the back-country areas of the county. These areas remained remote from community life, for communications westward from the lake had always been poor from earliest times. The flow of traffic and of cultural influence was along a north-south axis, to and from larger cities. But the community in the oak-openings was not over-whelmed by the larger cities. It remained a distinctive, vital center of institutions valued and defended by the local populace.

There had been conflicts in this system. An editorial writer at a local newspaper said: "We remember the depression vividly. The town was down cold. A lot of the labor organization stems from that period." But while people had commuted to jobs in the bigger cities during the depression, the revival of local industries found the skilled working force ready and available for the component part-making that was the economic strength of the community. This was work that perpetuated the image of skilled craftsmanship—more distinctively identified with a man's individual talent than work on mass assembly lines.

Strikes and local labor agitation had appeared. Even in prosperous times, home-grown executives could not satisfy their people completely with company pension plans and profit-sharing. One strike at the largest local plant had been particularly long and bitter. It had occurred just after the Second World War and coincided with the transition away from the old pattern of paternal ownership-management. During the '30s, the workers in this plant setting, which represented some of the less skilled local occupations, had learned to identify their interests with those of the union. And when postwar contract-bargaining began, the contrast between the point of view of a management that had formerly known its workers on a first-name basis and that of a greatly expanded working force that permitted its position to be formally represented by a union was greater than anticipated.

But conflict had not led to more conflict or bitterness between labor and management. It was interesting that the labor-management distinction—called the "upper and lower echelons of industry"—was the one most often made now in delimiting groups in the social system. (A Lutheran minister said that the most significant social distinction he noted in his church was that between the factory workers and the bosses.) However, the editor of the labor newspaper could say: "A lot of leading in community affairs comes from businessmen who are oriented to the town and have the time and money"; and the vice president and heir of the local (still nonunionized) home-products firm could admit: "Perhaps labor is becoming more sophisticated about their social responsibilities as a lasting element in the community." (He added, however, that he saw this growing social responsibility in the individual laborer who became involved in community activities more than in something called "organized labor.")

Thus, a common meeting ground for diverse points of view still existed: the industry all groups had helped to create, and the community all had helped to build.

There was another indication of points of conflict relating to those who had difficulties being encompassed by the interdependent "we" to which community leaders referred. Two ethnic segments had not really been transformed by the melting pot. One of these—the Mexican population—was fairly new to the community. Most had come as transient farm workers and remained, living in shacks in the wooded area west of town, cut off from participation in democratic institutions in town. When the Mexicans did come to town, it was only to work in the more menial jobs in the foundries. Their children did not attend the local schools. And the seniority and apprenticeship practices in industries and by unions made it difficult, in any case, for newcomers to break into better job positions. Still, the mayor considered it one of his greatest challenges to attempt to get sewage, water, and school systems to the rural-fringe area where the people still on the outside—"people of foreign extraction," as the mayor called them—lived.

The local Negro population was the other still very distinctive ethnic group. There had been a Negro population in the community from the pre-Civil War days when this Yankeeland strip was famous for its abolitionist sentiments. After that war, a few liberated southern Negroes had joined the small group of freedmen living in the community, and became respected citizens. Their families stayed and the offspring found employment in service occupations and in industry, although the industrial skills which were the source of greatest local pride were identified with European artisanship. This was not an expanding, open metropolis where a man could achieve a new identity on the basis of interests and special knowledge that transcended strictly local interests and locally prized skills. A clubwoman explained: "We used to have just a few well-liked and well-established Negro families here. But after World War Two things began to change. The foundries brought in Negroes from southern Illinois to work in the most menial industrial jobs. The numbers have increased greatly. I think we're becoming more conscious of our Negro population." A director of a local charity indicated that most of the migrants came between 1945 and 1949 when industry needed unskilled labor in the foundries and other places where "our" people didn't want to work.

The Negroes lived in more centralized areas than the Mexican families. They were attending the local schools. But their very visibility presented a difficulty to the melting pot. Their churches, whether Baptist or Methodist, remained "Negro" churches; their neighborhoods were *becoming* "Negro" neighborhoods. A community that had homogenized its population through the years was facing a reversal of its normal social processes with an expanding group toward which it was now "becoming more conscious."

The problem of any visible newcomer was dramatized by the chairman of the county board of supervisors. He described the board's practice of taking on the responsibility of managing a family's finances for a year. This seemed to occur, invariably, with newcomers to the community who were in a bad way financially. The assumption was made by the board of supervisors that the breadwinner could not manage his money. The man's paycheck would be assigned for a year and a budget set up for him. The board would take power of attorney and manage the family through the year. The chairman said: "This is done to help people who have not had the experiences with money that those of us who were tried in a harder school have had." In this way, a family that was not yet "in," could become a part of the interdependent "we"—by accepting the tutoring of those who had been through experiences the community prized.

"Man . . . and Citizen" in a Changing Context

The community on the lake shore increased in population by some 30 per cent between 1950 and 1960. It had expanded greatly since the days of the little community in which the early leader was noted for being a whole man who developed and applied his talents as "man and citizen." However, there were forces still operating to counter tendencies toward the multiple, impersonal contacts of urban life.[32]

The community resisted becoming a mass population center even as it grew in size. Life was still community centered. Big cities to the north and south drew professional people and others with big-city ambitions. A local psychiatrist said that people usually went to the big city for specialized services. The largest local professional group were in the law, while the medical profession was a distant second in numbers. (Perhaps legal matters were still, more often, affairs involving a person as man and citizen and much less as a specialized "case.") The nearness of large cities also made small retail businesses locally unprofitable. The community had few movie houses. People could go to the larger cities for entertainment, for shopping, and for temporary anonymity. Thus, many of the contract dealings local people had with others were reserved for temporary visits to larger urban centers. But this was no commuters' suburb; those who lived here also worked here. Most important activities and human relationships still took place within the county boundaries.

The predominant work activities revolved around the community's greatest success story: its industry. This was not a white-collar or professional man's town: it was a blue-collar town, and the people considered the color of the collar a rather light blue. An editor of a newspaper said: "Less than fifteen per cent of the news staff in this office came from the community; but all the clerical and printing staff are natives." Fifty per cent of the local labor force was employed in industry. Few of them were artisans of the type that gave the community an early reputation, but they were not mine or foundry or heavy-industry workers either. If with the advent of new machine processes, more persons had trouble maintaining pride in a prized skill, they could still feel some pride in the efficiency of a modern plant. Thus, there was a large measure of truth in slogans proclaiming that one of the community's greatest assets was its skilled and productive working force. And there was truth also in the statement of the Chamber of Commerce that "the man who runs the shop and the man who runs the machine work together off the job as well as on."

Shared activities outside of work also were common: ". . . something happens at Memorial Hall almost every night of the week," announced the Chamber of Commerce. The townspeople still had a place to meet; and while their meetings might not be over such dramatic issues as the freeing of a captured runaway slave or a debate over compulsory public education in the English language, they still brought cross-sections of the people together.

There were some communitywide activities in which citizens joined more passively. This community with the melting-pot heritage and the productive industry now called itself a "typically American" setting. It took great pride in its championship Boy Scout and Legion bands and marching units. The Fourth of July parade was the highlight of the year. The units participating had often won prizes in national competition. They too were a source of great pride to the community and were strongly supported by the populace.

Not everyone, however, was so immersed in the present that he did not foresee the possibility of different answers for the future. The director of the community chest felt that the community was moving from smalltown life to city life. It still was not developing its own specialists or attracting specialists in many professions. But the local liberal arts college now competed for students with a local center offering two years of accredited work for the University of Wisconsin. And there was a great influx of executive and management people who had not grown up in the community. Some family-run businesses were taking on outside managers from big industries. A new leadership was emerging, providing the first real break in the continuity of home-grown leadership.

The president of the home-products corporation could still speak of knowing many of his workmen personally, having attended public school with them; but his company was meeting increasing pressures from unions to allow employees to organize. Many other companies had become unionized. The home-products firm had found jobs for each of its employees during the Great Depression; but people were conditioned to different methods for meeting their problems in those years, particularly when these problems were impersonal and, apparently, irresistible—as the complex economic dislocations of the '30s appeared to the individual worker. The community now had strong labor organization and a weekly labor newspaper. And although labor had a deep commitment to the community and its way of life, labor organization also drew working people into a concern for labor issues that were not just local issues.

The home-products company had pioneered efforts to enable employees to become "part of the family" in a shared-business venture. Through the years, it had introduced a profit-sharing plan, a pension plan, and a hospitalization plan. A company booklet recalled that in the crash of 1929 "the loyalty and spirit of . . . employees carried the company through this period." Some years ago, this booklet was prepared as part of an attempt to recapture the small-business atmosphere and interpret the organization "rules of the game" to employees. The book explained its purpose:

> When our company was smaller it was natural and easy for all of us to keep in close touch with each other. . . . But today . . . we have grown to the point where we cannot depend on word-of-mouth explanation of our aims and purposes alone. So this little book is

designed to tell you things you should know about our company, something of our history and the products we make and the principles and rules which govern our relations with each other. . . .[33]

Earlier it was a matter of faith that people who grew up in the community would acquire naturally the ability to properly govern their relations with their fellows. Now this company believed it was necessary to formally introduce employees to the "rules which govern our relations with each other."

There were other evidences that tried and proved institutional answers would be strained in the future. The community moved slowly in the development of specialized answers to some of its problems. Psychiatrists and others in the mental-health field observed that the emphasis on recreational facilities as a cure-all to children's problems represented local shortsightedness. They said that the community provided only general and superficial answers to its social problems. Agencies which didn't affect the broad majority of people were badly neglected. Thus, the campaigns for funds for Boy and Girl Scouts, the YMCA, Little Leagues—and other programs aimed at recreational answers to local problems—were actually oversubscribed. A director of a family services agency said: "We have no facility for treatment of the twelve- to eighteen-year-old juvenile offender; but three and one-half million dollars was contributed for the new YMCA building. We are beginning to become aware of new problems of our older people, who are retiring from industry and can't always be easily accommodated in the families of our younger married people. But everyone says: 'Let's start a club for the aged.' People here feel that recreation or a social club of some kind will fix everything."

In a sense, the community on the lake shore recognized social problems but perceived only homogeneous answers. The normal procedure was for private donors, and for public solicitation, to provide funds for more and more recreational facilities. Many service organizations existed and concentrated on public issues and problems and responsibilities. People pointed to red-brick community centers the town had provided for its youth many years ago "when most towns were doing nothing." But a doctor complained: "Groups of citizens are still concerned, but they do very little in a coordinated manner. Sometimes," the doctor concluded, "I think this is the most disorganized organized community I've ever seen."

In this setting in the midland crossroads, some "typically American" dialogues occurred. The great issues of public education, of national Union, of new occupations in the midst of economic revolution, of accommodation of diverse groups to one another, of depression—all were experienced by those who came to this place and were caught up in the development of human institutions. The values of human controversy and compromise, of unique groups achieving concerted goals through interdependence, and of individual initiative in creative work were expressed here. A synthesis occurred that became a bit comfortable and doctrinaire. Events of the past decade have been less dramatic and challenging to the faith in public discussion. Colorful nationality groups—like the Danes, who are still numerous—now remain "different" more as a matter of nostalgic recognition (on special public occasions) of the melting-pot heritage of the community. And self-made executives and proud artisans are being replaced by managers who are new to the community and by workers whose pride must be identified more with their modern automated shops than with their individual skills.

There is still a broad and firm basis for individual dignity and the "good life" here. But old answers and new-found comfort may not provide adequate outlets for self-realization among a people who have always pursued the good life with enterprise and through vigorous discussions.

8

End of a Trail: Seattle

It is true that no such movement can be found in history where so great a number moved so great a distance as was witnessed in the immigration to the Pacific Coast in '52.

—A Puget Sound Pioneer[1]

"Whithersoever . . . Destiny May Lead"

In the spring of 1852 the migration westward reached the proportions of an army. One pioneer estimated that the caravan of wagons on the Oregon Trail that year was five hundred miles long and three columns deep.[2] Hints to travelers published in the East and the Midwest indicated: "The trip to Oregon is not a costly or expensive one"; "An individual can move here as cheap, if not cheaper, than he can from Tennessee or Kentucky to Missouri."[3]

The motives of those who joined in the movement were varied. In many cases people did not clearly perceive *why* they were leaving homes in cities and farms in older regions of the country to establish themselves anew. Some saw the opportunity of a lifetime in a relatively unoccupied territory "within the reach of the Pacific—within reach of the world's market." Reports on the climate were also a lure, particularly to those who had suffered from ague since moving to midwestern farms and had found their work activities curtailed because of periodic attacks of chills and fever.[4] For those who had lost farms during depression periods, Oregon was a second chance. And there were some who shared the feelings of one veteran of a wagon train from Missouri in 1852 who said, simply, "The object in coming was to go to a free country where negro slavery did not exist."[5]

Other men, in the higher councils of government, had expressed the nation's interest in the Far West in less personal terms. Even before the Oregon dispute between Britain and the United States was settled in 1846, these men encouraged a tide that soon became irrevocable. Senator James Buchanan spoke on the issue of expansion into Oregon to a Senate session in 1844:

I say, then, let us go on whithersoever our destiny may lead us. I entertain no fears for the consequences, even should Oregon become a State. . . . if . . . we adhere to our rights, we shall at least spread over her mountains and valleys a population identified with ourselves in religion, liberty and law. We shall at least bestow upon them the blessings of our own free institutions.[6]

The first great emigrant caravan over the Oregon Trail had made the trip in 1843, guided over the last stretch beyond Fort Hall by the returning missionary Marcus Whitman. Just four years later—one year after the boundary settlement with Britain had been reached—the Territory was shaken by the Cayuse Indian massacre at the Whitman mission. The war against the Indians of the next two years delayed the expansion of settlements within, and particularly beyond, the Willamette Valley for a time. But the march of a people to the western end of the trail, which had begun many miles and many generations before on rocky coasts and marshy tidelands at the other end of a continent, could not be halted for long. And even as the Whitmans died in the opening skirmish of a war, the number of settlers they had helped to attract to this western Territory already assured the outcome of the contest. Soon men with their families were leaving more protected settlements in the far Northwest and were pushing into still-unsettled areas.

In the fall of 1851, twelve adults and twelve children—most of them members of families that had crossed the plains from Illinois and Ohio the previous spring and summer—landed from a schooner at a point of land on a northwestern sound. Their voyage by ship from Portland had been short and uneventful and their arrival marked the beginning of major settlement in this region. Two of the overlanders had preceded the group into the area earlier that fall and had sent back word: "Come as soon as you can; we have found a valley that will accommodate one thousand families."[7] The following year some of the men in the group explored the east side of the bay on which the little party had landed and decided that this shore was the place to stake their claims. Later that fall of the first year of settlement the settlers adjusted their claims to permit a pioneer who owned a steam saw mill—enroute from Ohio—to occupy a site on the bay that would be the best location for his mill.[8] Soon the beginnings of commerce, particularly in trading with schooners coming to the area in search of timber, ensured the survival of the community. There was great demand at this time for piles for filling the city front of San Francisco. Men who engaged in this activity realized $20 per day. And men of vision and great optimism began to plan for a limitless future of growth and prosperity here on a Northwest sound.

Thus it was that the great migrations of 1852 and 1853 found a new region at the end of the Oregon Trail opening for settlement. While the best lands of the "old" Willamette Valley might already be taken, there were still places where a man could have his choice. Families pushed on to this less settled area. A trail through the mountains from the east was first attempted by a train of immigrants in August of 1853, lured over the route by the promise that in this undeveloped area one "can have the pick of the best." The first caravan had hardly completed the journey before people set to work building a wagon road through the mountains to attract others to the region.[9] Many who came settled on farms in shallow river valleys back from the sound, where land was not choked with timber and the soil was fertile. But men who had come to build a community and to use and control nature for their own ends continued to push back the forests and to carry on commerce that soon linked their activities and their interests to those of a larger world. From its beginning, the community at the far end of a continent was destined for bigness: a place where people learned the lessons of the modern industrial century.

A pioneer from Iowa described the community as he first saw

it, two years after the original settlement: "There was not much of a town, probably twenty cabins in all, with a few newer frame houses. . . . The mill, though, infused activity in the immediate vicinity and was really the life of the place."[10] An event in the first five years further concentrated the population for a time. An Indian war broke out, as local tribes resisted government efforts to turn them to agriculture on reservation lands. Trouble began in the valleys east of the sound, where orchards and vegetable farms had been developed for a distance inland of some twenty miles. Farms and homes were sacked and burned as the Indians moved on the town. The rural inhabitants fled to the protection of the stockade built next to the bay where, with the help of forces from a sloop-of-war standing by, the attack on the town was repulsed. The conscience of the pioneer was manifest even at the time, for there was no unanimity of strong feeling against the Indians, and in the legislature debates were long and vigorous over the Governor's action in declaring martial law.[11] The troublesome chief—who surrendered, was tried, and eventually hanged—had many defenders and later was honored by the community which built a park in his name.

The village on the sound soon crept up the hill from the bay. The owner of the steam saw mill estimated that nearly all the old settlers at some time or other were employed in connection with the mill, either at logging or as mill hands. Lumber was loaded for China and other foreign ports as well as for San Francisco.[12] It was said that the community ". . . was shipping timber to Australia and Singapore and importing goods from China and the Hawaiian Islands before there was a trail to the nearest village."[13] The Civil War passed with the formation of only a single volunteer military company. Even this was undertaken for the announced purpose of preparing to fight the Indians if any more trouble arose.[14] People here were too involved either with local problems or with international trade to be strongly affected by the great issues of Civil War. After the war, the village was described as a town of thirty or forty families.

The building of the railroads was the great issue across the West following the Civil War. As early as 1853 Congress had authorized exploration of four possible transcontinental routes.

But the Northern Pacific was not chartered until 1864, and by 1873 only five hundred miles had been completed. That was the year the community—waiting with anticipation for the Northern Pacific to announce where its western terminus would be—received word that the line would end near a little sawmill settlement many miles to the south. Whereupon, the citizens held a mass meeting and decided to build their own railroad. One day in 1874 the entire population turned out to begin the construction, starting eastward toward the mountain pass opened to wagons twenty years before. Their efforts could not begin to fulfill the original plan to reach the wheat country on the other side of the mountains: they managed to lay track only as far as the coal mines just east of town. Thus, for sixteen years after the northern route was completed to the Pacific Coast the community was virtually without railroad service. But the publicity of the fight against a great monopoly attracted national attention.

In 1876 population had grown to 3,600. "In spite of recession and business stagnation"—a report indicated—the community had slowly but steadily increased in "wealth, improvement and public confidence." Steamer service to San Francisco was available every ten days; there were now more than 1,000 houses; property valuation was more than double that of 1872.

There were two foundries in the community and steamer-repairing and mill-work came to these shops. Ship-building was a growing business. An investigation by a board of underwriters in San Francisco "proved" that materials from this area for building wooden vessels for deep-sea carrying were superior to any other timber. The salmon business was receiving some attention. And other services for the people were being developed. There were three schoolhouses. A community hospital had been established by a local doctor to care for the many accident cases in the logging camps and saw mills. This hospital served many small towns in the area as well as the city. Three daily and weekly newspapers now brought local and national news to the populace. A description for 1876 said: "If the three greatest factors of public intelligence and moral culture—the press, public schools, and churches—indicate anything, every citizen of this enterprising town has abundant reason for congratulations."[15]

The growth of cities in the latter nineteenth century was spectacular throughout a rapidly industrializing world. Even on the frontiers in America—in the Pacific Northwest—the process of urban concentration proceeded. The necessary conditions were present: communities were carved out of a wilderness of natural resources; and through the rapid development and expansion of markets for trading in these resources, a community actually fed on this natural wealth. Markets were far-flung from the very beginning in this region. There was no long, slow history of gradual growth. (The community never gave up in its fight with the railroads, although it did not actually win out as a western terminus until 1890; and in the decade following, a second transcontinental railroad reached the community.) In the '80s, the railroads were bringing west new, and different, throngs of people. One chronicler said: "There was no longer anything selective in the process of migration; all kinds of people took part in a great parlor-car trek across the plains. Among them were fine people; there were others who came with the outspoken intention of cashing in on the work of the pioneers and 'turning the crown into the pound,' or, more frequently, 'making their pile.' "[16]

In 1889 population was reported at about 20,000. A fire destroyed sixty city blocks, miles of wharves, and several great saw mills that year. A year later, growth had reached 43,000. Between 1890 and 1900 population doubled again. And between 1900 and 1910 it boomed from 80,000 to 200,000.[17]

There were always compensating events in those years to help the city ride out disaster. A report on effects of the national depression of 1893 said: "The city scraped along, dug clams and kept a weather eye open for some bright loophole in the pall of gloom."[18] The "bright loophole" was long in coming; but when it did appear the community received a momentum it never completely lost again. There had been gold strikes before: in Canada, along the Upper Columbia, in the inland basin region, even along rivers closer to the community. But gold in the Alaskan Klondike in 1897 started a rush that brought many dollars and many people to this jumping-off place for riches and fortune. Wise city fathers set out to publicize the community whence dispatches about gold in Alaska were sent. And a major business boom resulted when prospectors, who were convinced they would never find gold unless they started from this port, outfitted here and used the city streets to practice with their dog sleds and teams.[19]

The new metropolis in the Far West acquired gaudy hotels, bawdy-houses, and barrooms to rival any in America.[20] It was second only to New York in the number of live theaters performing. It developed "electric lights and cars, clubhouses and palace hotels, spacious parks, superb business blocks, and miles of handsomely built-up residence streets."[21] Until the great Alaskan gold rush, no one had come to the community to invest money and to bring substantial wealth. People had come to take land and to build a community. Wealth developed from local resources and not from investments by eastern financiers. And when the first millionaire made his fortune—from a construction contract given by one of the railroads—he gave much of it back to the community in philanthropies.

New Loyalties among a Heterogeneous People

Drastic contrasts and social conflicts were promoted by events in this setting of the Far West. At first glance, such developments seem incongruous with other forces at work here. The social openness, the lack of formality, the shirt-sleeves approach to community activities, the continuing arrival of streams of newcomers —usually unsponsored by others already on the scene—would not appear to contribute to a "class-conscious" society. One commentator wrote: "Actually, the average business man . . . well up into the nineties, could hardly be distinguished from the day laborers of other western cities."[22] An obituary of a pioneer businessman-citizen, written in 1912, is further revealing of the qualities deemed important in community-builders:

He was the type of the empire-builder—the aggressive, self-reliant, generous product that found its way to the coast at the dawn of American development. . . . he brought to bear in this region the ability and resourcefulness that have always been the chief glory of the American pioneer. . . . There was the stupendous calamity of the fire of 1889. . . . In that marvelous gathering of citizens . . . one of the best words of encouragement was given in the announcement

their favor, all Chinese had left the community. The Governor of the state reported on the events of 1886:

The fact is not to be disguised that the people of the Pacific Coast, with very few exceptions, possess a spirit of hostility towards the Chinese residents. . . . I may be permitted to urge the view which is naturally taken by residents of the Pacific Coast, that it is important to have that country settled by free American laborers, who have respect for the institutions and laws of our country, and who will establish permanent homes, and who will rear their families and train their children to have proper respect for labor in even its humblest sphere.[27]

The schism in the community left a wound that never completely healed. Periodically, in other times and under other stresses, similar issues could again draw class lines across the face of the community. But a vigorous, expanding center of heterogeneous people could eventually encompass many diversities and survive many conflicts. The prosperity of the '90s, once the railroad terminus had been established, not only revived a tone of optimism and openness, but brought Orientals back to the community. In 1896 a Japanese steamship line was convinced by the railroad baron of the Northwest that it should make the community the major port-of-call on this side of the Pacific. Thus, the community attitude toward the Oriental, in the space of less than two decades, came full circle and ". . . again the Asiatics were looked on, not as a menace, but as solemn symbols of the wealth of the Far East."[28] At the close of the century, the seaport frontier was attracting increasing numbers of Japanese, Chinese, and Filipinos into community life.

It is significant that, except for Orientals and, later, Negroes, ethnic names were not prominent in the story of this community of the Far West. Even the label "Yankee" or "Southerner" or "Midwesterner" was soon lost among these people. In spite of the tensions which threatened to replace older distinctions with a new class consciousness, this heterogeneous community was not destined to remain divided. There were too many forces working toward what could be called a "new differentiation" of the population. Conflicts were partly a symptom of the frustration of certain ideals of the American dream. When that dream dimmed, so that opportunities for the majority's fulfillment were frustrated, the tensions began to shape the outlines of a class war. This condition was natural to settings generally larger than the true melting-pot communities of midland America. It was a development of this setting of the West, which grew so fast that it did not experience the small paternalistic industry of skilled artisans where the owner conducted his business as a family affair. It was a development leading beyond the melting pot toward the multiple, more specialized social participations and grounds of personal identification typifying the urban metropolis.

The earliest indication of tensions over new identity and social conflict came with the Chinese issue. When the debate over Chinese expulsion was waxing hot, "older" Americans of this western community reflected on some Old World antecedents as things from which all Americans were now separated. A respected judge of the community spoke to the throng gathered at a meeting called to compromise the differences between the labor and business factions: "For the first time in the history of this territory an attempt is made to divide the community into two classes—laborers on one side and all other workers on the other. This attempt is as wicked as it is un-American. . . . The man who would now seek to divide us on Old-World lines is an enemy to all." And turning to his fellow Irish-Americans—for on this occasion the appeal to ethnic origins was made—the judge continued (speaking of the Irishman): "He will not deprive any of God's creatures, not even the defenseless Chinaman, of the protection of that law which found the Irishman a serf and made him a free man. . . . Those who come from other lands to live here must obey the laws and respect and honor the institutions of our country or go back to where they come from."[29] Thus some citizens maintained that perhaps the type of white European immigrant now entering the community was not properly in tune with the free institutions of this country. The search for causes of an "un-American" situation led to reflection on the origins of the "class-conscious" elements. One community father decided: "This agitation originated among and was fostered by the most undesirable element of European immigration, and not until recent years was congressional conscience or courage sufficiently aroused to properly legislate against this undesirable white immigration as well as against the men whose skins are yellow or black, but who are in many ways more desirable than most of the men who affect to despise them."[30]

There were other rounds in the contest between factions of people seeking new identity in the West. Eventually this population, relatively cut off from the past and starting anew on the Pacific Coast, found a basis for accommodation of group to group. In later prosperous times the community was described as "middle class"—indicating that even such a large population could achieve a kind of homogeneity, at least in their capacity to consume economic goods and services. However, through the years, often due to the economic cycle, the community fluctuated between open, democratic acceptance of diverse individuals and groups and a class conflict along labor-business lines that largely ignored older characteristics distinguishing groups.

One citizen described the situation he saw develop in the logging camps following the turn of the century. No one ever dreamed, he said, of the loggers doing anything as undemocratic as developing a class consciousness: "The rugged individualists of the skid road and the woods seemed the most unlikely candidates for such a thing—and then they developed class consciousness and began to speak in the language of Karl Marx . . . in numbers that doubled and quadrupled disturbingly."[31] The I.W.W. movement, originating in Chicago in 1905, found support for its anticapitalist ideology in the logging camps and mines of the West. Slogans began to appear on trees beside the road: INDUSTRIAL WORKERS OF THE WORLD. ONE BIG UNION. WORKERS OF THE WORLD, UNITE. Like the forest itself, the men who worked the camps had been used with little thought, at first, of "reseeding"— of nurturing their talents. An adequate labor supply seemed as limitless as the timber supply. But the rough, carousing, carefree men of the logging camps—whose trademark as individualists was the personal bedroll they carried, moving along the forest roads from job to job—were reached by the voices of the new organizers who were dissatisfied with mere craft unionism. These men proposed to upset and replace a system which had been guilty of exploitation of both natural and human resources. Soon the effects of strikes and agitation in the camps were apparent. Loggers began to get industrial insurance and better wages. Employers began to supply bedding and sheets, and the old bedrolls disappeared. But the movement was also felt through more tension. Incidents of violence occurred frequently when the "Wobblies" attempted to hold meetings to proclaim their doctrine.

There was strength in this movement at this time and in this place: it found a response among many who were disenchanted and had been exploited. But it did not capture as large a bloc of sentiment, proportionately, as had the earlier Anti-Chinese Congress. One socialist leader spoke of these men as "class warriors" and "direct inheritors of the fighting pioneer." But most Americans in the Far West were not ready to accept this perception of the new pioneer. In fact, most refused to give up on the dream that some day they too would be masters of their own personal empire, however small. The Wobblies set themselves off even more from the majority when they adopted a pacifist position during the First World War. There were more incidents of violence. And shortly after the war, the I.W.W. movement lost strength and in the '30s was finally absorbed in more conservative American unionism.

Organized labor continued to flourish in the community. It did not have to overcome a long tradition here of worker loyalty to small businesses and family-run industries. The great numbers who came and found work on the docks or in the forests were natural targets for organization. However, the great majority of union men carried A. F. of L. cards and were skilled craftsmen who had pride in their training and experience. Many were homeowners.[32] Pride and identity were no longer so linked to being a "Swede" or a "German-American" or to a loyalty to a trusted boss and businessowner, but to being a carpenter or longshoreman—and a homeowner. Men who came late had arrived with only their labor, skill, and ambition. They sought a means to parlay these things into a stake in a rapidly filling industrial community.

A Central Labor Council had been established to coordinate the actions of workingmen and their locals. After the end of the First World War, with many more workers attracted to the community's numerous shipyards, labor staged the first general strike ever attempted in the United States. The strike developed as a result of a postwar governmental policy to lower wages of local shipyard workers to bring them into line with wages in east-coast shipyards. All the union groups represented in the A. F. of L. voted to strike. Japanese unions—still kept off the Council by racial restrictions—sent delegates to say they would strike too. The sympathy strike which followed lasted for five days, while 60,000 workers went off their jobs and brought practically all business in a city of 300,000 to a stop. Again there were fears of class war. A union paper proclaimed: "The City Will Lie In Our Hands on Thursday. We shall have stopped the works and taken them over. What Shall We Do With Our Town? Shall we leave it alone until it falls to pieces and somebody else does something. Or shall we do something, plan it, organize it, and start it again, bit by bit, as we choose, fix it the way we want it. We are undertaking the most tremendous move ever made by labor in this country, a move which will lead—No One knows where! We need the Iron March of Labor!"[33]

But there *were* no plans to reorganize or to fix the works that had been stopped. The unions demonstrated their power; but they did not wish to destroy, to tear down and replace, existing institutions. Essential services were kept operating throughout the strike: a particular effort was made to ensure such things as milk deliveries and power supply to hospitals. And at the close of the strike the community went on about its business, perhaps a little more mature in a common knowledge of what all owed to one another. But a national reputation for strife and disorder had resulted. In the depression of the '30s there were other strikes— on the waterfront, among timber-workers, at the major newspaper. But one citizen has said that these disorders were largely a sign that the community had not lost its youthful energy. They caused more lifted eyebrows in other parts of the country than locally. For this, said the commentator, "was still a city where people did, or attempted, the things they wanted to do. . . . Those who shook their heads . . . should have remembered that the city has always been able to unite in a crisis."[34]

Perhaps it was natural that respectable, prosperous, unionized labor should develop in this new and untraditional community. Here organized labor even began to formulate a coherent doctrine of faith. In the strikes of the 1930s a line between laboring factions was drawn that eventually permitted the majority of

unionized labor to be embraced by the business community. Conflicts during the depression years between the unions on one side
and the representatives of the Chamber of Commerce on the
other resolved into conflicts between two major labor factions
and between them and the Chamber of Commerce. But finally a
pseudo-alliance occurred between the majority labor faction and
the Chamber of Commerce against a minority radical-labor faction. Since the General Strike, the approach of the larger labor
group had been to emulate business in outlook and to share its
profits. The leading organizer had found a new legitimate avenue
to the American success story. He reached out through his teamsters to organize the drivers of even the smaller businesses in the
community. And the reaction of businessmen was questioning
and uncertain: not the reaction of men who are sure of what they
should oppose as "un-American." Small businessmen revealed
their uncertainty when the teamster boss announced his intention to organize their businesses. A local chronicler recorded a
conversation following the meeting at which the labor organizer
revealed his plans: "I don't like to be told what I can do with
my own business. But I guess we are coming into a new age and
what I think doesn't count any more. I suppose it's as he says,
if I pay my men more, they live better and spend more, and make
business all around more secure and stable. But those drivers
will be making more than I do, some months. That's not fair, it
seems to me." To which another businessman reportedly responded: "Don't you get the idea? [He] . . . wants to make all
of his union members little millionaires and of course he will be
the big one."[35]

Slowly the point of view of a "successful" labor movement took
hold. The final seal to community approval came with the role
the labor boss played in settling a strike that had shut down the
community's largest newspaper. The guild calling the strike had
the support of Communists and other radicals in the laboring
ranks. The sentiment of most citizens in the community was
strongly in favor of settling this strike. Women picketed the
Labor Temple demanding that the newspaper be reopened. The
teamster boss not only proclaimed he was not behind the strike
—suing a newspaper which so accused him—but took on the task

of negotiating a settlement, organizing the striking workers into his own union. The settlement helped to legitimize the kind of role "respectable" labor sought. The labor leader wanted "a partnership between management and labor with labor getting a better cut of the profits" while keeping "the radicals out of the picture." He said: "They're trying to wreck both business and labor."[36] And on more than one occasion in subsequent years, local businessmen asked this labor boss to organize their shops before more radical organizers did the job. A local banker said: "He has a sense that it is part of his responsibility to keep the profit motive alive."[37]

The teamster head grew in local favor to become a regent of the state university. He also lived to see his own business practices investigated by the courts.

Wages are high in this community, and the cost of living is high. Workingmen and teachers and other professionals often live in the same neighborhoods: their children attend the same public schools and are pledged into the same fraternities and sororities at the university. There is a communitywide commitment to the benefits of the good life that most community participants feel they enjoy.

A representative of a local carpenters' union described the contribution of the labor movement to the growth of this "middle-class" attitude. He said the community is still more a blue-collar town than a white-collar town. But blue-collar occupations—providing good wages and the chance for homeownership—enabled workingmen to feel "successful" and "respectable." Now the carpenters' union no longer included the category of "race" on its membership or employment forms. Thus, respectable labor had attempted to be in the forefront of social change which seemed in line with the directions the community had moved and was moving. Union men said that a close relationship with business now existed. And in the community as a whole, a special day of labor recognition was observed in the public schools.

The conflicts of an era when old group identities were superseded by a new class consciousness were calmed in a prosperous community. And older visions of what a man must do and become in America in order to fulfill his destiny had also changed. But a new equilibrium was not a sign that a current concept of the good society would endure. For doubtless new tensions would grow out of pressures exerted by new malcontents.

Specialization and the Public Man

When a large and growing population sets about creating new vocations, a necessary interdependence develops among the people. The individual becomes less the complete master of his life. He comes to rely more on others, who provide him with many essential and some nonessential goods and services. Each individual finds his own vocational contribution and his own social participations more specialized and "partial." Many contrasts to the "whole-man-and-citizen" leader of the smaller community appear in the leading participants in the new, open, and expanding community.

A citizen of the Far West metropolis has described an "odd collection of burlesque characters" that dominated the political scene from 1909 into the First World War. And as for the accompaniment to these central performers, he said: "They were supported by a male chorus of ten thousand tramps that dreamed that they were 'Jack London,'" while the women in the cast were ". . . not to be mentioned except plurally and categorically." This commentator considered the show of which he spoke to have ended in the General Strike: ". . . a grand finale of a revolution that fuddled and flashed out. . . ."[38]

Even before 1909 the community of the post-Klondike era was an open town. "Little Egypt" was a major attraction, as were similar performers in the "Box-House" theater-bars that first appeared on the skid road during the easy-money Klondike days. Prostitution and gambling flourished. Vaudeville, the theater, and later movies also found an ample following. A newspaper listed in 1908 nine major theaters offering a varied fare to those on-the-town for entertainment. Thus new and different vocations were developed by enterprising people in the open community. And new concepts of a proper public role were introduced, tested, and refined. Perhaps it is significant that a degree of the anonymity which growth in community size permits was necessary to some of these vocations in the earliest phases of their development.

One of the enterprising men who became an important performer in local public affairs was described as a devout, church-going family man—and a man with great ambition to succeed. He began his business ventures by taking over and reviving one of the Box-Houses along skid road. Soon he was the proprietor of a thriving entertainment business which did not shy away from the vice that helped to make this an "open" town. During a political shakeup in which the chief of police resigned over frustration at not being able to touch powerful community figures like the Box-House czar, an altercation occurred and the ex-police chief was killed in a public gun battle with the business-man. In the trial that followed, public sentiment was far from unanimous in support of the defendant. But within a few months after acquittal, the entertainment king had a new, more legitimate line and was on his way to becoming one of the community's most successful men. Eventually he became the owner of a national chain of movie houses.

In the political arena also the "odd assortment" made itself known. The mayor who "opened" the town again in 1910, after it had been at least nominally closed for some years, explained his move as a blow at hypocrisy; and not only did the new mayor defend the "inevitable" vice of the big city, but he came close in his public statements to defending the graft that was scarcely hidden. Within a year, a campaign was under way for a recall election—the second recall election in the history of the country. Churches, labor unions, the YMCA, and some local department stores helped to circulate petitions to defeat the mayor. And defeated he was in a special election. Following the election, consensus seemed to be that the women's vote had been the chief element in this triumph of virtue over vice. Said a New York newspaper: ". . . the downtown precincts gave [the mayor] large pluralities, which were offset by the vote from the residence districts, where the influence of the women was mostly felt." A month after the election, it was estimated that one-half the skid-road women had left town.[39]

This did not end the public career of a mayor whose early

definition of his role brought down the wrath of many private citizens. Perhaps he mellowed his approach; and perhaps the attitudes of citizens were broadened a little in succeeding years. For the deposed mayor was re-elected in 1914 and again in 1916. By the time of his second defeat—in 1918—the community was wide open again, to such an extent that the commanding general of a nearby army camp declared it "off limits" to all his troops.

Even more new and untraditional public figures appeared at other times of great social stress. The community was no stranger to depression and poverty. The Great Depression came complete with a Hooverville and long lines of the unemployed and the hungry. A highly organized, specialized, twentieth-century technology wove a tight web of interdependence around large sections of a heterogeneous population and left only poverty as a common bond for many. The elections of 1932 turned up a conglomeration of parties, candidates, and platforms that made the somewhat exotic conditions of the post-Klondike era look "Early-Colonial-Traditional" in comparison. The Unemployed Citizens' League decided at its convention to back candidates filed under more orthodox banners. This seemed a wise course, considering the social and political factions prevalent at the time—resulting in candidates like the one who ran on a one-plank platform against hot foods. One commentator noted that the mayoralty race was swarming with "has-beens" and "never-wases."

The capstone of that depression-year election was the campaign a local newspaperman organized and publicized in an effort to demonstrate that practically anyone could run for mayor. He persuaded a local radio personality—proprietor of a night club, dance-band leader, radio M.C.—to enter the race. The newspaper made a mass-media publicity stunt out of the campaign, while the candidate burlesqued the common campaign slogans and hired gag writers to help compose his speeches. Although the "burlesque candidate" lost out in the primary, he acquired a taste for the political arena. The newspaper was ready to drop the whole matter, but the candidate now expressed his intention of running for Lieutenant-Governor on his own. In the state-wide election, he won the office and was reelected several times in subsequent years. At least one local historian maintains that this prompted one Governor to leave the state no more than once during his term of office in fear of the consequences should the Lieutenant-Governor become the acting chief executive. (On that one occasion, the Lieutenant-Governor had gone fishing in California; both men staged a race home when each heard of the other's travels. The Governor won.)[40]

Specialization and new public roles did not always imply the bizarre. In fact, in this new and expanding community, the specialized professional developed his talents and carved a niche that was as consistent and functional for the complex urban setting as could be found anywhere in America. As early as 1909 the community boasted: ". . . Lawyers Stand High in Ability . . . Members of Bench and Bar . . . Occupy First Rank in Judicial and Legal Annals of Northwest . . . Many Practitioners Would Have Been Powerful in Boston, New York, Philadelphia or Any Large City."[41] By the middle of the twentieth century specialized services here were on a par with those in any metropolis. Even the teamster boss (described as the dominant personality in the community in the late 1950s) became a "specialist" in conducting his business. His philosophy was: "Why should truck drivers and bottle washers be allowed to make decisions affecting policy? . . . That's what the officials are for, to sell what labor possesses, its own labor. Now to do that they must use business methods. That takes specialists . . . you can't just haul a guy in off the street and let him negotiate with a high-powered lawyer."[42]

In the development of social services here, general services became transformed more and more into specialized services. New agencies always sought to provide a specialized function, perhaps one not provided by any other agency. Usually the "treatment" approach to mental health and social problems was emphasized. An agency with a new program foundered recently because it had not actually chosen a function fitting the criteria of specialization. It had adopted a program that sought to serve "problem" children from what it perceived as a lower or working class of families. But mental health professionals in this community tended not to recognize ethnic or class categories of people— Negroes, lower class, Orientals etc. They screened a whole population through specialized, treatment categories.

Along with these tendencies went an emphasis on highly

trained professional staffs. The individual specialist who worked in these settings acquired and shared with his fellow professionals the outlook and special vocabularies of his profession. This meant, for example, that in integrated work settings the Negro professional—the social worker in the social agency, the doctor in the large hospital—became, for at least a large part of his day, a professional first and a Negro second. The process had touched a relatively small proportion of those who were still visibly different—like the Negro. But eventually it could have far-reaching repercussions.

The Strain toward Anonymity

Phrases often used to describe contemporary American culture can be applied to this metropolis. A heterogeneous population has become more uniformly content with a position in the expanding "middle class" of a social system. Suburbia has grown apace with postwar prosperity. The "masses" have increasing difficulty in forming groups for discussing and influencing community issues. But the very fact that many sophisticated people use this sociological jargon, often critically, bespeaks a desire to understand and control their own destinies. The individual who has known freedom and controversy, and who jealously guards against yielding to arbitrary authority, apparently does not like to be constrained even by a mold he has helped to create—once he recognizes the constraints. Still, the forces at work are often subtle, almost imperceptible. And certainly they are not in themselves "evil." They are neutral. They are . . . products of the physical and social situation of this population in this place at this time.

A community of this size is experienced more by participants as smaller "communities" through their particular relationships with others. However, people are still influenced by the characteristics of the larger entity. The characteristics of the whole determine the frequency and the nature of the encounters people have with one another in their daily lives. These characteristics also determine the events and the issues and the cultural names people share both through the mass media and in more personal situations.

One fact that is striking in the Far West metropolis is the larger loyalty most citizens have toward the local way of life. People do not seem to feel trapped by circumstances into staying here. They are here because they want to be here. This community pride has a homogenizing effect: it draws population elements together and lessens the outcries of the malcontents. Civic leaders emphasize this good feeling toward the community as a whole. Wherever a leader found it difficult to draw certain elements of his constituents into identification with the larger whole he would often pull away from these elements. This occurred in the period of labor strife, so that radical unionism was replaced by respectable unionism, accepting and selling a business ideology that captured the whole community. More recently, a Negro leader at the local Urban League expressed his disapproval of the reestablishment of a Negro newspaper by a newcomer. For the man at the Urban League, this move was a step backward—against the grain of normal social processes in the community. (But among many Negro newcomers the phrase could be heard: "That older leadership has run away and left us.")

There were other signs of the tendency toward homogeneity, and evidence also of some tensions that kept pace with this tendency. Figures gathered at the Council of Churches showed that new churches were growing rapidly, particularly in the suburbs. The strongest move among the Protestants was toward the non-denominational church. A staff member said that sometimes a new church would be affiliated with a particular denomination, but more often it would become a community church and remain interdenominational. These community churches were typical of the outlying areas. A Lutheran minister said that his denomination had grown in numbers along with the growth of what he called the "middle class." "At one time," he explained, "the local Lutheran welfare services operated a skid road mission for Scandinavian seamen. They were also concerned for the welfare of the many unmarried Scandinavian domestics who worked in homes here." But now Lutheran welfare services attempted to reach the broader community first—motivated by the traditional Lutheran social concern—and secondarily felt an obligation to give priority to Lutheran families in need. This same minister mentioned that interracial congregations were appearing in the Lutheran churches in the community, thus providing other situations in which the person who was visibly different from the majority could be confronted, naturally, on the primary basis of his beliefs.

A prominent Catholic businessman pointed to changes he had noted in the community during his lifetime. He said: "When I was a boy a Catholic was pointed out more—was set apart from the majority. But I married a non-Catholic; and so did most of my brothers and sisters. I came from a big family and that used to identify a person as a Catholic. But now everyone is raising a larger family than in the old days." This layman was still active as a member of his church. He said that the Catholic bishop of earlier days in the community was noted for being a "separatist" who wanted to keep his flock distinct and different. But the emphasis of the new bishop was on communitywide cooperation, although some concern was expressed within the church hierarchy that the middle-class Catholic might lose completely his distinct religious identity.

A Jewish professional spoke critically of the effects of homogenization. He described how the Jews had come to the community along with the earliest immigration of the 1880s and 1890s, and that, therefore, there was no distinct class division among Jews based on different layers of immigration. In older American cities, he said, this split is usually based on a distinction between the German and the non-German Jew, with the former considering himself superior. In this western community the social processes affecting the whole population had operated strongly on the Jewish population. This Jewish professional had purchased a home in the suburbs where he lived in a neighborhood side-by-side with fairly prosperous white-collar workers and professionals. "But I haven't joined the Reformed synagogue in the suburbs," he said, "because, I think, it is too subject to the 'cliquishness' and conformity that typifies so much social participations in suburbia." He was particularly concerned that his teenage son not become involved in the same social tendencies on the Sabbath that affected him in school during the week. So this man sent his son into the city to attend the Orthodox synagogue.

At the Council of Churches an informant said that highly visible ethnic groups, like the Orientals, still stayed much to their own congregations. Japanese-Americans were no longer concentrated in downtown ethnic neighborhoods—they had been diffused tremendously throughout the community following the Second World War. But Japanese-American families still attended mostly Japanese-American churches, although a majority attended Christian churches rather than Buddhist or Shinto churches. Old ties and loyalties to the extended family and the older generation were still strong. However, for this minority, too, the future seemed to indicate greater assimilation, even though the break with the past had not been violent. The younger families were accommodating respectfully to the older generation while moving toward broader participation in the larger community and toward more complete "Americanization." The form of services at a Japanese Christian church illustrated this pattern: the church was established for Japanese-Americans and had formerly held services in the Japanese language; but now two services were held on Sunday, one in Japanese for the old folks, and one in English for the younger people.

The school system had been a great source of pride to this community—a symbol and a major vehicle of democratization. Newcomers both learned and helped to develop many of the distinctive ways of the community through the public schools: the children through participation in these local models of democratic institutions and their parents through PTA and other participation and support. The Japanese-Americans were particularly proud of the academic records of their children in the school system. The Nisei often had earned high honors in the public schools and, far out of proportion to their numbers in the total population, had been named valedictorians of graduating classes. A high school principal described the social situation as he saw it in this school system: "You can't really associate a particular social class or ethnic group with a particular school any more. This was possible in the old days; and recent Negro immigration has threatened to introduce a 'separatist' pattern again. But where segregated schools have developed inadvertently, because of population mobility and housing patterns, both whites and Negroes have become concerned because this tendency is really counter to the normal direction we have moved in this community." Generally, schools had become more cross-sectional, with the "less-privileged" schools increasingly sending more children to college and the "more-privileged" schools getting more children from lower economic groups. The principal said that school clubs were based almost completely on service and academic standing. The HiY had died out some years ago—and there were no plans to revive it. The boys at his school, he said, told him they felt everyone belonged to the "whole school community."

Some people in the community viewed the disappearance of traditional group loyalties and the growth of specialization with much concern if not alarm. It appeared that the homogenization process coupled with specialization contributed to the tendency for a large population to become merely a "mass." And the individual—particularly one who was least secure economically and a newcomer—could become lost in the crowd and lose all sense of direction and dignity, and control over his future.

A juvenile judge voiced these fears. He said that he had to guard against allowing dependent or delinquent children to be "sovietized," as he called it, by social agencies, particularly public agencies. He did not wish to see an impersonal arm of the state crowd out other facilities for caring for children. This judge took it on himself to encourage local religious groups to take more active interest in particular segments of the population. Other people who worked with delinquents expressed the opinion that Protestant groups could help a great deal to claim troubled children from the urban mass if they would develop programs aimed at particular publics. The Lutherans—and the Catholics—were less remiss in this regard because they did gear their programs more toward identifiable publics. The juvenile judge had encouraged the opening of a Protestant Home for semi-delinquent boys. The judge believed a community conscience could best be expressed by encouraging and supporting groups that retained a basis for personal concern for "their own." The child or any person who became merely a "case" or a treatment category was in danger of losing personal dignity in the urban mass.

There were many symptoms of this quite natural process in

this complex community. A psychiatrist who helped to evaluate families for a social agency said he had ruled himself out from screening Negro families applying for adoption. "My professional training has conditioned me," he said, "so that it is difficult to approve of any of the Negro families I see." These were families naturally subjected to greater tensions in their situations in the city. The number of Negro children defined as dependent and delinquent in the community was highly disproportionate to the size of the Negro population. Available professional services found it difficult to treat and rehabilitate these children when the specialized approach to treatment and care was heavily weighted against considering the problems of individuals in a group as cultural problems at least in part unique to that group. In addition, the very size and complexity of organizations tended to shape the outlook of professional workers, making it difficult for the professional from his vantage point in the large organization to retain a concept of "a case" as a whole and valued personality.

The conditions described here represent just one facet of "anonymity" in the human dramas of community life. It is significant that counterirritants were at work within the system. Dialogue had not been shut off completely. The tradition of broad participation in public affairs through membership in private guilds helped to give structure to publics formulated out of the larger mass of population. However, it seemed that people as a whole were more often stirred, now, merely as a listening audience when the community conscience was quickened. The greatest danger appeared to be that people immersed in situations that threatened basic values would be unable, from a narrowed vantage point *within* these situations, to recognize threats to those values and confront them with new answers.

Pursuit of the More Perfect Union

The pressures of an expanding, moving, restless, and diverse population continued to build up and find release in the new metropolis. Manifestations of these pressures were not new to the community. In the early days of the Second World War a commentator wrote: "In this far corner of the United States, there are refugees from the dust bowl of Oklahoma and Arkansas and many more from South Dakota. . . ." These people usually settled in the agricultural region which was still, according to this commentator, "divided into small communities and farms where the human touch is never lost and nothing is impersonal." In open areas of the county, it was said: ". . . no one hears 'Okie' or 'Arkie' or any other propaganda word designed to separate people from their rights as human beings and Americans." The valley was the scene of friendships between whites and Indians in the earliest days when even the leader of the Indian revolt had his ardent defenders among the pioneer settlers. There were memories in this area too of the experiences of pioneers of the last century who arrived "ragged and destitute" and were welcomed and helped by those who had preceded them.[43] But even these less crowded areas had difficulties at times ensuring the rights of Americans of all colors and origins. And with the concentration of 100,000 newcomers attracted by war industries and the postwar migration of thousands of Negroes to urban areas of the open metropolis, new problems and new tensions were faced throughout the community.

The story of the wartime Japanese-Americans is a poignant chapter in the compromises and uncertainties that accompany a democratic experiment. In the agricultural areas of the community the Japanese constituted 10 per cent of the population and controlled 90 per cent of the truck farming. In the central urban areas they were small-business owners—operating grocery stores, cleaning and dye works, restaurants, small hotels, and apartment houses. A Nisei who studied this population group just prior to the Second World War noted that most of them had come, in the early years of this century, without intending to stay. The elders were mostly from a commercial class that sought opportunities not available in those years in a still semi-feudal Japan. Like others who settled this frontier—and other frontiers in America—they intended to achieve success, then return to a place where they would be "somebody" amid familiar institutions they revered. Many, through the years, returned to the old country to visit; but few remained there. They and their offspring became a part of a new pattern of institutions they had helped to build in a new country. At first they were very clannish, maintaining a tightly-knit subculture in their own neighborhoods and retaining the Japanese language. But the American-born generations, who went on to capture honors in the public schools, became "Americans" through their broader participation in the community. By the beginning of the Second World War most of them hardly spoke Japanese. They were entering professions and beginning to move into many neighborhoods in the city.[44]

At the time of Pearl Harbor, 63 per cent of the Japanese-Americans were American born. As new versions of old racial fears swept the West Coast, the community resisted hysteria for a time. But the same forces at work in California found echoes in the Northwest too. Locally the issue became enmeshed with matters of politics and economics—expediency and business jealousy. For those most closely involved, the problems remained both matters of abstract principle and intimately human matters. The Japanese American Citizens League prepared a report for a Congressional Committee on National Defense Migration. They emphasized that the Japanese had grown up with the country, aiding in its development, and that their immigration was no different than that from various parts of Europe. This report made an impassioned plea that would have done justice to any American revolutionary. It said: "This is not a war of races. To consider it so is to be taken in by Tokyo propagandists. . . . If the loyalty of citizens as a group is to be questioned, in what may the American people have faith and confidence? . . . We are Americans. We want to do our duty where we can serve best. We make these statements, not because we fear evacuation, but because we believe, to the bottom of our hearts, that the best interests of the United States, our nation, are to be served by being permitted to stay, work, fight, and die for our country if necessary here where we belong."[45]

Perhaps it is a tribute to the institutions the Japanese-Americans were forced to forsake for a time that so many fought and died, while many others returned after the war to take up their homes and vocations again in the community.

The Negro population in the community increased by some 300 per cent in a ten-year period following the Second World War. This influx was another expression of that same restlessness which throughout American history has kept the unsatisfied and the discontented on the move in search of new opportunity and new experience. These people came in large groups. They concentrated in central neighborhoods. Their problems were far different from those faced by the first Negro to settle this region.

In 1845 the Provisional Government of Oregon Territory had passed a law forbidding slavery but also prohibiting Negroes from settling in the region. This ruling caused a free-Negro immigrant from Pennsylvania to move his family to the northern areas of the Territory. Thus, a free Negro was the head of one of the first two American families in Washington Territory and already had a flourishing farm under cultivation when the great immigration of 1852 hit this area. He helped newcomers with supplies, without charge, during the first hard years. But shortly after, he and his family were threatened with the loss of their farm, because in those pre-Civil War days Negroes were not allowed to own land in the United States and no claim could be filed. In that early day the settlers who had been recipients of the personal hospitality and help of the Negro settler raised an outcry to the federal government. As a result, Congress passed a special act allowing the free Negro from Pennsylvania and his heirs to hold title to their land forever.

The problems of a large aggregate of people—easily lumped together by others because of common, visible, physical characteristics—were not the problems of that first Negro in the Territory. The early settler was confronted, personally and individually, as a man who shared with his fellows and neighbors the danger and the challenge inherent in the effort to overcome the forces of nature. It is out of such encounters that men's perceptions of groups of people change, influenced by specific experiences with a particular representative of a group. In the crowded, competitive, urban arena the process is often reversed: encounters with a categorical group of people—usually impersonal, perhaps in normal day-to-day situations unpleasant and colored by mutual suspicion—influence men's perceptions of every individual in the group. Such confrontations also influence the way men on either side of these encounters perceive themselves—as "superior" or "inferior," as "privileged" or "deprived." In a community which emphasized that all should be able to achieve the good life through participation in interdependent institutions, a highly visible group of people who had hardly shared in the creation of these institutions was at a distinct disadvantage in gaining acceptance.

A Negro professional social worker who had lived in the community for over twenty years said that when the Negro population was small—around 3,000—they could live any place or go any place they could afford, although work opportunities were restricted. The unions once had clauses restricting employment to whites. Negroes had worked mostly on the boats and trains and in small businesses like shoeshine stands. But many "traditionally" Negro jobs—like that of redcap—were held by Orientals. Gradually the color line in employment was broken during the war, influenced by the fair employment clauses of government contracts. The large war plants had hired both Negroes and Orientals, and the unions, too, had instituted nonsegregation clauses in their charters.

Ten years after the war the Negro population was estimated to have risen to around 55,000. Now the problems were not so much restrictions on employment, but restrictions on where one could live. And with the older Negro residents, who had grown up with the community, these became major problems, since these people now sought complete acceptance into the open metropolis. They tried, increasingly, to supersede a general identification with the Negro subculture by participations that transcended color lines. And within the Negro population the major criterion of status seemed to be based on how long one had been a resident in the community. One professional said that this "length of residence" criterion was a stronger basis for cliquishness than any solidarity based on common occupation or a shared profession. A high school counselor noted that there was real concern in some central neighborhoods that because of changed housing patterns, and subtle real estate pressures and restrictions, some schools were becoming all-white or all-Negro. "In our schools with large Negro populations," she said, "the school authorities have had a real problem getting the longer-resident, middle-class Negroes to help the newcomers from the South to learn the ways and the rules of our public schools." But now these young people were taking on this responsibility, perhaps more willing than their parents to serve as a bridge between the old and the new.

The two extremes to the problem of Negroes as a group in this community can be dramatized in two stories told by different local professionals.

A social worker explained the problems her agency had in finding homes for Negro dependent children. "At first," she said, "we made the mistake, in trying to form a guild to promote interest in adoption among the Negro middle class, of asking someone to get together a group of her 'Negro friends.' But this very use of the term 'Negro' seemed to keep people away." The agency achieved success when it asked a Negro clubwoman merely to get together a "group of friends," ignoring the label "Negro" or "colored." Yet, the problem for the agency was still one of placing Negro children in adoptive homes in a community which had not become completely interracial.

The other story was told by a psychiatrist. He described the case of a Negro teenager who had gotten into trouble for stealing. The boy was from a family of recent arrivals who lived in one of the crowded central neighborhoods. Adjacent to this neighborhood was an exclusive, older residential area, set apart as "Private—No Trespassing" by a high wall. The boy had been apprehended by police for stealing a bike. Interestingly, he had gone to the trouble of scaling the wall to retrieve a bicycle and bring it back over the wall. The psychiatrist said: "In this act, far more significant than the desire of a deprived teenager for a material object was the symbolic importance of where he went to obtain the object." In the open metropolis, a man's worth was based on what he could acquire and achieve. Walls in this setting of opportunity were meant to be scaled. And walls were particularly obnoxious and challenging when erected by those who already "had it made."

The pressures of a growing population were not, of course, solely manifested as racial pressures. The juvenile judge reported that problem families had formerly been located on the fringe of town—"out in the sticks." Now they tended to be in crowded and changing central neighborhoods. "Old neighborhood loyalties are being destroyed," he said. "There seems to be less neighborly tolerance of families for one another now." A principal at a central high school said that while the school had once been stable, now families were moving in and out constantly. "Every Monday we have half a dozen new enrollees, and there are many dropouts during a semester. Families seem to have money to spend; but lots of families are deeply in debt to loan companies." A counselor at the sheriff's office reported that teenage vandalism had increased in recent years.

The problems of unrooted "masses" were becoming increasingly apparent. One solution sought by those who worked with these problems was to attempt to encompass the various parts of the population within at least a partial circle of concern.[46] An aspect of this renewed effort was an appeal to the churches to attempt to reach out to those who formerly had denominational ties. But the greatest force in the growth of the churches themselves—toward nondenominationalism—worked counter to these efforts to help those still struggling at the vital center of the community.

The open metropolis presented this moving picture of continued change and increasing specialization of human participations. People in the privacy of the suburbs were forming homogenized communities; the central areas, where masses now congregated and old neighborhood loyalties were disappearing, were becoming scenes of conflict, where visibly different and excluded people often fought the symbols of the "respectable" society.

The Oregon Trail was closed now. Most men had to seek their destinies within geographical limits in which nature no longer played a significant part. But there were new problems to tax men's continued faith in the basic values of democratic living.

PART III. *Diversity: Peril and Promise*

Geographical areas like those described once encompassed most of men's perceptions of social reality. But conditions have changed in both physical and social environments. In the former, man no longer sees himself opposite an untamed nature, but largely encounters structures created by man. The conditions relating man to other men also have changed. It has become more difficult to describe a context for human communication—a community—as an entity circumscribed by geographical boundaries. In new types of social participation "the people" may become an undifferentiated "mass": a confusion of human objects who use one another for expediency.

But there on the prairies of central Illinois people who felt common needs committed their talents to one another, for a time.

The tall, rough frontiersman was twenty-two years old when he first came to New Salem. He had completed a flatboat journey from central Illinois and down the Mississippi all the way to New Orleans that spring of 1831; and he stopped on his return in the little village on the Sangamon River, ". . . for the first time . . . by himself. . . ." He was a wanderer that year, "a piece of floating driftwood," he later said, ready for growth and new experience in the world beyond his parental home. The young man was not sure where he was headed or what he would become. But the community sensed his bent for leadership just in the talents and enthusiasm he brought to life on the prairie frontier. He *was* sure of their support while he was among them. He would grow here. And others in New Salem would grow too, through knowing him and helping him.

In this trading post on the Sangamon the young man was never among the most successful citizens. In fact, he was one of the least stable in occupation. He did not bring a trade with him to New Salem, so he had to look for odd jobs. Tending store for a local merchant, he slept in the store and boarded out for his meals in homes in the community.

Store-keeping was a social experience here as well as a vocational one. And with his droll stories and imitations, the clerk kept his patrons amused and interested in other things than the buying and selling of goods. On the other hand, there were many occasions in New Salem specifically set aside for socializing. Saturday afternoons there were horse races and foot races, boxing and wrestling matches, and shooting contests. Election days and trial days were special occasions for games and talk and contests. Religious revivals came "as the spirit moved," while dances and feasts followed every special social affair.

The young clerk proved his prowess in the skills prized on this frontier. Thus, he could afford to be gentle and kind—and studious too, for this also was his inclination. So he read; and he talked. (There was time for talk in New Salem.) And there must have been times when his boss at the store wondered about the gain for his business in employing such a loquacious young man.

He also joined the New Salem Debating Society, and to the surprise of the other members, showed that behind the droll stories was a mind ready for formal argumentation.

When a war with the Indians came to the prairies, a volunteer company was raised locally and the young man was elected its captain. Unskilled in the ways of the military, he gave little thought to the army as a career. But in his own way, and with his own men, he demonstrated a flair for leadership of rough, pleasure-loving individualists. When his brief service was up and he announced his candidacy for the state legislature, his old comrades-in-arms were among his chief backers.

The campaign on the stump in the backwoods carried the candidate into a larger world. But New Salem remained the home base for his life. When he announced: "Fellow Citizens, I presume you all know who I am" in the clearings where people gathered to listen to political speeches, there were few who answered "no." Although his popularity in New Salem was overwhelming, in the district it was not quite enough to elect him. So, out of work again, he became a partner in a new business venture, initially raising his share through his good personal credit rating. And he continued to meet his fellow citizens.

He began to take on formal grammar studies with the town schoolmaster in his spare moments. The schoolmaster sent his grown pupil across the prairie to another town to borrow books from the collection in a private library there. The business venture folded—one partner lost in books, the other in drink—and the young man owed twelve hundred dollars after the intemperate partner died. (He eventually paid off the debt in full.) Soon there were many worries and painful doubts about himself. But he also had more time for his friends. One friend said: "His case never became so desperate but a friend came out of the darkness to relieve him."

They found him a job as postmaster; and for a while he had a second job as deputy surveyor, covering the area around New Salem. Thus, he continued to meet old and new friends, daily, in his work, while in his private hours he continued to study, seeking to acquire the knowledge he needed for the surveying work. And throughout the countryside where he appeared with compass and chain as he surveyed new townships and roads and tracts, he was soon a familar figure.

Successful in his next try at public office, he served quietly but attentively through a term as assemblyman, then returned to his "home" community to take up former duties as postmaster and deputy surveyor. Now his personal ambition and his self-image were taking clearer form. To move toward the goals he was formulating for himself he must study the law. And his friends would help him. Not that there were any in New Salem that he could "read with"; but if he could obtain the books, the community would be there to surround him with its subtle approval of his ambitions.

They helped him through some dark days of personal trouble. And as election time came and he announced himself a candidate for the assembly again, his friends in the community sent him back to the legislature. This time he showed himself a smart parliamentarian, taking an active part in legislation, discussion, and debate. It would be expected of him. Didn't his community have a vital stake in matters of new courts, education, the development of travel? And hadn't it been the sounding-board for his developing verbal and literal talents—the social milieu where dim perceptions formed into ideas relevant to his experience of himself and his fellows?

When he returned from the legislature this time, he had served with distinction. During this term he had been enrolled to practice law before the bar of the state of Illinois. Now he would move on to a broader stage—to Springfield—looking for new challenges for his developing talents. For seven years he had grown in New Salem. There was no thought of exploitation as he moved on. He had been a part of the community and its institutions, and those who had shared his years there would always be a part of him.

The town on the Sangamon soon died out. The people moved on to form other communities. The most famous citizen of New Salem went on to become a Congressman and a President of his country. But these were merely niches that provided new opportunities for the *man* he had become. He became shrewd in the

games of social and political life, or he would not have advanced
to the broader stages on which he applied his talents. But these
games never were the only ends-in-themselves he knew and
served. The things that grew and developed within the man—
nurtured in the seven years in New Salem—enabled him to leave
his distinctive mark in history.

At times his résumé didn't look very good; but his credit with
his friends always stood high. His experience of freedom was immediate and real but tempered by disciplines implied by his
responsibilities to himself and others. His vision of what he
might become and where he might direct his restless energies
was both expanded and focused by a sense of the unfinished tasks
still facing a people. And his experience of "the people" and of
himself as a part of the people was carved indelibly on all that
he later did and said and wrote. It was *their* revolution that the
citizen of New Salem cherished and advanced.

Charades of Homogenization

The great urban complexes of America and their large work
organizations have replaced villages and towns of the prairies
and plains as domestic frontiers of a free people. They have become the most prominent settings for the human encounters and
social experiments of the democratic revolution. And particularly
in young, open cities where history has been covered by asphalt
and space is not filled with permanent and constraining lines,[8]
the problem of the individual in establishing reference points for
identity is greatest. The search for challenge and opportunity
finds some returning along older trails to more traditional settings
where young organizations have located and sends others beyond the bounds of country and continent. But most who are
there remain in the great terminals, and more arrive every day.
In such a setting the participant in the community encounters
others as fleeting impressions from the overpopulated surfaces[9]
of daily life.

The number of others encountered has increased tremendously
since the prairie years on the Sangamon. One's fellow citizens
are met in numerous ways: many are only offensive objects on
freeways; others are mute strangers jostled on sidewalks; some

Eventually a call came that took him to the Far West and a higher salary and position in an older, more stable corporation. He relaxed a bit in his guarded struggles at work. A better position in the organization hierarchy provided a built-in insulation from the dangers of communication with many others. He began to take an interest in outside activities other than the company bowling league, which had served to provide a feeling of physical achievement and an outlet for harmless friendships. The sense that he and his family had reached the end of a trail, for a time, quickened his interest in affairs of the local community: in schools, recreation, even politics. And in the early years of the 1960s he sensed the growing sentiment that private pursuits in the organization were not the only careers for men of talent and education. There was even talk of a Congressional candidacy for him, backed largely by other organization professionals—mostly newcomers also seeking involvement in public affairs in their suburban district.

But what of the conditioning of this latter-day pioneer as he prepared for service to local community, state, and nation? A history of participation in charades of achievement left him without much experience in shared human purposes. He had known little of people using "their worth to make a community together." He had been almost lost without human identity in a stream of events over which he and his cohorts had only pretended to exert a measure of control.

Discontents of Segmentation

Frustrations of the year of Khrushchev's visit also revealed problems of "massness" in another guise. The steel strike of that year called forth more soul-searching. The labor writer of the *New York Times* envisioned that "behind the steel dispute lies the danger of class war."[11] Groups were forming irreconcilable lines in public, pursing "proximate goals," heedless of any commitment to defend institutions of which all were a part. James Reston observed: "Dave McDonald of the steelworkers union has to get more money for his men every time a contract ends or lose control of his union; or so he thinks."[12] In the mass society, it seemed that when individuals did reappear from private anonymity to align themselves with distinctive groups, they did so merely to use these groups for expedient purposes.

There was nothing basically new about conflict in a restless society among turbulent, visible groups. Tocqueville described the problems faced in 1830 by cities like Philadelphia and New York, with their "freed blacks" and "a multitude of Europeans who have been driven to the shores of the New World by their misfortunes or their misconduct. . . ." Having no civil rights, he said, "they are ready to turn all the passions which agitate the community to their own advantage. . . ." He warned:

> . . . I look upon the size of certain American cities, and especially on the nature of their population, as a real danger which threatens the future security of the democratic republics of the New World. . . . I venture to predict that they will perish from this circumstance, unless the government succeed in creating an armed force, which . . . will be independent of the town population, and able to repress its excesses.[13]

In 1961 *Time* magazine commented on attacks in American cities directed against the police, asking: "Is There No Respect?" "Philadelphia and Detroit . . . reported an alarming increase in the number of attacks against policemen," said *Time,* adding, "In Los Angeles, where such assaults have tripled in recent years, some 300 cop fighters were prosecuted in the past year. . . ."[14] Evidence indicated that violence was precipitated not over property or the effort to acquire goods or things but over the perceptions of people that they were being penned in and deprived of their rights, watched over by a modern counterpart of Tocqueville's "armed force" which had been left behind to maintain order by the more genteel peoples who now cut themselves off from community relationships with these "different" others. This condition also contributed to the increased invisibility of the deprived in the affluent society, as they ceased to be a part of the immediate experience of the majority. Only the threatening effects of their situations were noted when reported in the mass media.[15]

In the past, America had lived through many group conflicts. It had amalgamated most "Europeans . . . driven to the shores . . . by their misfortunes . . . ," often in interior cities where groups could begin on a more equal footing. Tocqueville had not seen the American melting pot in true operation. Nor had he paid much attention to settings where even separated groups maintained unique identity and commitment to a common whole. He did not dwell long on the "great separation" imprinted on a large part of rural America by slavery, since in Tocqueville's day the slave segment was denied even the dream of becoming.

It was this last most firm and visible manifestation of segmentation that was destined to remain the persistent dilemma of an experiment predicated on human equality. For while the dream of equality was not damaged in communities where unique groups flourished, where separation was categorical and implied unchanging inferiority of a whole classification of human beings, the dream was shattered and institutions were warped.

Then one hundred years after they were legally recognized as *human* participants—at a moment of crisis and uncertainty over values in America—representatives of the nation's most enduring segment became active agents of a revived revolution. Perhaps years of conditioning in frustration permitted the discontents of America's Negroes to ripen more maturely. Phases in their discontents can be seen against some of the varied backgrounds laid out in preceding chapters.

The Negro came to the tidelands of America as property of a Western man who sought and found ways to conquer nature. And to this white man, the Negro in his static African culture seemed a part of nature. The opening of the New World had presented vast new regions to be tamed, and offered new possibilities for individual independence. The idea of "property" received great impetus from this opening of new regions. Increasing numbers aspired to this right of possession which set them apart, uniquely, from their fellows.

In a society where property ownership was the chief determinant of relationships between men, the Negro as an object of possession was actually excluded from human relationships. He was a pawn with almost no points of reference for human identity. But the white man on the tidelands had a penchant for orderliness. He arranged the independent, private world of his domain into an organic whole: each part had a place and there were reciprocal obligations between the parts. Thus the plantation owner took on the responsibility of teaching his religion to his slaves, recognizing at least that they possessed human souls. And through this religion, which he transformed with his tribal cadences, the Negro began to find a voice in a society in which he was merely an object.

Within the little world of the plantation the slave had been wrenched from his tribal culture, and the constant shattering of his family ties made continuity in identity almost impossible. The house servant could become more "human" than the field hand in this little world by staying closer to the master's family and serving it over a span of generations while he built an identity within this family and acquired a distinctive role in it. A few slaves—sometimes by accident, often by the volition of a master— were freed from plantation bondage and remained at liberty in the city on the tidelands. It was in the city that the slave revolt of 1822 occurred, led by a self-educated freed slave and organized through classes meeting in the African church. And it was in the city that great tensions arose when the plantation worlds were torn by the Civil War so that freed slaves flocked to urban centers; because in the city the individual Negro exchanged his slave status for identification with a population group which labeled him inferior and subservient by reason of color. In the midst of efforts to shore up the semblance of older organic little worlds under new conditions, the white men of the tidelands directed their strongest energies to constructing the wall of separation between white and Negro. And with their tradition of independence and privacy and emphasis that human relationships were before all else *personal* matters, the men of the tidelands were suspicious of the city and the new human situations arising there.

The urban setting was a place of public encounters; thus in key institutions and at other crucial points throughout the city the symbols of the great separation were proclaimed. The system was fashioned and managed by just one side of the community: there could be little rationale for the allegation that the great separation could also imply equality. Yet, on the tidelands, the voice of discontent from a deprived segment was low and muffled. Tradition weighed heavily on the Negro too; and the uncertainty involved in breaking an old pattern together with a lack of models of what the new would be, pressed him to maintain the unchanging role prescribed for him. As the Negro minister-leader said: "People here get to a certain point, they are on the verge of achieving something, and then there is a withdrawal." They remained in cliques and accepting little internal leadership, their side of the community so depressed and lacking in means for growth and change that even the professions required to service its separated institutions were almost caricatures of the white man's counterparts. Internal energies that could vitalize were siphoned off as the Negro who did attain more education left the community. If there was to be movement toward new opportunity and new self-definition, the energies must come from without. But how could they penetrate a community where both white and Negro resisted the outsider?

When the plantation culture reached the bayou lands of the Southwest it soon was confronted with the realities of another segmentation. The clash of Anglo and Mexican cultures left another gulf running through communities on the bayou, thus modulating the polarization of the great separation. In addition, the bayou lands were not so constraining. Land was plentiful in the early days so that the first colonists with their slaves settled over a wide area: there was no city to serve as a focus for their activities and to contain the distilled essence of their culture. When the city was formed—as a promotion scheme—it became and remained a place of movement and change, of open opportunity for men of wits.

The process of movement on the tidelands—from city to country in quest of property status—was reversed in the vital years of community growth on the bayou. The great activities of the most successful in the boom years were financial activities that brought men from the country to the city where property took forms other than land. There seemed to be an indefinite extensibility to the forms which property could take as new resources were tapped for wealth and shrewd men built new industries. There were many kinds of activities to be performed in the community and many social roles fashioned in their performance.

The slaves freed on the bayou also left the plantations for the city. And in a setting of turbulent individualism there was more violence inflicted by them and upon them in this community than occurred on the tidelands. But the bayou people did not dwell long on the lost splendor of their plantation days. The growing city provided room for the freedman to find new outlets and opportunities. The community erected by and for the Negroes was separated in its major institutions from the white, but there were points of contact around more different kinds of activities. Even beginning from a menial occupation, an individual Negro could, in a moneyed economy where goods and services flourished, acquire means for elevating himself so that financially he could surpass many whites. He could help to support better schools and even a college for his own, and these institutions could produce an articulate leadership internally.

Separation still left a gulf that made Negro institutions, on the whole, second-class. And "traditional" occupations were still reserved to most Negroes, with vocational training in newer technical areas omitted from curricula in their high schools. But there was enough economic growth and social space to permit expansion of a fairly broad repertory of social roles at different social levels in his own community—to elicit aspirations for achievement from the Negro. In the expanding market place he was not walled off but sensed the same stimuli and in large numbers acquired many of the same ambitions as did whites. As the Negro professor said: ". . . A man is a man when he's a consumer."

Conditions were more fluid on the bayou for changing the implicit inequality of categorical separation. Sounds of discontent were mixed with other sounds of competing groups on the turbulent stage. The Negro had already become more than a category; and he had lessened the gulf between his institutions and the white by education and economic attainment. He was encountering the white in daily activities—in the market place—more under conditions of equality. The voice of the Negro had been heard here for many generations. Fifty years ago it spoke through articulate leadership—largely religious—that seemed to accept "social and racial barriers imposed by a beneficent Jehovah." But contemporary leadership took note of the strength of the local Negro "middle class" as consumers of goods and services. Education for a broader role in a larger world was a key issue to the stimulated Negro on the bayou. His new leadership would join the move to change the separated society.

In spite of local reaction and stop-gap measures in the school system, this community as a whole would move toward public recognition of human equality, at least where men came together as consumers and in the institutions where they prepared themselves for such participation. Still, there would remain a carry-over of pride in the achievements of the local Negro community[16] in its years of separated growth.* A revolution would find men both adherents of change and conditioned to pride in the past among discontented segments on the bayou.

In settings in America remote from the plantation economy and scarcely touched by the institution of slavery, the discontents of the Negro have a different history and reflect different current conditions. Since Colonial days, communities outside the South have never legally sanctioned the delegation of a population group to the category of slave.[17] Yet all communities of any size experienced social inequalities as their populations were stratified at different times and with varying degrees of finality. And in every setting—in this experiment originally undertaken by white men—the heaviest weight was borne by those who least resembled the Founding Fathers. To the American Negro was added the further burden of a national memory of his former condition of servitude.

It appears that history is on the side of the Negro in non-southern communities, in that a long history in the local community serves to legitimize his commitment to the whole. However, a long history for a few and a short local history for their more numerous brethren—particularly in a community where the Negro population is swelled constantly by migration—may cause a gulf to develop separating Negroes most able to lead in participation in local institutions from those most in need of leadership and most likely to be lost in a mass. Basically, the problem

---

* The local Negro college became more attractive in recent years, not only to local residents but to Negroes from settings like cities in the Far West where distinctive group identity had been shunned in the past as a barrier to achievement. In developing a high-caliber track team, noted for its relay championships, the college recruited heavily among Texas Negro high schools and more than held its own in attracting boys sought by big Midwest universities.

of discontent is tied to the visibility of the Negro in the local population, the type and extent of his participations in the activities of daily life, and the relative degree of deprivation he considers to be the result of his segment-identification.

In the coastland community the Negro appeared early—in small numbers—as a participant in community life. The Quakers in the township went on record in the majority at a monthly meeting (1716) as forbearing to purchase any slaves. Other records indicate that local slave-holders released their slaves under pangs of conscience. A census of male population in 1777 showed that "Blacks," along with "Quakers," were distinguished from "Popular" in the township and were thirty in number that year of Revolution. Records also indicate that some Negroes took part in the war, both at sea and on land. Then in the vigorous years of community growth, Negroes were engaged in activities like those which occupied all others as the whaling industry was built into a great institution. That both amalgamation and separation occurred at this time is indicated by the recorded facts that one of the great whaling captains employed by white owners was a Negro, while at one time local Negroes financed and manned their own whaling ship. Through Civil War years abolition sentiment was strong, especially among Quakers; and apart from his local presence in somewhat varied roles, the Negro was a general symbol of a human cause to many of these New Englanders and their religious leaders.

As the community of the coastland became crowded with a heterogeneous population, the Negro was not highly visible or so visibly different from men clustered in other separated groups. He learned new trades and was conditioned in the urban ways he had helped to develop. Newcomers were not pressing in to swell the group and threaten an older stability by weight of numbers. Negroes had a history in the community predating most other groups—except the Yankee. If some felt discontent at disinheritance from the "Yankee strata" with whom their forebears had shared the past, they all could look about at the majority of other distinctive groups in the community with a relatively lessened sense of social and economic deprivation within the whole.

Farther west—in much younger communities—history is less important, while population numbers and pace of movement become more important in assessing the character of discontent. On the midlands, although white foreigners were accepted quickly into full citizenship, the constitutional convention for the state failed to pass a resolution to recognize full civil and political rights for the free Negro. In the vigorous melting pot on the lake, the Negro cast hardly a shadow as a local participant in the years when institutions acquired their distinctive characteristics. He was largely an abstract symbol of a cause: appearing in events like the freeing of the imprisoned fugitive slave by local citizens, which is venerated in community history. The community was called a "hotbed of abolitionism" in pre-Civil War years and numbered a few free Negroes in its population then, as after the war. However, the numbers of Negro participants in community life continued to be small, and those mentioned as long-time residents in local histories were former slaves from border states who came after the Civil War and took up menial-service occupations. They were respected and their talents given a place in an interdependent society.

But the community's great experience of amalgamation—in which foreign immigrants became "Americanized" in a generation —left the already American Negro largely on the outside. He could not lose his differences readily. The occupational skills prized in the building of new industries were skills he did not possess and he could hardly acquire them in this setting where an apprenticeship system was combined with family continuity in occupation. As his numbers did increase, he was left to the most menial tasks on the shop floor. In fact, the great increase in numbers came in post-Second World War years when industry needed unskilled labor for the foundries where, as other citizens phrased it, "*our* people didn't want to work." And in a community which stressed interdependence, the Negro did not, as his numbers increased, develop a subcommunity requiring even Negro professional services and a concomitant pluralism of roles. Occupation figures showed that as their numbers increased, Negroes became more concentrated in the least prized and least skilled occupations. They also became more visibly concentrated in central neighborhoods which became "Negro neighborhoods."

Local white citizens who spoke of the "few well-liked and well-established Negro families" the community once had, sensed a growing local consciousness of a visibly different population sector. The Negro segment itself had not given clear voice to local discontents around a local leadership. The community as a whole was small enough and stable enough to manage its own affairs through the institutions which most of its citizens—or their forebears—had created. And there was not the expansiveness of new and open opportunity in this milieu that could agitate discontent. "Massness"—irresponsibility, lack of commitment—in any population sector went against the grain of this community pattern. But energies from a broader movement could be a strong element in enervating local discontent and agitating change within the community pattern for meeting problems.

In the Far West, the open metropolis was often the third or fourth stop in the Negro's migration from the South. Many arrived after years spent in midwestern cities, conditioned to urban living and frequently the recipients of college education. The Negro was not present in sufficient numbers in the years of great racial and labor unrest to be a prime object of conflict. By the time his numbers had increased greatly, labor unions had begun to pride themselves on their nondiscriminatory membership clauses and industry was able to provide employment opportunities. Negroes penetrated the occupation system at many levels, although they were unevenly distributed; and some professionals occupied key positions that dramatized their commitment to the whole community. High schools and the university were proud of their growth in an atmosphere that eroded racial barriers. The occupations and professions for which they prepared the young to serve the whole community became more and more specialized —indifferent to color, family background, history. The Negro could find increasing freedom and equality through specialized roles in an urban society.

The great expansion in numbers in the Negro population following the Second World War threatened the older equilibrium and stirred discontent. The phenomenon of visible concentration in nonskilled occupations and in central neighborhoods occurred here also. Many of the newcomers came directly from the South and were without previous urban conditioning. The stimulations of the open metropolis found them ill-prepared to manage affairs of an urban home and to budget the income that could be acquired by marketing one's labor. The longer-resident Negroes tried to remain distinct from these newcomers and maintain identification with the larger community where occupation, church membership, even place of residence had become less separated by race. And this drawing apart by Negroes—no less natural than the escape of the homogenized to the suburbs—also threatened to permit the discontents of a deprived segment to well up from a purposeless mass.

However, the open metropolis had a history that had not been swept away by events: it retained a structure of institutions and means for participation in them. The separation of suburb from central area had not been extreme. The schools of most city areas were not all-Negro or all-white—and school principals said schools had become more cross-sectional in socio-economic class. The community resisted pressures toward "massness" because enough of its citizens remained concerned about changing situations and committed to seeking new solutions. And somehow violent group conflicts had always in the past been absorbed in a new identification with the whole community.

The great metropolitan areas—East or West—are settings where sheer pressures of population numbers and growth blend the discontents of segmentation with the problems of anonymity in a mass society. Mass populations lack a history, and individuals and groups in them lack a sense of directed movement toward long-range goals. Participants move aimlessly, or where a segment is formed its adherents may rush headlong toward expedient ends.

Where all sense of local community has broken down, perhaps the example of a purposeful national movement can be a rallying point for local commitments to new values. Such a movement may be a catalyst for new reciprocal obligations of local community. Where community traditions and historical memories are strong, what would local differences mean to the movement for rights and freedom that mobilized the discontents of the American Negro on a national scale?

Obviously, varied settings contributed people and ideas to the national movement. And in all these locales the mass media performed an important function in drawing Negroes out of their local insulations to a broader identification that was a source of pride and strength. For example, on the tidelands the new models of a different Negro could penetrate the community and not be rejected directly as the personal work of "outsiders." Perhaps this was the most important consequence (in all settings) of the energies generated by the Negro movement. But the concrete realization of "rights" and "freedom" would still have to be institutionalized in local areas, where people of all hues enacted roles in the day-by-day dimensions of community life.

Energies and Channels for a Revolution

Evidence began to appear in the 1960s that the American social experiment was on the move again. An interesting phenomenon was occurring. It was as if a visible segment with a long history of disenchantment and categorical denial in the American dream had somehow revitalized that dream. Protestant spokesmen began to speak out from priviliged suburban sanctuaries to their genteel congregations. Catholic and Jewish spokesmen began to sanction, and join, the movement of the discontented ones. Even the "respectable" college student showed cognizance of a cause and moved to support it.

A nation's conscience was quickened, and a chief means of its quickening through the dramatization of events and their principal characters were the very media which earlier had contributed so much to the deadening process. It became clear that aspects of a national community could take form and content from the mass media and allow for participation in dramas that were not just charades.*

What were the significant characteristics of the new dramas and their major participants?

The American Negro was projecting a new image of himself in

---

* The assassination tragedy of November 22, 1963, brought home most clearly the possibilities of television in knitting together a national community. Said columnist Marya Mannes: "This was not viewing. This was total involvement. . . . I stayed before the set, knowing—as millions knew —that I must give myself over entirely to an appalling tragedy, and that to evade it was a treason of the spirit." ("The Long Vigil," *The Reporter*, Dec. 19, 1963.)

American life—*as a member of a visible segment*—and fashioning a new history in America of which he could be proud. The Rev. Dr. Martin Luther King, Jr., said: "Today's Negro has a new sense of some-bodiness. . . . there is a new Negro on the scene with a new sense of dignity and destiny."[18] The new Negro leadership called on all men to be maladjusted to a society that allowed segregation. It said that men were "sleeping through a revolution"; for the world had been made a neighborhood by man's scientific genius and ". . . through our moral and ethical lives, we must make it a brotherhood." The chief spokesmen ruled out violence in the effort to end white supremacy.[19]

Other spokesmen took a different tack and offered a minority view on the Negro's quest of dignity. The Black Muslims held that the white man's sins were irrevocable and asked that a Negro area be set aside as a homeland in the United States. Malcolm X told his Negro listeners: "You are wasting your time begging for integration and civil rights. . . . If the white man wanted to integrate, we'd have been integrated a long time ago."[20]

An older political demagogue played a little of both major themes as he maneuvered to retain the support of Harlem masses. Congressman Adam Clayton Powell displayed the conspicuous triumphs of his own entree and assimilation into the larger society, yet advocated a militancy that smacked of "dignity" through "separation." Taking on both his critics in the larger society and the new nonviolent Negro leadership, he told the one that his political junkets and exploitations were no more flagrant than their own excesses at the public expense, and warned the other to purge their movement of white-liberal interlopers in leadership positions. An acquaintance noted that Powell used race "as a club or shield, depending on the situation." Sometimes the Congressman's charges seemed justified, the critic said, but often he had no evidence on which to base them. "But he makes them . . . to gain some momentary advantage or provide himself with an escape hatch."[21]

The significant point in these variations was that a new movement was organized around the assertion of group identity. The Negro, who in the past had difficulty locating grounds for dignity and pride in family and in a personal history of achievement, was beginning his new assertions of pride in broader identifications with his group. From this base in new pride *as an American Negro* he would turn to renewed efforts at individual discipline and family pride. For some extremists—the racists in reverse, for example—the process reached great lengths of personal discipline and self-sacrifice, worthy of an individual agent of a divinely commissioned group.

The young American Negro, with the eyes of the whole nation on him, had set about building and participating in a new history. In a southern city one spring morning in the centennial year of emancipation a tract was distributed among Negro children near their schools:

> Fight for freedom first then go to school. . . . Join the thousand in jail who are making their witness for freedom. . . . It's up to you to free our teachers, our parents, yourself and our country.[22]

Some youthful marchers actually ran to waiting patrol wagons: "'Freedom! Freedom! Freedom!' chanted the Negro girls and boys as the school buses swept by the commissioner on the way to jail." In the yellow brick church where the demonstration had begun, Rev. Dr. King admonished his followers to keep to the nonviolent approach, saying, "The world is watching you." And in the streets the march went on. A newsman reported: "As one group stepped off the curb . . . two patrolmen stepped out with their nightsticks and gently cut off a little boy bringing up the rear who appeared to be less than 5 years old. Chanting their freedom songs, the Negroes marched gaily toward the waiting police as older Negroes watching . . . applauded or sang softly a verse from 'We Shall Overcome.' . . ."[23]

In the days following the arrests of the schoolchildren reporters sought stories in the jails and the courtrooms. A twelve-year-old girl spoke from a jail cell: "My mother told me I had to serve my time."[24] A mother told a judge that his lecture to her boy was in vain: "I know this, judge—these younger people are not going to take what we took. I have another son in Oberlin [college], and he'll never want to come back here."[25] A probation officer noted: "Some of the parents won't come for their children. They're leaving them here. Why? It's for the movement I suppose."[26]

"The movement" was the vehicle for new pride. And it was truly a people's movement, meant not for the few but for the many. The young man who integrated a Deep South university explained that he was battling the feeling that only exceptional Negroes can succeed: "Maybe that was all right in the past . . . but it doesn't help America now. . . ." James Meredith said he would feel greater need to explain if he got all A's than if he got all F's in his courses: "That would mean I was either inhuman or super-human, neither of which I want to be."[27] And the movement had many heroes that were not merely racial heroes. Some would remain unsung in the battles against the firehoses and police dogs of old orthodoxies. At least one, however, in his martyrdom drew wide attention to the cause. Medgar Evers had said of this cause just ten days before he died by an assassin's bullet: "I've been fighting for America. . . ."[28] And the leader of the cause—Dr. King—said of him: "America has lost one of those pure patriots whose paramount desire was to be an American and to live as an American."[29] At the seat of national government, the president of the National Council of Churches urged that the steeple bells of member churches be rung at noon on the day of the funeral as a memorial to the fallen hero. The membership division of a Jewish Labor Committee passed a resolution calling on the President of the United States to proclaim a day of mourning for "this modern Patrick Henry."[30]

There were other perturbations of these events in the Negro revolt, some nationwide, others more local. The image of the Negro and his roles in America as well as the image of his revolt was changing, certainly more slowly in some places than in others. And more importantly, the Negro's image of himself was changing. As could be expected, the waves from the revolt spread unevenly. But most local communities of any size had their counterpart of "the movement." On the tidelands, teenagers and children formed at the old African Methodist Episcopal Church for a demonstration march through the downtown business district. (The church was the same one that served, in 1822, as the site for preparation of the slave revolt.) Most whites did not "recognize" these marchers as "our Negroes" and were sure that outsiders were responsible for the unrest. But old interrace friendships were strained, for one of the most firmly held beliefs on the tidelands was that the role prescribed for the "old friend" was the one desired by him. Now there was evidence of particular exceptions—individuals known personally by local white citizens. The mayor tried to minimize the extent of local Negro participation in the agitation: "It is tragic that a very few local citizens, incited by out-of-town agitators, and aided and abetted by street idlers and irresponsible children, should inflict this wrong upon us." But the local minister-leader who directed the community movement had probably received more help from the broader events of the spring and summer of 1963 than from the physical presence of "outside agitators." Now he had new models and new examples toward which to point his people.[31] (On the bustling bayou, where new social models were already filled by Negroes on the local scene, change had proceeded against less inertia. In April of 1962—the year before the centennial upswing for emancipation—all major convention hotels in the bayou community were integrated. The change was effected quietly to avoid conflict and mass agitation. "Newspapers have made no mention of the action," a report stated, adding: ". . . and newspapers and radio stations had been asked not to mention it unless there were incidents.")[32]

North and South, East and West the new energies of a revolution made their presence felt. Some evidence indicated that the energies were controlled more responsibly in the South than elsewhere: the Negro and his leaders there resisted the tendency to be lost in a population mass. There was no counterpart in the South to New York's Harlem.[33] It was in Harlem that Dr. King became the target of a few eggs thrown during a speaking tour.[34] An aide later said "there is no real nonviolent leadership in the North" and indicated the nonviolence leader "will have to come North and lead the civil rights movement." He added: "In the South, there is a resurgence of religious feeling because of the civil rights movement. . . . The whole atmosphere is becoming more religious. . . ."[35]

Before the summer was over the diffuse energies of discontent had been given concentrated display in Washington, D.C., in "the greatest assembly for redress of grievances" the capital had ever seen. Represented along with the Negro leaders on the steps of the Lincoln Memorial and later in the session with the President were white Catholic, Protestant, and Jewish religious spokesmen and a labor leader. The movement was seen at its best on this day when it was receiving its broadest support. Newspapers noted "there was no violence to mar the demonstration"; and television cameras were present to record this fact—giving the demonstration better coverage (said James Reston) than any event since the Presidential inauguration.[36] Reston noted the summation of the day given by James Baldwin, the author:

> . . . He was convinced that the country was finally grappling with the Negro problem instead of evading it; that the Negro himself was "for the first time" aware of his value as a human being and was "no longer at the mercy of what the white people imagine the Negro to be."[37]

Here was no mass seeking expedient ends but a responsible body of the people. Perhaps the great awakening of The March was that these people did not seem to wish to manipulate or use one another or other groups as mere means: they were linked to common purposes. Two aspects of the Negro movement were discernible and only the first had made great strides by the centennial summer. As a population sector, visible across the whole of America via the mass media, Negroes raised issues of equality and dignity and quickened the national conscience. But as participants in specific local communities where daily human confrontations occurred in normal living, they had only begun to use the aroused national conscience to create new local conditions that could lead to more dignified workaday roles.

Of course, these manifestations of a people addressing their unfinished tasks would always confront the problem that the re-creation of institutions to meet new conditions might be more difficult than the initial creation of institutions in a land with an open frontier. Old orthodoxies would be difficult to challenge when the alternative for the group or individual was not moving on to start anew but was staying on. Old, strong, and hallowed social and cultural residues could not be ignored. In fact, it might well be that the history-filled setting in this country presented more promise for responsible revolution than did the completely "open" setting. In the former there might, in the long run, be a greater sense of responsibility of participants to one another and perhaps to a larger whole.

The basic processes in the continuing revolution permitted variety in response by the people in meeting new challenges. Thus there could be infinite variability in local styles for confronting shared human problems: for example, in conditioning for personal or impersonal relationships, in the stress on group and individual interdependence or on separateness. In the thesis presented here it is not any particular pattern of social accommodation in any community that represents the true "American pattern" or the "ideal." The major lesson of the preceding stories is that variety has been vital to the American heritage but that unifying values that impel new experiments continue to appear across the whole—if not woven into local institutions, then irritating an established equilibrium and provoking change. The questions of equality and dignity for the individual and the perpetuation of the imperfect dialogue through which answers are explored move the cause of freedom in this country and around the world.

In America's domestic efforts in behalf of freedom and self-determination, diversity has been a constant challenge. For truly no people has ever continued to form institutions out of such heterogeneous human elements. And no other democratic experiment has been forced back more on the primitive assessment of the worth of each participant. Still, from the time when the Pilgrim Fathers admitted "stranger-adventurers" into their religious colony and thus risked to "break the course of communitie," the recurring questions of each epoch and generation have been: Can diverse populations find grounds for community? What are the intrinsic values around which community is newly achieved?

Evidence indicates that community is achieved and that the value of equality of individuals does still find expression in "frontier" experiments. It would be wrong to believe that the hearts of Americans are any purer than those of other men. But "changing the hearts of men" is at least in part a matter of changing the conditions under which men "experience" one another.

In American history, a frontier always provided new settings for men to meet as equals. As Tocqueville noted, the boundless continent for our energies gave us the means of remaining equal and free. Military historians (as well as anthropologists) have observed that under stress in the Second World War and in Korea diverse American populations achieved common commitments around a primary regard for the individual human life.[38] Surely the Peace Corps provides more recent examples of the basic values projected by Americans under other primitive conditions.

But apart from exceptional experiments in which heirs of the Founding Fathers are transplanted to new ground: Can freedom and equality find new outlets for expression within the confines of a conquered continent? Those who continue to listen to the restless and discontented ones may not find an answer to this question but they will sense an imperative. For the sounds of the American revolution will continue to be the sounds of men and women at their unfinished private and public tasks. They are the sounds of imperfect, unsatisfied human beings, impatient with constraints and asserting unique selves that resist regimentation. They are the sounds of the people in communication with one another, continuing to create and re-create the institutions of diverse communities.

Appendix I. Population Facts

A Note on Census Facts and Community Histories

Population facts suggest the way population is differentiated and the context for social encounters in given spatial settings. However, the U.S. Census of Populations is not tailored for social-psychological analyses. The facts set down here are merely illustrative.

In addition, to analyze a community system, population facts must be viewed through historical time. Thus, varying rates of growth or decline, swift or gradual changes, occupation and income-distribution shifts through time, and the types of population groups involved in these shifts and changes must be considered by looking at many censuses and at other records in the life history of the community. Indications of these processes are set down in the narrative portions of the book.

Data in the table following are based on *counties* as geographical units with the exception of the community of Chapter 1 where a "Standard Metropolitan Statistical Area" was substituted. (The county unit in Massachusetts was not comparable, as a population base, to this unit in other states.) These same units were the basis of historical and contemporary discussions, in the text, of social forms and processes in communities.

The job of the scientist, of course, begins where the hunches set down in this book leave off: relating historical and census data to conceptualized patterns of social process; and noting the interrelatedness of the concepts when the scheme presented here is used as a guide to further data.

Table 1. Differentiation of Population in Eight Communities[a]

Community of Chapter	Total Nos. Approx., 1960	Ethnicity				Nativity	
		% White	% Spanish Surname[b]	% Negro	% Oriental or Indian	% Native-born American	% Native of Foreign or Mixed Parents
1	143,000	97	—	3	—	84	35
2	216,000	64	—	36	—	99	3
3	45,000	97	54	—	2	99	4
4	1,243,000	80	6	20	—	98	7
5	21,000	100	—	—	—	98	15
6	93,000	99	—	—	—	98	9
7	142,000	96	—	4	—	93	21
8	935,000	95	—	3	2	92	19

Income and Aspiration

Community of Chapter	All Population				Nonwhite Population Alone				
	Median Income of Families	% under $3,000	Persons 25 Years and Older, median, school years completed	% Employed Persons in "Highest" Census Occupation Group[c]	Median Income of Families	(% of Median of All Population)	% under $3,000	Persons 25 Years and Older, median, school years completed	% Employed Persons in "Highest" Census Occupation Group[c]
1	$5,217	20	8.6	8	$4,139	(79)	36	8.4	4
2	4,518	33	10.1	11	2,149	(48)	66	6.3	5
3	5,182	26	11.7	18	—	—	—	—	—
4	6,040	18	11.3	13	3,386	(56)	43	8.8	5
5	4,979	29	9.8	10	—	—	—	—	—
6	5,868	16	12.2	13	—	—	—	—	—
7	6,722	11	10.5	11	5,414	(81)	16	8.6	1
8	7,084	10	12.2	16	5,563	(79)	20	11.1	11

[a] Figures in tables taken from 1960 U.S. Census of Populations. Percentages are rounded to nearest whole per cent.
[b] "Spanish" population is included in count of white population but is also differentiated in a separate count of "Spanish Surnames" in the Southwest.
[c] Highest occupation group represents mainly "professionals." Negro professionals serve largely a Negro subcommunity in communities 2 and 4; while in 7, for example, they have no subcommunity and seldom rise to serve the whole community.

Table 1. Differentiation of Population (cont'd)
Plot of Percentages in Predominant Four Occupation Groups in Each Community:

All Employed Population

Community of Chapter	Professional, Technical, and Kindred	Managers, Officials, and Proprietors, including Farmers and Farm Managers	Clerical and Kindred, and Sales	Craftsmen, Foremen and Kindred	Operatives and Kindred	Private Household Workers	Service Workers except Private Household	Laborers, including Farm Laborers and Farm Foremen
1	11		17	13	37		8	
2	18		20	15	15			
3	13	12	25	11				
4		28	24	14	14			11 (rural)
5		17	17	14				
6	13		25	13	25			
7	11		21	17	12			
8	16		27	15				

Nonwhite Employed Population Alone

Community of Chapter	Professional, Technical, and Kindred	Managers, Officials, and Proprietors, including Farmers and Farm Managers	Clerical and Kindred, and Sales	Craftsmen, Foremen and Kindred	Operatives and Kindred	Private Household Workers	Service Workers except Private Household	Laborers, including Farm Laborers and Farm Foremen
1	—	—	—	7	47	8	11	7
2	—	—	—	—	18	26	14	22
3	—	—	—	—	—	—	—	—
4	—	—	—	—	18	17	22	16
5	—	—	—	—	—	—	—	—
6	—	—	—	—	—	—	—	—
7	—	—	—	9	38	—	18	—
8	11	—	14	—	15	—	21	15

Generally, occupations shift from "higher" to "lower" in moving from left to right in the Table. However, the variable of size of community is obviously important to comparisons. Also, size of nonwhite population should be considered in comparisons in the lower part of the Table and between the upper and lower parts. In community 8, about 2 out of 5 nonwhites are Oriental. Even so, this community compared to others shows a remarkable dispersion of predominant occupations for nonwhites.

Appendix II. Definitions

Basic Concepts

COMMUNITY: This term is used to designate the geographical entities studied as bases of population. However, bases of population were primarily considered as contexts for human communication. Thus, the term "community" also connotes—as it is used in this book—any human aggregate as a communication system where participants are conscious of their identity, and relationships to others, in the whole.

CULTURE: An aggregate of population considered as participating in and organizing a field of significant symbols. As a cultural milieu, a community is viewed as a field of "names" which have significant meaning and value to participants.

SOCIAL SYSTEM: The patterns of interrelationship between the elements—individuals and groups—of a designated aggregate of population.

ROLE: The basic unit for analyzing the attitudes and behaviors of participants in the culture and the social system. Thus, membership in a differentiated group and the "names" accruing to such membership tend to prescribe attitudes and behaviors for participants, as does relative position within a group.

Forms of Population Differentiation
(Tendencies in the way population is broken down and clustered in a given aggregate)

HOMOGENEITY: Lack or absence of distinct population differentiation; sameness and similarity.

(Corollary) NONSTRATIFICATION: Evaluations of "higher" and "lower" not significant (or played down where differentiation is apparent).

SEGMENTATION: Clustering of population into a few major, visible, and significant groupings. Implies firm boundaries between conspicuous clusters of population.

284

(Corollary) Class Bifurcation: Strong evaluations dividing "higher" and "lower" social groups.

Heterogeneity: Multiple groupings of population. Less firm boundaries and less gross clustering of groups.

(Corollary) Multiple Strata: Many degrees of evaluation of higher or lower social position, such as "less high," "less low," etc.

Orientations to the Social Forms

(Tendencies in the way participants perceive themselves and others as they occupy positions, and enact roles defined by these positions, in the social structure)

Ascribed: Individual and group characteristics, and expectations based on them, are believed inherent and "given."

Achieved: Individual and group characteristics, and expectations based on them, are believed acquired through present efforts and geared to continued strivings.

Separated (*or* Independent): Groups and individuals expected to keep to themselves.

Interdependent: Groups and individuals believed to owe more to one another and to the larger whole.

Realms of Social Participation

(Tendencies in the extent of role participations)

Private-Public Blending: No clear distinction between micro and macro social realms; or distinction is resisted.

Private-Public Split: Distinct separation between micro and macro social realms and between roles played in each.

Private-Public Multiplicity: Many shades of micro and macro participation, implying many possible roles for the participant.

Orientations in the Realms of Social Participation

(Tendencies in the way participants encounter one another as they enact the more micro and the more macro social roles)

Contractual: Relationships on a more specialized and partial basis, under conditions like those of a market place.

Personal: Relationships involve whole persons who are experienced more completely as "wholes."

SPECIFIC: Relationships geared more to the particular situation or to the particular person. (Roles can be more easily shaped by participants in the course of events.)

GENERAL: Relationships geared more to categorical role-types. (Participants have less freedom to reshape roles.)

Additional Concepts (Not Part of the Theoretical Scheme)

INSTITUTION: A social and cultural subsystem in which values and roles are clearly defined and defended. The term is used in social science to refer to an articulated and valued pattern of roles and role-expectations in the social structure.

MASS *or* "MASSNESS":   This item is used in this book to indicate a human aggregate lacking a clear social structure with valued and defended roles. Used as an adjective for describing states or conditions of an institution, the term indicates alienation of participants from one another in their reciprocal role obligations and alienation from the long-term values of the institution.

A Classification Scheme

The preceding definitions provide an outline that can be used as a gross classification scheme for the communities studied. The four concepts under the classifications of "Forms" and "Realms" pattern bipolar tendencies. For example: A community as a whole may be classified as *Segmented* and as tending to an *Ascribed* more than an *Achieved* orientation and as tending to a *Separated* more than an *Interdependent* orientation; and it may be further classified as *Blending* the Private-Public realms and as tending toward *Personal* more than *Contract* participations and more toward *General* than toward *Specific* role orientations.

My gross classification of the eight communities *as wholes* (without noting directions of change) appears as follows:

1. Heterogeneous: Ascribed, Separated. Multiplicity: Contract, General.
2. Segmented: Ascribed, Separated. Blending: Personal, General.
3. Segmented: Ascribed, Separated. Split: Contract, General.
4. Segmented: Achieved, Separated. Split: Contract, General.
5. Homogeneous: Ascribed, Separated. Blending: Personal, General.
6. Homogeneous: Achieved, Interdependent. Blending: Personal, Specific.

7. Homogeneous: Achieved, Interdependent. Multiplicity: Contract, General.
8. Heterogeneous: Achieved, Interdependent. Multiplicity: Contract, Specific.

Notes

The quotation on the title page from Dr. Benjamin Rush, a signer of the Declaration of Independence, is taken from Herbert Agar, *The Price of Union* (Boston: Houghton Mifflin Co., 1950), pp. 36–37.

Introduction

1. From the Preface of *Leaves of Grass*, quoted in *The Britannica Library of Great American Writing*, I (ed. by Louis Untermeyer), (Philadelphia and New York: J. B. Lippincott Co., 1960), p. 759.

2. Reinhold Niebuhr, "What Alternative to Communism?" *Current*, Sept., 1961, p. 67.

3. For a broad discussion of the importance of ideas in human history, see Alfred North Whitehead, *Adventures of Ideas* (New York: New American Library, 1955). Note particularly Part One for a discussion of key sociological ideas.

4. The thesis that economic forces determined the structure of the American Constitution is probably most closely identified with Charles A. Beard. See *An Economic Interpretation of the Constitution of the United States* (New York: The Macmillan Co., 1936). One does not have to accept Beard's thesis (that landed interests in the early American aristocracy determined the political forms decided upon at Philadelphia) to agree upon the relevance of the socioeconomic situations of men as constraining their perceptions of the "good" society. A point to note, however, is that men of varied interests reached compromises that permitted an apparatus of government to be created which was flexible enough to give room, through the years, for varied expression and interpretation of the key ideas.

A different thesis to that of Beard has been formulated by Robert R. Palmer. See *The Age of Democratic Revolution* (Princeton: Princeton University Press, 1959). Palmer holds that it was not economic forces reflected in *particular* representative institutions that gave the American Revolution its force in western democracy; it was the *idea* of a sovereign people delegating authority over themselves to elected representatives who decided what the apparatus of government should be. Thus Palmer emphasizes the revolutionary importance of long-term dynamic ideas rather than the specific impact of short-term perceptions.

5. Men who write of Jefferson invariably have difficulty in trying to tie his thoughts together into a prescription for democratic government. Perhaps Jefferson's Declaration is his finesh epitaph. It does not tell us where we are heading or what means we will need to get there but sets us out on a venture in human freedom and self-determination. For a recent discussion of the idealistic impact of Jefferson see Merrill D. Peterson, *The Jefferson Image in the American Mind* (New York: Oxford University Press, 1960).

6. Alexis de Tocqueville, *The Republic of the United States of America* (trans. by Henry Reeves), (New York: A. S. Barnes and Co., 1851), pp. 178–179, 105.

7. This social-psychological orientation can be traced basically to the works of Cooley and Mead. For example, see Charles Horton Cooley (with an introduction by Robert Cooley Angell), *Two Major Works: Social Organization. Human Nature and the Social Order* (Glencoe, Ill.: The Free Press, 1956); George Herbert Mead (ed. and with an introduction by Anselm Strauss), *The Social Psychology of George Herbert Mead* (Chicago: University of Chicago Press, 1956). A recent refinement of the social-psychological orientation can be found in works by Erving Goffman. Goffman limits his definition of an "encounter" to "one type of social arrangement that occurs when persons are in one another's immediate physical presence. . . ." See Erving Goffman, *Encounters* (Indianapolis: Bobbs-Merrill, 1961), pp. 17–18. In the present book, "encounter" is used more generically to refer to any meeting between people, whether direct or indirect, in which participants are cognizant of stimuli from one another as individuals or as representatives of groups.

Also the concepts of George Homans are basic to the analysis here of communities as systems. The focus upon the attitudes ("sentiments") toward self and others engendered by "activities" and "interactions" of individuals and groups in community settings was a guide, borrowed from Homans, to relevant facts. See George C. Homans, *The Human Group* (New York: Harcourt, Brace, and World, 1950).

8. The point of view represented in this discussion of human involvement in history (through which men become, in part, creatures of the institutions they create) is expressed in the philosophy of Reinhold Niebuhr. See *The Self and the Dramas of History* (New York: Charles Scribner's Sons, 1955).

The present author is aware of the oversimplifications of social-scientific analysis. The social scientist believes he can make significant but imperfect and partial statements about human behavior by reference to patterns of social relationship. His frame of reference is one that focuses on the constraints upon human behavior imposed by the structures that man has created. That this does not leave man a completely analyzable object and "creature of culture and society" is attested to by discussions like those by Niebuhr.

9. The psychologist Edward Tolman said of the culture of a human group: "Culture has 'names.' It has . . . symbolic ways of focusing the attention of its participants upon the particular discrimination and generalization units and beliefs that it favors." See Talcott Parsons & Edward A. Shils (eds.), *Toward a General Theory of Action* (Cambridge, Massachusetts: Harvard University Press, 1952), p. 345.

10. For some commentaries on the changing quality of human relationships see: David Riesman, *The Lonely Crowd* (New Haven: Yale University Press, 1961); Erich Fromm, *The Sane Society* (New York: Holt, Rinehart and Winston, 1955); William H. Whyte, Jr., *The Organization Man* (New York: Simon and Schuster, 1956); Walter Lippmann, *The Public Philosophy* (Boston: Little, Brown, and Co., 1955); and Erich Kahler, *The Tower and the Abyss* (New York: George Braziller, 1957). Two books which deal specifically with the problems of "community" in the modern world are Robert A. Nisbet, *The Quest for Community* (New York: Oxford University Press, 1953) and Maurice R. Stein, *The Eclipse of Community* (Princeton, N.J.: Princeton University Press, 1960). Nisbet analyzes the problems generally as the breakdown of "intermediate associations" in a world in which the powers of the modern state usurp the functions of socializing agencies. Stein discusses the "eclipse of community" in America against the backdrop of changing approaches to the study and analysis of the community in social science literature.

11. Frederick Jackson Turner's historical essay, written in 1893, on the significance of the American frontier provides many insights into the dynamics of a continuing experiment. The focus in this book on communities as diverse settings of American culture borrows the orientation of Turner's essay, that ". . . American development has exhibited not merely advance along a single line, but a return to primitive conditions on a continually advancing frontier line, and a new development for that area. American social development has been continually beginning over again on the frontier. This perennial rebirth, this fluidity of American life, this expansion westward with its new opportunities, its continuous touch with the simplicity of primitive society, furnishes the forces dominating American character." See

Frederick Jackson Turner, *The Significance of the Frontier in American History* (El Paso: Academic Reprints, Inc., 1960).

Chapter 1

1. From William Bradford, *Bradford's History of Plymouth Plantation, 1606–1646* (ed. by William T. Davis), (New York: Charles Scribner's Sons, 1908), p. 107.

2. From a letter of Robert Cushman, who carried on negotiations with London merchants for the colony at Leyden, Holland; quoted in *ibid.,* p. 73.

3. *Ibid.,* p. 106.

4. William Bradford, *Pilgrim Courage* (Selected Episodes from His Original History of Plimouth Plantation), adapted and edited by E. Brooks Smith and Robert Meredith (Boston, Toronto: Little, Brown, and Co., 1962), pp. 15, 19.

5. *Ibid.,* p. 29.

6. *Ibid.,* p. 59.

7. From John Quincy Adams (1842), "The New England Confederacy of MDCXLIII," in *Collections of the Massachusetts Historical Society,* Vol. IX of the 3rd Series (Boston: Freeman and Bolles, 1846), p. 202.

8. Bradford, *Bradford's History of Plymouth Plantation, 1606–1646, op. cit.,* pp. 107–08.

9. *Ibid.,* p. 293.

10. *Ibid.*

11. *Ibid.,* p. 294.

12. *Ibid.,* p. 299. The colony at Plymouth generally proved more tolerant of dissent and social aberration than did the quickly populated settlements at Massachusetts Bay and the austere congregation at Salem. Bradford commented on Roger Williams (who came to Plymouth after troubles at Massachusetts Bay and left to go to the church at Salem, whence he was finally banished to the hinterlands): ". . . and his teaching well approved, for the benefite whereof I still bless God, and am thankfull to him, even for his sharpest admonitions and reproufs, so farr as they agreed with truth. He this year begane to fall into some strang oppinions . . . which caused some controversie between the church and him. . . . Yet after wards sued for his dismission to the church of Salem. . . . But he is to be pitied, and prayed for, and so I shall leave the matter, and desire the Lord to shew him his errors, and reduce him into the way of truth, and give him a setled judgment and constancie in the same; for I hope he

belongs to the Lord, and that he will shew him mercie" (p. 299). From 1643, and continuing some forty years, the various colonies in New England—Massachusetts Bay, Plymouth, Connecticut, and New Haven—associated together in a loose confederation for mutual protection. John Quincy Adams later wrote: "The Union . . . consisted of four separate, independent communities, in a great measure self-formed; the vital principle common to them all being religious contention. . . ." However, the "contention" of Roger Williams was not acceptable to this "one small religious sect of Christians" in their separate communities, and Rhode Island was excluded from the confederation (John Q. Adams, in *Collections*, IX, *op. cit.*, p. 210).

13. In 1661 a church teacher wrote: "It is the Commandment of the Lord, that a people should enter into Covenant with the Lord to become his people even in their Civil Society. . . ." Thus, civil rules should "compel men to their undoubted duty, and punish them for their undoubted sins. . . ." From "The Christian Commonwealth: or, The Civil Policy of The Rising Kingdom of Jesus Christ," by Mr. John Eliot, Teacher of the Church of Christ at Roxbury in New-England (1661), in *Collections*, IX, pp. 143, 154.

14. Deed (recorded in 1664) cited in Leonard Bolles Ellis, *History of New Bedford and its Vicinity 1602–1892* (Syracuse, N.Y.: D. Mason and Co., 1892), p. 19. John Q. Adams points out: "Of the European settlers on the American Continent, the colonists of New England were the first who ever held themselves bound to respect the right of prior occupancy of the Indian savage, and to purchase it of him for an equivalent" (*Collections*, IX, p. 197).

15. Quoted in Ellis, *op. cit.*, p. 18.

16. Quoted in *ibid.*, pp. 44–45.

17. Quoted in *ibid.*, p. 24.

18. Quoted in *ibid.*, p. 21. In negotiating for a termination of hostilities, the Plymouth authorities had promised amnesty to the Indians. However, this promise was broken, and 178 Indian captives, including the chief's (King Philip's) wife and son were marched to Plymouth and sold into slavery. Records indicate that in spite of the suffering incurred by them during the war, the nonconformist dissenters led the protests against this treachery (*ibid.*, p. 28).

19. Quoted in New Bedford Board of Trade, *New Bedford, Massachusetts* (New Bedford: Mercury Publishing Co., 1889), p. 13.

20. John Stetson Barry, *The History of Massachusetts, II, The Provincial Period* (Boston: Privately published, 1857), p. 18.

21. Records from Ellis, *op. cit.*, pp. 42–51.

22. *Ibid.*, p. 41.

23. From the Preamble to the articles declaring the New England Confederation; quoted in *Collections,* IX, p. 215.

24. Charles Henry Pope, *The Pioneers of Massachusetts* (Boston: Charles H. Pope, 1900), p. 7. Data (pp. 523–24) on occupations of 1,725 pioneers for whom occupation was recorded, show (partial list):

323	Tillers of soil (from landholders to plowmen)
210	House and ship carpenters
115	Tailors
103	Merchants
91	Ministers
81	Shoemakers
75	Seacaptains
62	Weavers
54	Coopers
41	Tanners
39	Blacksmiths
34	Fishermen
30	Innholders
28	Millers
23	Bricklayers and makers
21	Physicians, surgeons

25. Journal of Rev. Paul Coffin, quoted in *Centennial in New Bedford, Historical Address by Hon. William W. Crapo* (New Bedford: E. Anthony and Sons, 1876), p. 29.

26. Elmore P. Haskins, *The Story of Water Street* (New Bedford: Old Dartmouth Historical Sketches No. 15, 1906), p. 9.

27. Figures from Ellis, *op. cit.*

28. A local newspaper of Sept. 18, 1924, quoted on "The Fairhaven Taxes 1771," in John M. Bullard, *The Rotches* (Milford, New Hampshire: The Cabinet Press, 1947), p. 15.

29. Description taken from "Tea Leaves" (a book by Francis S. Drake, published in 1884), cited in Bullard, *op. cit.*, p. 47.

30. Quoted in Ellis, *op. cit.*, pp. 78–79.

31. Facts on local companies from *ibid.*, pp. 140–41, 67.

32. *Ibid.*, p. 72.

33. Account quoted in *ibid.*, p. 71. High spirits apparently prevailed in these early, exhilarating days of war. The account told, humorously, how the single carriage gun—a captured piece—aboard the Yankee ship "having lost its trunnions, was then loaded to a timber head, and when chance brought it in range, fired, but proving yet loyal to the king, it kicked out of the traces and went overboard at first fire."

34. *Ibid.*, p. 102.

35. From accounts in *ibid.*, and in Emma L. Gartland (ed.), *New*

Bedford's Story (New Bedford: Emma L. Gartland, 1934), pp. 9–10.

36. Ellis, *op. cit.*, p. 143.

37. Gartland (ed.), *op. cit.*, p. 11.

38. Local newspaper, quoted in *ibid.*, p. 163.

39. *Ibid.*, p. 161.

40. Local newspaper, quoted in *ibid.*, p. 171.

41. Local newspaper, quoted in *ibid.*, p. 227.

42. Quoted in Daniel Ricketson, *New Bedford of the Past* (Boston and New York: Houghton, Mifflin and Co., 1903), p. 92.

43. *Ibid.*, p. 53.

44. Excerpts from Zephaniah W. Pease (ed.), *Life in New Bedford a Hundred Years Ago* (The Diary of Joseph R. Anthony), (New Bedford: George H. Reynolds, 1922), pp. 16, 20–22, 25–27, 31, 33, 34, 39, 43, 62, 69.

45. Gartland (ed.), *op. cit.*, p. 28.

46. *The New Bedford Mercury, One Hundredth Anniversary Supplement*, Aug. 7, 1907, p. 13.

47. *Ibid.*, p. 10.

48. *Ibid.*, p. 12.

49. Local newspaper, April 21, 1851, quoted in Gartland (ed.), *op. cit.*, p. 30.

50. Daniel Ricketson, quoted in Robert Grieve (ed.), *New Bedford Semi-Centennial Souvenir* (Providence, R.I.: Journal of Commerce Company, 1897), p. 10.

51. *The New Bedford Mercury, One Hundredth Anniversary Supplement, op. cit.*, p. 12.

52. *Centennial in New Bedford, Historical Address by Hon. William W. Crapo, op. cit.*, p. 132.

53. *Diary of Rev. Moses How* (No. 59 in Series of Sketches of New Bedford's Early History), (New Bedford: Reynolds Printing, 1931), p. 18.

54. Ellis, *op. cit.*, p. 326.

55. *Diary of Rev. Moses How, op. cit.*, p. 20.

56. Daniel Ricketson, *New Bedford of the Past, op. cit.*, p. 9.

57. Zephaniah W. Pease, *op. cit.*, pp. 26, 27.

58. Quoted in *Centennial in New Bedford, Historical Address by Hon. William W. Crapo, op. cit.*, p. 150.

59. Haskins, *op. cit.*, p. 10.

60. Words used by Ellis, in *op. cit.*, p. 246.

61. Excerpts from *Diary of Rev. Moses How, op. cit.*, pp. 12, 13, 14.

62. Quoted from Benjamin Rodman, *A Voice from the Prison* (New Bedford: Benjamin Lindsey, 1840), pp. 6 and 51.

63. *The New Bedford Mercury, One Hundredth Anniversary Supplement, op. cit.,* p. 12.

64. *Ibid.,* p. 5.

65. New Bedford Board of Trade, *op. cit.,* pp. 141–142.

66. Free Public Library, New Bedford, Mass., *Some Facts about New Bedford, 1906.*

67. Grieve (ed.), *op. cit.,* p. 14.

68. *The New Bedford Mercury, One Hundredth Anniversary Supplement, op. cit.,* p. 15.

69. Articles of incorporation quoted in Ellis, *op. cit.,* p. 144.

70. From Grieves (ed.), *op. cit.,* p. 63.

71. *Diary of Rev. Moses How, op. cit.,* p. 5.

Chapter 2

1. From a correspondence between Lord Ashley and Captain Halsted, December, 1671. In "The Shaftesbury Papers and Other Records Relating to Carolina and the First Settlement on Ashley River Prior to the Year 1676," *Collections of the South Carolina Historical Society* (Charleston: South Carolina Historical Society, 1897), V, 364.

2. *Collections,* V, 361 (words of Lord Ashley in a letter to Sir John Yeamens of Barbadoes).

3. *Ibid.* (Quotations are excerpts from Locke's "Fundamental Constitutions," pp. 95 ff.).

4. *Ibid.,* p. 32.

5. Figures quoted in William Francis Guess, *South Carolina: Annals of Pride and Protest* (New York: Harper & Row, 1960), p. 31.

6. *Collections, II,* compiled by B. R. Carroll (New York: Harper & Row, 1836). Quotations from a "Brief Description of the Cape Feare Expedition of 1666," pp. 16, 17.

7. *Collections,* V, 182.

8. *Ibid.,* p. 361.

9. *Ibid.*

10. Quoted in Charleston News and Courier, *The Centennial of Incorporation* (Charleston: The News and Courier Book Presses, 1884), p. 66.

11. W. J. Cash, *The Mind of the South* (New York: Alfred A. Knopf, 1941), p. 33.

12. Quoted in Charleston News and Courier, *op. cit.,* pp. 62–63.

13. Quoted in Verner W. Crane, *The Southern Frontier 1670–1732* (Durham: Duke University Press, 1928), p. 109.

14. *Ibid.,* p. 108.

15. Quoted in Robert G. Rhett, *Charleston, An Epic of Carolina* (Richmond: Garrett and Massie, 1940), p. 25.

16. *Ibid.*, p. 41.

17. *Collections*, II, 156.

18. *Ibid.*, p. 161.

19. From *Collections*, V, ix (quoted in an address of Joseph W. Barnwell, "Dual Governments in South Carolina").

20. Cash, *op. cit.*, p. 96.

21. Described and quoted in W. F. Guess, *op. cit.*, p. 58.

22. Figures from Richard Walsh, *Charleston's Sons of Liberty* (Columbia, S.C.: University of South Carolina Press, 1959), pp. 24–25.

23. Described in Mrs. St. Julien Ravenel, *Charleston, the Place and the People* (New York: The Macmillan Co., 1931), pp. 385–386.

24. *Ibid.*, p. 399.

25. *Collections*, IV (1887), 8. From a 21st anniversary address before the South Carolina Historical Society by William J. Rivers, delivered May 19, 1876.

26. Walsh, *op. cit.*, p. X.

27. John Rutledge, quoted in *ibid.*, p. 68.

28. Quotation from the historian Bancroft in Rhett, *op. cit.*, p. 108.

29. Quoted in Ravenel, *op. cit.*, p. 193.

30. Quoted in *Bulletins of the South Carolina Historical Commission, No. 9*, "Delegates to the Continental Congress from South Carolina, 1774–1789, with Sketches of the Four Who Signed the Declaration of Independence," by A. S. Salley, Jr. (Columbia, S.C.: The State Company, 1927), p. 3.

31. Ravenel, *op. cit.*, pp. 189–190.

32. *Ibid.*, p. 387.

33. *Encyclopedia Americana*, XXII, 688.

34. Cash, *op. cit.*, pp. 60–61.

35. John Drayton, *A View of South Carolina* (Charleston: W. P. Young, 1802), pp. 144–145.

36. James Hamilton, Jr., *An Account of the Late Intended Insurrection among a Portion of the Blacks of this City* (2nd ed.; Charleston: A. E. Miller, 1822), p. 8.

37. Ravenel, *op. cit.*, p. 453.

38. *Ibid.*, pp. 464, 485.

39. Warning given by Barnwell Rhett (at the time of the nullification proceedings), described in Guess, *op. cit.*, p. 191.

40. By "A Westindian," *Charleston, South Carolina, A Satiric Poem; Shewing That Slavery Still Exists in a Country, Which Boasts, above All Others of Being the Seat of Liberty* (London: S. Y. Collins, 1851).

41. Cash, *op. cit.*, p. 80 (quoting Dr. J. H. Thornwell, later president of the college of South Carolina).

42. Alice Hopton Middleton (ed.), *Life in Carolina and New England During the Nineteenth Century* (Bristol, R.I.: Privately printed, 1929), pp. 76–79.

43. *Ibid.*, pp. 60–61.

44. Letter reacting to statements of northern abolitionists, in *ibid.*, pp. 113–114.

45. Quoted in John Porter Hollis, *The Early Period of Reconstruction in South Carolina* (Baltimore: The Johns Hopkins Press, published monthly, Jan.-Feb., 1905, Johns Hopkins University Studies in Historical and Political Science, Series XXIII, Nos. 1–2), note, pp. 18–19.

46. Quoted in *ibid.*, pp. 17–18.

47. Quoting Nathaniel R. Middleton, Jr., in Middleton (ed.), *op. cit.*, p. 174.

48. *Ibid.*, p. 169.

49. Hollis, *op. cit.*, pp. 40–49.

50. *Ibid.*, note, p. 57 (quoting a speech by Wade Hampton in the *Charleston News and Courier* of March 23, 1867).

51. James S. Pike, *The Prostrate State* (New York: D. Appleton and Co., 1874), p. 11.

52. *Ibid.*, p. 53.

53. *Ibid.*, pp. 11–12, 16–17, 20–21, 62–63.

54. *Collections*, V (Barnwell address), p. iii.

55. William Watts Ball, *The State That Forgot* (Indianapolis: The Bobbs-Merrill Co., 1932), p. 149.

56. Cash, *op. cit.*, p. 107.

57. *Ibid.*, p. 124.

58. Cf. quotation in Hollis, *op. cit.*, p. 81.

59. Pike, *op. cit.*, p. 67.

60. *Collections*, IV, 21.

61. Ball, *op. cit.*, p. 265.

62. F. Gray Griswold, *Plantation Days* (Norwood, Mass.: privately printed, 1935), p. 14.

63. Cash, *op. cit.*, pp. 35, 97.

64. Archibald Rutledge, *The World around Hampton* (Indianapolis: The Bobbs-Merrill Co., 1947), p. 14.

65. Archibald Rutledge, *God's Children* (Indianapolis: The Bobbs-Merrill Co., 1947), p. 108.

66. National Urban League, *A Study of the Social and Economic Conditions of the Negro Population, Charleston, South Carolina* (Community Relations Project, 1946).

67. Elizabeth Verner, *Mellowed by Time* (Columbia, S.C.: Bostick and Thornley, Inc., 1941), pp. 33–34, 2–3.

68. Dubose Heyward, quoted from his *Carolina Low-Country* in R. G. Rhett, *op. cit.*, pp. 74–75.

69. Figures quoted in National Urban League, *op. cit.* (from 1940 Census survey).

70. Quotation from *ibid.*, p. 55.

71. *Ibid.*, p. 56.

Chapter 3

1. From Josiah Gregg, *Commerce of the Prairies* (5th ed.; Philadelphia: J. W. Moore, 1851), I, 109–110.

2. Friar Marcos, "Cibola Seen from Afar," in Maurice Garland Fulton (ed.), *New Mexico's Own Chronicle* (Caldwell, Idaho: The Caxton Printers, Ltd., 1950), pp. 22–23.

3. Paul Horgan, *The Centuries of Santa Fe* (New York: E. P. Dutton and Co., 1956), p. 310.

4. *Ibid.*, p. 311.

5. M. G. Fulton, *op. cit.*, p. 46.

6. *Ibid.*, p. 47.

7. Cleve Hallenbeck, *Land of the Conquistadores* (Caldwell, Idaho: The Caxton Printers, Ltd., 1950), p. 128.

8. *Ibid.*, p. 141.

9. *Ibid.*, pp. 158–159.

10. *Historical Society of New Mexico, Publication #7, the Franciscan Martyrs of 1680* ("Funeral Oration over the 21 Franciscan Missionaries killed by the Pueblo Indians, August 10, 1680, preached by Dr. Ysidro Sarinana y Cuenca, March 20, 1681"), (Santa Fe: New Mexican Printing Co., 1906), pp. 16–17, 27.

11. Gregg, *op. cit.*, p. 113.

12. Hallenbeck, *op. cit.*, p. 303.

13. Fulton (ed.), *op. cit.*, p. 85.

14. *Ibid.*, p. 293.

15. Quoted in L. Bradford Prince, *Historical Sketches of New Mexico* (New York: Leggat Brothers, 1883), p. 255.

16. Fulton (ed.), *op. cit.*, p. 97.

17. Gregg, *op. cit.*, p. 219.

18. *Ibid.*, pp. 257–258.

19. *Ibid.*, pp. 242–243.

20. *Ibid.*, pp. 226–227.

21. Quoted in Fulton (ed.), *op. cit.*, p. 137.

22. *Historical Society of New Mexico, Publication #10* ("Journal

of New Mexico Convention of Delegates to Recommend a Plan of Civil Government, September, 1849"), (Santa Fe: New Mexican Printing Co., 1907), p. 21.

23. Quoted in Fulton (ed.), *op. cit.*, p. 153.

24. From *Historical Society of New Mexico, Publication #20,* ("Historical Sketch of Governor William Carr Lane . . ."), (Santa Fe: New Mexican Printing Co., 1917), pp. 12–16.

25. Quoted in Fulton (ed.), *op. cit.*, p. 227.

26. *Ibid.*, p. 183.

27. *Ibid.*, p. 184.

28. Newspaper account from Oliver LaFarge, *Santa Fe, the Autobiography of a Southwestern Town* (Norman, Okla.: University of Oklahoma Press, 1959), pp. 31–34.

29. From Fulton (ed.), *op. cit.*, p. 246.

30. *Ibid.*, p. 285.

31. Paul A. F. Walter (for Santa Fe Board of Trade), *Santa Fe County, New Mexico* (Santa Fe: The New Mexican Printing Co., 1909), p. 35.

32. Hallenbeck, *op. cit.*, p. 332.

33. Cleofas M. Jaramillo, *Shadows of the Past* (Santa Fe: Seton Village Press, 1941), p. 15.

34. Gregg, *op. cit.*, pp. 232, 226, 256.

35. Ruth Laughlin, *Caballeros* (Caldwell, Idaho: The Caxton Printers, Ltd., 1945), p. 54.

36. Gregg, *op. cit.*, pp. 91–92, 236, 226.

37. *Historical Society of New Mexico, Publication #20, op. cit.*, p. 15.

38. Jaramillo, *op. cit.*, p. 96.

39. Walter (for Santa Fe Board of Trade), *op. cit.*, p. 19.

40. *New Year's Edition, Santa Fe New Mexican,* Jan., 1910.

41. Quoted in the Foreword to LaFarge, *op. cit.*, p. viii.

42. From Fulton (ed.), *op. cit.*, p. 223.

43. From *ibid.*, p. 339.

44. Horgan, *op. cit.*, pp. 325, 331.

45. LaFarge, *op. cit.*, p. 417.

46. Laughlin, *op. cit.*, p. 399.

47. Horgan, *op. cit.*, discusses this later tendency toward "nonobjective representation" by the New Mexico artists (pp. 314 ff.).

48. Laughlin, *op. cit.*, pp. 392–393.

49. Dorothy L. Pillsbury, *Roots in Adobe* (Albuquerque: University of New Mexico Press, 1959), p. 3.

50. Jaramillo, *op. cit.*, p. 97.

Chapter 4

1. Proclamation of General Sam Houston from his headquarters at Nacogdoches, Texas, quoted in Mattie Austin Hatcher, *Letters of an Early American Traveller* (Dallas: Southwest Press, 1933), p. 57.

2. Colonel William Travis, quoted in Ernest Wallace and David M. Vigness (eds.), *Documents of Texas History, 1528–1846* (Lubbock: The Texas Tech Press, 1960), I, 96.

3. Local newspaper, quoted in Federal Writers' Program, *Houston, A History and Guide* (Houston: The Anson Jones Press, 1942), p. 31.

4. Order by Sam Houston, quoted in *ibid.*, p. 32.

5. Henry Austin letter, quoted in Hatcher, *op. cit.*, p. 58.

6. Quoted from an address delivered in Philadelphia by Sam Houston (1851), in Amelia W. Williams and Eugene C. Barker (eds.), *The Writings of Sam Houston, 1813–1836* (Austin: The University of Texas Press, 1941), V, 274–275.

7. Local newspaper, quoted in Federal Writers' Program, *op. cit.*, p. 38.

8. *Ibid.*

9. Moses Austin to J. E. B. Austin, April 8, 1821, in *Austin Papers;* quoted in Samuel Harman Lowrie, *Culture Conflict in Texas 1821–1835* (New York: Columbia University Press, 1932), p. 39.

10. Stephen Austin to Hawkins, July 20, 1821, in *Austin Papers;* quoted in Lowrie, *op. cit.*, p. 23.

11. S. Austin letter, quoted in Mallie Phegley, *The Father of Texas* (San Antonio: The Naylor Company, 1960), p. 69.

12. Governor Martinez, quoted in Jose Thomas Canales (ed.), *Bits of Texas History*, Part II: "Native Latin American Contribution to the Colonization and Independence of Texas" (Brownsville: J. T. Canales, 1957), p. 82.

13. Seguin to Austin in 1825, quoted in Canales, *op. cit.*, p. 86.

14. Phegley, *op. cit.*, p. 73.

15. One historian estimates, after scanning records of various local censuses of the period, that in 1834–35 the Anglo-American element constituted more than three-fourths of the "civilized white population" of Texas, and that about three-fourths of this Anglo-white population was born in slave states of the U.S. In the census of 1850, the ratio of whites to slaves in Texas was about 3 to 2. See Lowrie, *op. cit.*, p. 36.

16. Quoted in Barker, *op. cit.*, p. 41.

17. *Ibid.*, p. 53.

18. *Austin Papers,* Oct. 30, 1823, quoted in Lowrie, *op. cit.,* p. 42.

19. Lester G. Bugbee, *The Texas Frontier 1820–1825* (Harrisburg, Pa.: Harrisburg Publishing Company, 1900), p. 107.

20. "The 'Prison Journal' of Stephen F. Austin," *The Quarterly of the Texas State Historical Association,* Jan., 1899, Vol. II, No. 3 (Austin: Published Quarterly by the Association), pp. 189, 196–197.

21. J. Frank Dobie, *The Flavor of Texas* (Dallas: Dealey and Lowe, 1936), p. 64, repeats a story set down in Clarence R. Wharton's *San Jacinto: The Sixteenth Decisive Battle.*

22. Max Freund (ed. and trans.), *Gustave Dresel's Houston Journal* (Austin: University of Texas Press, 1954), pp. 32–33.

23. A woman visitor in the 1840s, quoted in Herbert Fletcher (ed.), *Harris County, Republic of Texas 1839–45* (Houston: The Anson Jones Press, 1950), p. 28.

24. Fletcher, *op. cit.,* pp. 29, 9–10.

25. Quoted in Joseph William Schmitz, *Texas Culture 1836–1846* (San Antonio: The Naylor Company, 1960), p. 13.

26. Fletcher, *op. cit.,* pp. 23, 24.

27. Impressions of travelers, set down in Federal Writers' Program, *op. cit.,* pp. 62–63.

28. *Ibid.,* p. 63.

29. William Curry Holden, *Alkali Trails* (Dallas: The Southwest Press, 1930), p. 55.

30. *Ibid.,* notes, p. 56 (quoting *Northern Standard* of Clarksville, Texas).

31. Figures from Arthur Coleman Comey, *Houston, Tentative Plans for Its Development* (report to the Houston Park Commission, 1913), p. 13.

32. Barker, *op. cit.,* pp. 80–85, presents views of Stephen Austin on slavery.

33. Federal Writers' Program, *op. cit.,* p. 70.

34. Sam Houston speaking at Galveston; quoted in *History of Texas together with a Biographical History of the Cities of Houston and Galveston* (Chicago: The Lewis Publishing Co., 1895), p. 89.

35. Figures from *ibid.,* p. 89.

36. Quoted in D. Fisher Allen, *The City of Houston from Wilderness to Wonder* (Temple, Texas, 1936), pp. 48–49.

37. Description of the last days of the Civil War taken from Charles W. Ramsdell, "Texas From the Fall of the Confederacy to the Beginning of Reconstruction," *The Quarterly of the Texas State Historical Association* (Austin: Published by the Association, 1908), XI, 202–206.

38. Quoted in Federal Writers' Program, *op. cit.,* p. 81.

39. See Charles W. Ramsdell, "Presidential Reconstruction in Texas," *The Quarterly, op. cit.,* XI, 286.

40. John F. Elliott, *All About Texas: A Hand Book of Information* (Austin: Hutchings Printing House, 1888), pp. 11–13.

41. Quoted in Federal Writers' Program, *op. cit.,* p. 84.

42. *Ibid.,* p. 87.

43. Wm. Brady, *Glimpses of Texas: Its Divisions, Resources* (Houston: A. C. Gray and Co., printers, 1871), pp. 5–6.

44. Statewide figures from Frank Goodwyn, *Lone-Star Land* (New York: Alfred A. Knopf, 1955), p. 4.

45. City and county figures from Comey, *op. cit.,* p. 13.

46. Federal Writers' Program, *op. cit.,* p. 96.

47. Elliott, *op. cit.,* pp. 46–47.

48. Katie Daffan, *Texas Hero Stories* (Boston, New York, Chicago: Benj. H. Sanborn and Co., 1908), p. 146.

49. From Federal Writers' Program, *op. cit.,* pp. 110–113.

50. *Ibid.,* p. 112.

51. *Ibid.,* p. 115.

52. Clarence Peckham Dunbar and William Hunter Dillard, *Houston, 1836–1936, Chronology and Review* (Houston: W. H. Dillard and C. P. Dunbar, 1936), p. 35.

53. Goodwyn, *op. cit.,* pp. 4–7.

54. Ed Bartholomew, *The Houston Story* (Houston: The Frontier Press, 1951), p. 7.

55. Amber and Barker (eds.), quoting Sam Houston speech in Philadelphia in 1851, *op. cit.,* p. 272.

56. George Fuermann, *Houston: Land of the Big Rich* (Garden City, N.Y.: Doubleday and Co., 1951), p. 23.

57. Wallace and Vigness (eds.), quoting Col. Travis, *op. cit.,* p. 97.

58. Ruben Rendon Lozano, *Viva Tejas* (San Antonio and Houston: Southern Literary Institute, 1936), pp. 6, 50.

59. Wilson Little, *Spanish-Speaking Children in Texas* (Austin: The University of Texas Press, 1944); statistics pp. 37, 41. The study reported was based on a census of Texas school districts which enrolled over 75 per cent of the total school population in the state.

60. Federal Writers' Program, *op. cit.,* p. 83.

61. Quotations, in order, from *The Red Book of Houston, A Compendium of Social, Professional, Religious, Educational and Industrial Interests of Houston's Colored Population* (Houston: Sotex Publishing Company, 1915), pp. 3, 189, 185, 184, 116.

62. Henry Allen Bullock, *Pathways to the Houston Negro Market* (Ann Arbor: J. W. Edwards, distributors, 1957), p. 1.

63. Most comparisons were made on four income groups clustered

as follows: Under $2,000; $2,000–$3,999; $4,000–$5,999; $6,000 and over. Highest percentages of the 44,225 households surveyed fell in the following income ranges: $3,500–$3,999 (16.1%); $4,000–$4,499 (15.7%); $4,500–$4,999 (11.0%); $3,000–$3,499 (10.3%). Only 1.5 per cent earned less than $1,000; 1.4 per cent fell in the $8,000 and over bracket. Data on preferences and attitudes are from Bullock, *op. cit.*, pp. 215, 217, 227.

64. *Ibid.*, p. 191.

65. *Ibid.*, pp. 65, 67.

66. Federation of Women's Clubs, *The Key to the City of Houston,* I, No. 1 (Houston: State Printing Co., 1908), pp. 11–12.

67. The U.S. census of populations does not include data on religious affiliation. The estimates at the Council of Churches in the late 1950s were: Baptists, 27 per cent of the total city population (over ½ of these Southern Baptists); Methodists, 18 per cent; Presbyterians, 7–8 per cent; Catholics, 12–14 per cent. The latter figure contrasts with the figure of 23 per cent Catholics in the total population provided by the Monsignor at the local Catholic social services agency. It seemed that where clustering and segmentation were predominant tendencies in a shifting, growing, competing population, representative spokesmen of "clusters" tended to overestimate the size of the cluster.

Chapter 5

1. John B. Newhall, *A Glimpse of Iowa in 1846* (Iowa City: State Historical Society of Iowa, 1957), p. vi.

2. These and other historical census facts in the narrative are taken from Union Publishing Co., *History of Butler and Bremer Counties, Iowa* (Springfield, Ill.: Union Publishing Co., 1883).

3. Newhall, *op. cit.*, p. 59.

4. *Ibid.*, p. 62.

5. Isaac Galland, *Galland's Iowa Emigrant* (Chillicothe, Iowa: Wm. C. Jones, 1840), p. 3.

6. This chronology of basic facts and significant events was provided by the Chamber of Commerce of the local community.

7. Union Publishing Co., *op. cit.*, p. 827.

8. *Ibid.*, p. 804.

9. *Ibid.*, p. 938.

10. *Ibid.*

11. The brief descriptions of the early and later Civil War perceptions of slavery and the Negro of the western soldier was gleaned from Bruce Catton's *Grant Moves South* (Boston: Little, Brown, and

Company, 1960), particularly Chapter 14, "To Be Terrible on the Enemy"; and from Catton's *This Hallowed Ground* (Garden City, N.Y.: Doubleday and Co., 1956), pp. 78 ff., 305 ff., 374.

12. Ray A. Wilson, *Trails and Trials* (Creston, Iowa, 1959), p. 20.

13. As it is represented in Appendix I, the county unit is used in this book as the delimited area which is described as a sociocultural entity. In the description of a rural community, the distinction between a town—the largest center in the county—and the whole county which includes several smaller towns is more apparent than in descriptions of other communities in this book. In other community descriptions, county and city almost coincide in area or in population; or one town or city has more population than has all the rest of a county. In the rural analysis, the "way of life" is a phenomenon of the activities and interactions of people in a county area which is dominated by a major trade center. Where town life is described it is the life in this county seat.

14. Galland, *op. cit.*, p. 5.

Chapter 6

1. Charles S. Walgamott, *Six Decades Back* (Caldwell, Idaho: The Caxton Printers, 1936), p. 21.

2. *Ibid.*, p. 128.

3. *Ibid.*, p. 140.

4. *Ibid.*, p. 151.

5. J. L. Campbell, *Six Months in the New Gold Regions* (Chicago: John R. Walsh, 1864), p. 39.

6. George A. Bruffey, *Eighty-One Years in the West* (Butte, Mont.: Butte Miner Co., 1925), p. 51.

7. Walgamott, *op. cit.*, p. 134.

8. Local newspaper, Oct. 13, 1863, quoted in Annie L. Bird, *Boise, the Peace Valley* (Caldwell, Idaho: The Caxton Printers, 1934), p. 149.

9. Local newspaper, Dec. 5, 1863, quoted in Federal Writers' Project, *Idaho Lore* (Caldwell, Idaho: Caxton Printers, 1939), p. 165.

10. Local newspaper, Feb. 6, 1864, quoted in Federal Writers' Project, *op. cit.*, p. 165.

11. Local newspaper, Feb. 18, 1865, quoted in Bird, *op. cit.*, p. 135.

12. Local newspaper, Aug. 4, 1864, quoted in Bird, *op. cit.*, p. 194.

13. Local newspaper, Aug. 16, 1864, quoted in Bird, *op. cit.*, p. 194.

14. Local newspaper, Dec. 27, 1864, quoted in Bird, *op. cit.*, p. 198.

15. Local newspaper, Oct. 1, 1864, quoted in Bird, *op. cit.*, p. 204.

16. *The Idaho Statesman, Holiday Number,* Jan. 1, 1890 (Boise, Idaho: Statesman Printing Co., 1890).

17. *Ibid.*

18. Interestingly, this same man had been superintendent of schools in both of the similar-sized but quite different communities discussed in Chapters 3 and 6. His perceptions of the problems of performing in a public role in the two settings bear witness to the reality of socio-cultural dynamics—and testify to the difficulty different individuals have in adjusting to participation in different social arenas.

19. This does not mean conditions did not exist for the individual "delinquency" that may be a product of teenage adjustment problems to authority figures in any setting of American culture. However, these problems were not reacted to as problems of a deviant, rebellious group, visible in public. Thus, they were not symbolized as formal problems, and juvenile acts defined as "delinquent" elsewhere may have been under-represented on local police records. In addition, a "middle class" community of this size did not present the conditions for the formation of a delinquent subculture of "working class boys," in rebellion against middle class values and institutions. The latter condition is the type described by Cohen in his analysis of the culture of delinquency. (See Albert Cohen, *Delinquent Boys* [Glencoe, Illinois: The Free Press, 1955].)

20. Nelle P. Davis, *Stump Ranch Pioneer* (New York: Dodd, Mead and Co., 1942), p. 240.

Chapter 7

1. From Michel Chevalier, *Society, Manners, and Politics in the United States* (Boston, 1839), quoted in Joseph Schafer, *The Yankee and the Teuton in Wisconsin* III (Reprinted from the *Wisconsin Magazine of History*, VI, No. 4, June, 1923), p. 19.

2. Chevalier, *op. cit.,* quoted in Joseph Schafer, *The Yankee and the Teuton in Wisconsin* II (Reprinted from the *Wisconsin Magazine of History*, VI, No. 3, March, 1923), note, p. 263.

3. Described in Reuben Gold Thwaites, *Wisconsin: The American-ization of a French Settlement* (Boston: Houghton Mifflin Co., 1908), p. 246.

4. Local newspaper, March 10, 1838, quoted in Western Historical Co., *The History of Racine and Kenosha Counties, Wisconsin* (Chicago: Western Historical Co., 1879), p. 364.

5. Described in Thwaites, *op. cit.,* p. 257.

6. From a description of "Marshall Mason Strong, Racine Pioneer,"

by Eugene W. Leach, in the *Wisconsin Magazine of History,* V, No. 4, June, 1922, p. 21.

7. *Ibid.,* p. 6.

8. *Ibid.*

9. Thwaites, *op. cit.,* p. 256.

10. Western Historical Company, *op. cit.,* p. 362.

11. Local newspaper, Dec. 3, 1843, quoted in Joseph Schafer, *Four Wisconsin Counties* (Madison, Wis.: State Historical Society of Wisconsin, 1927), p. 207.

12. Quoted in Schafer, *Four Wisconsin Counties, op. cit.,* p. 171.

13. Quoted in Thwaites, *op. cit.,* p. 321.

14. Local newspaper, quoted in Western Historical Company, *op. cit.,* p. 373.

15. Thwaites, *op. cit.,* p. 321.

16. Eugene W. Leach, *Racine County Militant* (Racine, Wis.: E. W. Leach, 1915), p. 45.

17. Local newspaper, April 17, 1861, quoted in Leach, *op. cit.,* p. 48.

18. *Ibid.,* pp. 49–50.

19. Local newspaper, July 31, 1861; quoted in Leach, *op. cit.,* p. 61.

20. Thwaites, *op. cit.,* pp. 172–173.

21. Milwaukee newspaper, Oct. 11, 1848, quoted in Sister M. Justille McDonald, *History of the Irish in Wisconsin in the 19th Century* (Washington, D.C.: The Catholic University of America Press, 1954), p. 10.

22. *Ibid.,* p. 15.

23. The description of this process is taken from Schafer, *Four Wisconsin Counties, op. cit.,* pp. 183 ff.

24. Quoted in Thwaites, *op. cit.,* p. 408.

25. Wisconsin newspaper, Oct. 16, 1890, quoted in McDonald, *op. cit.,* p. 173.

26. Figures from Schafer, *Four Wisconsin Counties, op. cit.,* p. 180.

27. See Joseph Schafer, *The Yankee and the Teuton in Wisconsin* III & IV (Reprinted from the *Wisconsin Magazine of History* VI, No. 4, June 1923 and VII, No. 1, Sept. 1923).

28. Quoted in Fred L. Holmes, *Old World Wisconsin: Around Europe in the Badger State* (Eau Claire, Wis.: E. M. Hale and Co., 1944), p. 317.

29. Sketches are based on brief biographies in *Dictionary of Wisconsin Biography* (Madison, Wis.: Wisconsin State Historical Society, 1960).

30. *Ibid.,* p. 192.

31. Quoted from a brochure and map provided by the Racine, Wis., Chamber of Commerce.

32. This tendency is described by C. Wright Mills in his *White Collar: The American Middle Classes* (New York: Oxford University Press, 1953). Mills says: "The prestige market of the big city is often a market of strangers, a milieu where contacts having relevance to prestige are often transitory and fleeting. . . . The metropolitan man is a temporary focus of heterogeneous circles of casual acquaintances, rather than a fixed center of a few well-known groups. . . . One has contacts, rather than relations, and these contacts are shorter lived and more superficial. . . . Rather than cohesion there is uniformity, rather than descent or tradition, interest . . ." (pp. 251–254).

33. S. C. Johnson and Son, Inc., *This Company of Ours* (Racine, Wis.: S. C. Johnson and Son, Inc., 1944).

Chapter 8

1. Ezra Meeker, *Pioneer Reminiscences of Puget Sound* (Seattle: Ezra Meeker, 1905), p. 5.

2. *Ibid.*

3. Charles Marvin Gates (ed.), *Readings in Pacific Northwest History* (Seattle: University Bookstore, 1941), p. 172.

4. Meeker, *op. cit.*, attributes these elements, particularly, as contributing to the "motive prompting the movement [which] had been gathering force for years" (p. 6).

5. Clarence B. Bagley, *History of King County, Washington* (Chicago, Seattle: The S. J. Clarke Publishing Co., 1929), II, 72.

6. From a speech by Senator James Buchanan in the United States Senate, March 12, 1844; quoted in C. M. Gates (ed.), *op. cit.*, p. 113.

7. Quoted in Emily Inez Denny, *Blazing the Way* (Seattle: Rainier Printing Co., 1909), p. 47.

8. Description taken from an account in Frank Hadley Cass (ed.), *Looking Northwest* (Portland: Binfords and Mort, 1938), p. 29.

9. Meeker, *op. cit.*, pp. 133 ff., describes the early lures and conditions of travel in the far Northwest and the opening of this more direct overland trail.

10. *Ibid.*, p. 66.

11. See Gates (ed.), *op. cit.*, p. 143.

12. Denny, *op. cit.*, p. 68. The millowner's views on the centrality of his business to the community are quoted on pp. 443–444.

13. Archie Binns, *The Roaring Land* (New York: Robert M. McBride and Co., 1942), p. 50. Binns notes that the first mill never made a great profit but left a great city. Later mills, established on the west

side of the sound, "made fortunes but left nothing but dwindling villages" (p. 53).

14. J. Willis Sayre, *This City of Ours* (Seattle: J. W. Sayre, 1936).

15. The description of the community in 1876 is from Gates (ed.), *op. cit.*, pp. 310–315.

16. Binns, *op. cit.*, p. 109.

17. Figures from *ibid.*, pp. 164–165.

18. *Ibid.*, p. 164.

19. *Ibid.*, p. 165.

20. *Ibid.*

21. From an account in Gates, *op. cit.*, p. 320.

22. Ralph B. Potts, *Seattle Heritage* (Seattle: Superior Publishing Co., 1955), p. 25.

23. Local newspaper account, quoted in Bagley, *op. cit.*, pp. 76–77.

24. Potts, *op. cit.*, p. 25.

25. The description of community attitudes at the time of the Chinese agitation was obtained from Murray Morgan, *Skid Row* (New York: The Viking Press, 1951), pp. 82–92.

26. Quoted in *ibid.*

27. Quoted in Bagley, *op. cit.*, I, 349–350.

28. Morgan, *op. cit.*, p. 106.

29. Quotations from *ibid.*, pp. 91–92.

30. Quoted in Bagley, *op. cit.*, I, 341.

31. Binns, *op. cit.*, p. 85.

32. Description from Potts, *op. cit.*, p. 130.

33. Quoted in *ibid.*, p. 72.

34. Binns, *op. cit.*, p. 168.

35. From Potts, *op. cit.*, p. 134.

36. Quoted in *ibid.*, p. 142.

37. Morgan, *op. cit.*, p. 266.

38. Potts, *op. cit.*, p. 48.

39. Morgan, *op. cit.*, p. 180.

40. *Ibid.*, pp. 240 ff.

41. *Seattle Daily Times, Anniversary Number*, Feb. 14, 1909.

42. Morgan, *op. cit.*, p. 221.

43. Binns, *op. cit.*, pp. 145–149.

44. Shotaro Frank Miyamoto, *Social Solidarity among the Japanese in Seattle* (Seattle: University of Washington Publications in Social Science, 1939).

45. Japanese American Citizens League, *Report Submitted to Tolan Congressional Committee on National Defense Migration* (Seattle, 1942, unpublished).

46. A recent study by two American sociologists (Carle C. Zimmerman and Lucius F. Cervantes) indicated a new, achieved pattern of adjustment by "successful" families in responding to the pressures of modern urban life. Successful families were seen to be forming friendship enclaves to insulate themselves from urban din and the forces toward atomization and anonymity. In other words, groups of families that share many life activities and values are banding together for mutual support to replace the kinship bonds of the older extended family typical of rural America and of older ethnic neighborhoods in American cities. This finding is particularly relevant to the bayou community of Chapter 4, and its lessons of segmented insulation and personalization, as well as to the open metropolis. Adaptable man seems to create new anchors for the self, building new structures to provide the experience of "community" where community has otherwise broken down. (Reported in an article by Jack Harrison Pollack, "What Makes Happy Families Happy?" *This Week Magazine,* Sept. 13, 1959; publication based on the study not located by present author.)

Chapter 9

1. From Paul Horgan's essay on Lincoln: *Citizen of New Salem* (New York: Farrar, Strauss, 1961), pp. 24, 30.

2. Some second thoughts on the press handling of the tour appeared soon after the guest had departed. A column by Doris Fleeson (*Denver Post,* Oct. 6, 1959) included this comment: "It was during these indecisive moments [in the administration] that Vice President Richard Nixon preached his 'talk back' gospel at the White House which was to stick U. N. Ambassador Henry Cabot Lodge with his truth squad role, one of the trip's major fiascos."

3. Jack Gould in the *Denver Post,* Nov. 1, 1959.

4. Quoted in a column by Andrew Tully, *Rocky Mountain News,* Oct. 9, 1959.

5. Quoted in *ibid.*

6. Column by James Reston in the *New York Times,* Nov. 8, 1959.

7. Margaret Mead, *New Lives for Old* (New York: William Morrow and Co., 1956), pp. 177–178.

8. The author recalls post-Second World War undergraduate days at UCLA when the imminence of change and movement was daily represented on campus by the chugging of heavy earth-moving equipment, preparing the way for new parking lots that were soon bases for new buildings. This occurred amid the setting where young Californians learned, impatiently, to partake of the past. (The rush of

many toward the future was slowed and confused by the Korean War.)

9. The phrase "overpopulation of the surfaces" is used by Erich Kahler to describe the modern human condition in which a new callousness has developed along with increased sensibility as events are crowded in the domain of our vision and consciousness. See *The Tower and the Abyss* (New York: George Braziller, 1957), pp. 96, 138.

10. In the case of newscasters and commentators, an important screening and organizing function *is* performed—with varying degrees of skill and integrity in selection and presentation.

11. Article in the *Sunday Denver Post*, Dec. 13, 1959, by A. H. Raskin.

12. Reston column, *op. cit.*

13. Alexis de Tocqueville, *The Republic of the United States of America* (trans. by Henry Reeves), (New York: A. S. Barnes and Co., 1851), note, pp. 316–317.

14. *Time*, Sept 8, 1961.

15. In his analysis of the American "culture of poverty" Michael Harrington states:

"These, then, are the strangest poor in the history of mankind.

"They exist within the most powerful and rich society the world has ever known. Their misery has continued while the majority of the nation talked of itself as being 'affluent' and worried about neuroses in the suburbs. In this way tens of millions of human beings became invisible" (*The Other America* [New York, The Macmillan Co., 1963], p. 174).

Interesting, too, is the fact that most studies of the poor are based on statistics that cut across the whole society, looking at population groups like the aged, the unskilled, the Negro, etc. This tends also to blur the understanding of the problems of segmentation as grounded in specific local communities and their social systems. It is in such local areas that change in the dynamics of a particular system must be explored—in a manageable context for democratic dialogue and institutional re-creation.

16. See *Sports Illustrated*, April 16, 1962, "Record-Breaking Day in Austin," by Tex Maule. In 1962, the first time a Negro college was allowed to enter the Texas Relays at Austin, the bayou college swept all five races it entered. The coach explained his success in recruiting: " 'Midwest schools have come down here recruiting! . . .' But some of the boys who went from the Negro high schools to integrated big schools there found the social adjustment hard to make.' " The boys on the relay teams seemed, at Austin, to be winning their spurs as Texans: "As the afternoon wore on, the almost all-white crowd cheered TSU

more and more enthusiastically. After the loudest cheer, when the time of the mile relay was announced, [coach] Wright turned from his athletes, looked past the stands and said, 'That's a wonderful sound, isn't it?' . . ."

17. Slavery existed and increased in New England during the colonial period. *Colliers Encyclopedia* estimates the Negro population of Massachusetts as growing from 2,000 to 5,000 between 1715 and 1764 (Vol. XVII, p. 279). Individual slaveholdings were usually quite small, and men of conscience released many slaves during this period.

18. Rev. Dr. Martin Luther King, Jr., *New York Sunday Times Magazine*, Aug. 5, 1962 (article adapted from a speech at the Washington Press Club).

19. Rev. Dr. Martin Luther King, Jr., *New York Times*, April 30, 1962 (sermon at a Princeton religious conference on integration, in which Dr. King also expressed some satisfaction at the growing awakening of the churches).

20. Malcolm X at a Muslim rally in Chicago, reported in the *New York Times*, Feb. 28, 1963.

21. Article on "The Perils of Powell," by Raymond Robinson, *New York Times*, May 5, 1963.

22. Quoted in account of Birmingham demonstrations by Claude Sitton, *New York Times*, May 7, 1963.

23. *Ibid.*

24. From an article on Birmingham demonstrations by Philip Benjamin, *New York Times*, May 9, 1963.

25. *New York Times*, May 9, 1963.

26. *Ibid.*

27. James Meredith, quoted in the *New York Times*, Dec. 4, 1962.

28. Medgar Evers, quoted in the *New York Times*, June 13, 1963.

29. Rev. Dr. Martin Luther King, Jr., quoted in *ibid.*

30. *New York Times*, June 15, 1963.

31. Quotations from article by Claude Sitton on Charleston racial unrest, *New York Times*, July 22, 1963.

32. *New York Times*, April 10, 1962.

33. A description of a Harlem riot in June, 1963, indicated that a minor street incident involving the police—the formal symbol of oppression—brought on clashes that left this scene: "At midnight, central Harlem was relatively quiet, but it looked like an armed camp, with helmeted patrolmen stationed at intervals of 5 to 10 yards for blocks from 125th Street" (*New York Times*, June 19, 1963).

34. "Dr. King Is Target of Eggs in Harlem" (*New York Times*, July 1, 1963).

35. Rev. Andrew J. Young, quoted in the *New York Times,* July 22, 1963.

36. Descriptions of the civil rights march taken from the *New York Times,* Aug. 29, 1963.

37. From a column by James Reston in the *New York Times,* Aug. 29, 1963.

38. S. L. A. Marshall has noted that person-to-person communication had to be learned in the situation of stress by "the mutest army that we ever sent to war." (See *Men against Fire* [New York: William Morrow and Co., 1947] p. 136.) He attributes this muteness, in an army that did not sing and did not talk, to the conditioning in passivity by years of movies and radio. His concern was with the consequences of this for the functional transfer of information in military formations. A social psychologist would be even more interested in the phenomenon as symptomatic of the break in human linkages in a society and the weakening of the symbols that evoke common sentiments in a human group. The American soldier saw himself as a standardized object: "Government Issue." Real-life "experiments" indicated, however, that the G.I. achieved human linkages around the basic values of his society: the concern of one valued individual for the value of the others who shared his situation.

Bibliography

N.B. Limited to References Specifically Cited in Notes

Books, Studies, Historical Journals

AGAR, HERBERT. *The Price of Union.* Boston: Houghton Mifflin Co., 1950.

ALLEN, O. FISHER. *The City of Houston from Wilderness to Wonder.* Temple, Texas, 1936.

BAGLEY, CLARENCE B. *History of King County, Washington,* II. Chicago-Seattle: The S. J. Clarke Publishing Co., 1929.

BALL, WILLIAM WATTS. *The State That Forgot.* Indianapolis: The Bobbs-Merrill Co., 1932.

BARKER, EUGENE C. *Mexico and Texas, 1825–1835.* Dallas: P. L. Turner Co., 1928.

BARRY, JOHN STETSON. *The History of Massachusetts: The Provincial Period,* II. Boston: Privately published, 1857.

BARTHOLOMEW, ED. *The Houston Story.* Houston: The Frontier Press, 1951.

BEARD, CHARLES A. *An Economic Interpretation of the Constitution of the United States.* New York: The Macmillan Co., 1936.

BINNS, ARCHIE. *The Roaring Land.* New York: Robert M. McBride & Co., 1942.

BIRD, ANNIE L. *Boise, The Peace Valley.* Caldwell, Idaho: The Caxton Printers, 1934.

BRADFORD, WILLIAM. *Bradford's History of Plymouth Plantation, 1606–1646* (ed. William T. Davis). New York: Charles Scribner's Sons, 1908.

———. *Pilgrim Courage* (Selected Episodes From His Original History of Plymouth Plantation, adapted and edited by E. Brooks Smith and Robert Meredith). Boston, Toronto: Little, Brown, and Co., 1962.

BRADY, WM. *Glimpses of Texas: Its Divisions, Resources.* Houston: A. C. Gray and Co., printers, 1871.

BRUFFEY, GEORGE A. *Eighty-One Years in the West*. Butte, Montana: Butte Miner Co., 1925.

BUGBEE, LESTER G. *The Texas Frontier 1820–1825*. Harrisburg, Pa.: Harrisburg Publishing Co., 1900.

BULLARD, JOHN M. *The Rotches*. Milford, New Hampshire: The Cabinet Press, 1947.

Bulletins of the South Carolina Historical Commission, No. 9. Columbia: The State Company, 1927.

BULLOCK, HENRY ALLEN. *Pathways to the Houston Negro Market*. Ann Arbor: J. W. Edwards, distributors, 1957.

CAMPBELL, J. L. *Six Months in the New Gold Regions*. Chicago: John R. Walsh, 1864.

CANALES, JOSE TOMAS (ed.). *Bits of Texas History*. Brownsville: J. T. Canales, 1957.

CASH, W. J. *The Mind of the South*. New York: Alfred A. Knopf, 1941.

CASS, FRANK HADLEY (ed.). *Looking Northwest*. Portland: Binfords and Mort, 1938.

CATTON, BRUCE. *Grant Moves South*. Boston, Toronto: Little, Brown, and Co., 1960.

———. *This Hallowed Ground*. Garden City, N.Y.: Doubleday and Co., 1956.

Centennial in New Bedford, Historical Address by Hon. William W. Crapo. New Bedford: E. Anthony and Sons, 1876.

CHARLESTON NEWS AND COURIER. *The Centennial of Incorporation*. Charleston: The News and Courier Book Presses, 1884.

COHEN, ALBERT. *Delinquent Boys*. Glencoe, Ill.: The Free Press, 1955.

Collections of the South Carolina Historical Society, II (compiled by B. R. Carroll). New York: Harper & Row, 1836.

Collections of the South Carolina Historical Society, IV. Charleston: South Carolina Historical Society, 1887.

Collections of the South Carolina Historical Society, V. Charleston: South Carolina Historical Society, 1897.

Collections of the South Carolina Historical Society, Vol. IX of the 3rd Series. Boston: Freeman and Bolles, 1846.

COMEY, ARTHUR COLEMAN. *Houston, Tentative Plans for Its Development*. (Report to the Houston Park Commission, 1913.)

COOLEY, CHARLES HORTON, *Two Major Works: Social Organiza-*

tion. Human Nature and the Social Order (with an introduction by Robert Cooley Angell). Glencoe, Ill.: The Free Press, 1956.

CRANE, VERNER W. *The Southern Frontier 1670–1732.* Durham: Duke University Press, 1928.

DAFFAN, KATIE. *Texas Hero Stories.* Boston, New York, Chicago: Benj. H. Sanborn and Co., 1908.

DAVIS, NELLE P. *Stump Ranch Pioneer.* New York: Dodd, Mead and Co., 1942.

DENNY, EMILY INEZ. *Blazing the Way.* Seattle: Rainier Printing Co., 1909.

Diary of Rev. Moses How (No. 59 in Series of Sketches of New Bedford's Early History). New Bedford: Reynolds Printing, 1931.

DOBIE, J. FRANK. *The Flavor of Texas.* Dallas: Dealey and Lowe, 1936.

DRAYTON, JOHN. *A View of South Carolina.* Charleston: W. P. Young, 1802.

DUNBAR, CLARENCE PECKHAM and DILLARD, WILLIAM HUNTER. *Houston, 1836–1936, Chronology and Review.* Houston: W. H. Dillard and C. P. Dunbar, 1936.

ELLIOTT, JOHN F. *All about Texas: A Handbook of Information.* Austin: Hutchings Printing House, 1888.

ELLIS, LEONARD BOLLES. *History of New Bedford and Its Vicinity 1602–1892.* Syracuse: D. Mason and Co., 1892.

ENGLER, RICHARD E., JR. *A Systematic Approach to the Study of Morale in an Organization.* University of Southern California, Unpublished Doctoral Dissertation, 1956.

FEDERAL WRITERS' PROGRAM. *Houston, A History and Guide.* Houston: The Anson Jones Press, 1942.

FEDERAL WRITERS' PROJECT. *Idaho Lore.* Caldwell, Idaho: The Caxton Printers, 1939.

FEDERATION OF WOMEN'S CLUBS. *The Key to the City of Houston,* I, No. 1. Houston: State Printing Co., 1908.

FLETCHER, HERBERT (ed.). *Harris County, Republic of Texas 1839–45.* Houston: The Anson Jones Press, 1950.

FREE PUBLIC LIBRARY (New Bedford, Mass.). *Some Facts about New Bedford, 1906.*

FREUND, MAX (ed. and trans.). *Gustave Dresel's Houston Journal.* Austin: University of Texas Press, 1954.

FROMM, ERICH. *The Sane Society.* New York: Holt, Rinehart and Winston, 1955.

FUERMANN, GEORGE. *Houston, Land of the Big Rich.* Garden City, N.Y.: Doubleday and Co., 1951.

FULTON, MAURICE GARLAND (ed.). *New Mexico's Own Chronicle.* Caldwell, Idaho: The Caxton Printers, 1950.

GALLAND, ISAAC. *Galland's Iowa Emigrant.* Chillicothe, Iowa: Wm. C. Jones, 1840.

GARTLAND, EMMA L. *New Bedford's Story.* New Bedford: Emma L. Gartland, 1934.

GATES, CHARLES MARVIN (ed.). *Readings in Pacific Northwest History.* Seattle: University Bookstore, 1941.

GOFFMAN, ERVING. *Encounters.* Indianapolis: The Bobbs-Merrill Co., Inc., 1961.

GOODWYN, FRANK. *Lone-Star Land.* New York: Alfred A. Knopf, 1955.

GREGG, JOSIAH. *Commerce of the Prairies* (5th ed., Vol. I). Philadelphia: J. W. Moore, 1851.

GRIEVE, ROBERT (ed.). *New Bedford Semi-Centennial Souvenir.* Providence: Journal of Commerce Co., 1897.

GRISWOLD, F. GRAY. *Plantation Days.* Privately published, 1935.

GUESS, WILLIAM FRANCIS. *South Carolina: Annals of Pride and Protest.* New York: Harper & Row, 1960.

HALLENBECK, CLEVE. *Land of the Conquistadores.* Caldwell, Idaho: The Caxton Printers, 1950.

HAMILTON, JAMES, JR. *An Account of the Late Intended Insurrection among a Portion of the Blacks of This City* (2nd ed.). Charleston: A. E. Miller, 1822.

HARRINGTON, MICHAEL. *The Other America.* New York: The Macmillan Co., 1963.

HASKINS, ELMORE P. *The Story of Water Street.* New Bedford: Old Dartmouth Historical Sketches No. 15, 1906.

HATCHER, MATTIE AUSTIN. *Letters of an Early American Traveller.* Dallas: Southwest Press, 1933.

Historical Society of New Mexico, Publication #7. Santa Fe: New Mexican Printing Co., 1906.

Historical Society of New Mexico, Publication #10. Santa Fe: New Mexican Printing Co., 1907.

Historical Society of New Mexico, Publication #20. Santa Fe: New Mexican Printing Co., 1917.

History of Texas together with a Biographical History of the Cities of Houston and Galveston. Chicago: The Lewis Publishing Co., 1895.

HOLDEN, WILLIAM CURRY. *Alkali Trails.* Dallas: The Southwest Press, 1930.

HOLLIS, JOHN PORTER. *The Early Period of Reconstruction in South Carolina.* Baltimore: The Johns Hopkins Press, 1905.

HOLMES, FRED L. *Old World Wisconsin: Around Europe in the Badger State.* Eau Claire, Wis.: E. M. Hale and Co., 1944.

HOMANS, GEORGE C. *The Human Group.* New York: Harcourt, Brace, and World, 1950.

HORGAN, PAUL. *Citizen of New Salem.* New York: Farrar, Straus, 1961.

———. *The Centuries of Santa Fe.* New York: E. P. Dutton and Co., 1956.

JAPANESE AMERICAN CITIZENS LEAGUE, *Report Submitted to Tolan Congressional Committee on National Defense Migration.* Seattle, Wash., Unpublished, 1942.

JARAMILLO, CLEOFAS M. *Shadows of the Past.* Santa Fe: Seton Village Press, 1941.

JOHNSON, S. C. AND SON, INC. *This Company of Ours.* Racine, Wis.: S. C. Johnson and Son, Inc., 1944.

KAHLER, ERICH. *The Tower and the Abyss.* New York: George Braziller, Inc., 1957.

LAFARGE, OLIVER. *Santa Fe, the Autobiography of a Southwestern Town.* Norman, Okla.: University of Oklahoma Press, 1959.

LAUGHLIN, RUTH. *Caballeros.* Caldwell, Idaho: The Caxton Printers, Ltd., 1945.

LEACH, EUGENE W., *Racine County Militant.* Racine, Wis.: E. W. Leach, 1915.

LIPPMANN, WALTER. *The Public Philosophy.* Boston, Toronto: Little, Brown, and Co., 1955.

LITTLE, WILSON. *Spanish-Speaking Children in Texas.* Austin: The University of Texas Press, 1944.

LOWRIE, SAMUEL HARMAN. *Culture Conflict in Texas 1821–1835.* New York: Columbia University Press, 1932.

LOZANO, RUBEN RENDON. *Viva Tejas.* San Antonio and Houston: Southern Literary Institute, 1936.

MAAS, HENRY S., and ENGLER, RICHARD E., JR. *Children in Need of Parents.* New York: Columbia University Press, 1959.

MARSHALL, S. L. A. *Men against Fire.* New York: William Morrow and Co., 1947.

MCDONALD, SISTER M. JUSTILLE. *History of the Irish in Wisconsin in the 19th Century.* Washington, D.C.: The Catholic University of America Press, 1954.

MEAD, GEORGE HERBERT. *The Social Psychology of George Herbert Mead* (ed. and with an Introduction by Anselm Strauss). Chicago: The University of Chicago Press, 1956.

MEAD, MARGARET. *New Lives for Old.* New York: William Morrow and Co., 1956.

MEEKER, EZRA. *Pioneer Reminiscences of Puget Sound.* Seattle: Ezra Meeker, 1903.

MIDDLETON, ALICE HOPTON (ed.). *Life in Carolina and New England during the Nineteenth Century.* Bristol, R. I.: Privately published, 1929.

MILLS, C. WRIGHT. *White Collar: The American Middle Classes.* New York: Oxford University Press, 1953.

MIYAMOTO, SHOTARO FRANK. *Social Solidarity among the Japanese in Seattle.* Seattle: University of Washington Publications in Social Science, 1939.

MORGAN, MURRAY. *Skid Road.* New York: The Viking Press, 1951.

NATIONAL URBAN LEAGUE. *A Study of the Social and Economic Conditions of the Negro Population, Charleston, South Carolina.* Community Relations Project, 1946.

NEW BEDFORD BOARD OF TRADE. *New Bedford, Massachusetts.* New Bedford: Mercury Publishing Co., 1889.

NEWHALL, JOHN B. *A Glimpse of Iowa in 1846.* Iowa City: State Historical Society of Iowa, 1955.

NIEBUHR, REINHOLD. *The Self and the Dramas of History.* New York: Charles Scribner's Sons, 1955.

NISBET, ROBERT A. *The Quest for Community.* New York: Oxford University Press, 1953.

PALMER, ROBERT R. *The Age of Democratic Revolution.* Princeton: Princeton University Press, 1959.

PARSONS, TALCOTT, and SHILS, EDWARD A. (eds.). *Toward a*

General Theory of Action. Cambridge, Mass.: Harvard University Press, 1952.

PEASE, ZEPHANIAH W. (ed.). *Life in New Bedford a Hundred Years Ago.* New Bedford: George H. Reynolds, 1922.

PETERSON, MERRILL D. *The Jefferson Image in the American Mind.* New York: Oxford University Press, 1960.

PHEGLEY, MALLIE. *The Father of Texas.* San Antonio: The Naylor Company, 1960.

PIKE, JAMES S. *The Prostrate State.* New York: D. Appleton and Co., 1874.

PILLSBURY, DOROTHY L. *No High Adobe.* Albuquerque: University of New Mexico Press, 1950.

———. *Roots in Adobe.* Albuquerque: University of New Mexico Press, 1959.

POPE, CHARLES HENRY. *The Pioneers of Massachusetts.* Boston: Charles H. Pope, 1900.

POTTS, RALPH B. *Seattle Heritage.* Seattle: Superior Publishing Co., 1955.

PRINCE, L. BRADFORD. *Historical Sketches of New Mexico.* Kansas City: Ramsey, Millett and Hudson, 1883.

Quarterly of the Texas State Historical Association, The, II, No. 3. Austin: Published Quarterly by the Association, Jan. 1899.

Quarterly of the Texas State Historical Association, The, XI. Austin: Published Quarterly by the Association, 1908.

RAVENEL, MRS. ST. JULIEN. *Charleston, the Place and the People.* New York: The Macmillan Co., 1931.

Redbook of Houston, The (A Compendium of Social, Professional, Religious, Educational and Industrial Interests of Houston's Colored Population). Houston: Sotex Publishing Co., 1915.

RHETT, ROBERT G. *Charleston, An Epic of Carolina.* Richmond: Garrett and Massie, 1940.

RICKETSON, DANIEL. *New Bedford of the Past.* Boston: Houghton, Mifflin and Co., 1903.

RIESMAN, DAVID. *The Lonely Crowd.* New Haven: Yale University Press, 1961.

RODMAN, BENJAMIN. *A Voice from the Prison.* New Bedford: Benjamin Lindsey, 1840.

RUTLEDGE, ARCHIBALD. *God's Children.* Indianapolis: The Bobbs-Merrill Co., 1947.

———. *The World around Hampton*. Indianapolis: The Bobbs-Merrill Co., 1960.

SAYRE, J. WILLIS. *This City of Ours*. Seattle: J. W. Sayre, 1936.

SCHAFER, JOSEPH. *Four Wisconsin Counties*. Madison, Wis.: State Historical Society of Wisconsin, 1927.

———. *The Yankee and the Teuton in Wisconsin*. II, III, & IV. Reprints from the *Wisconsin Magazine of History*, VI, No's 3, 4, VII, No. 1, 1923.

SCHMITZ, JOSEPH WILLIAM. *Texas Culture 1836–1846*. San Antonio: The Naylor Company, 1960.

STEIN, MAURICE R. *The Eclipse of Community*. Princeton: Princeton University Press, 1960.

THWAITES, REUBEN GOLD. *Wisconsin: The Americanization of a French Settlement*. Boston: Houghton Mifflin Co., 1908.

TOCQUEVILLE, ALEXIS DE. *The Republic of the United States of America*. New York: A. S. Barnes and Co., 1851.

TURNER, FREDERICK JACKSON. *The Significance of the Frontier in American History*. El Paso, Tex.: Academic Reprints, Inc., 1960.

UNION PUBLISHING CO. *History of Butler and Bremer Counties, Iowa*. Springfield, Ill.: Union Publishing Co., 1883.

UNTERMEYER, LOUIS (ed.). *The Britannica Library of Great American Writing, I*. Philadelphia and New York: J. B. Lippincott Co., 1960.

VERNER, ELIZABETH. *Mellowed by Time*. Columbia, S.C.: Bostick and Thornley, 1941.

WALGAMOTT, CHARLES S. *Six Decades Back*. Caldwell, Idaho: The Caxton Printers, 1936.

WALLACE, ERNEST and VIGNESS, DAVID M. (eds.). *Documents of Texas History, I, 1528–1846*. Lubbock: The Texas Tech Press, 1960.

WALSH, RICHARD. *Charleston's Sons of Liberty*. Columbia, S.C.: University of South Carolina Press, 1959.

WALTER, PAUL A. F. *Santa Fe County, New Mexico*. Santa Fe: The New Mexican Printing Co., 1909.

WESTERN HISTORICAL COMPANY. *The History of Racine and Kenosha Counties, Wisconsin*. Chicago: Western Historical Co., 1879.

WESTINDIAN, A. *Charleston, South Carolina, A Satiric Poem; Shewing That Slavery Still Exists in a Country Which Boasts, above All Others of Being the Seat of Liberty.* London: S. Y. Collins, 1851.

WHITEHEAD, ALFRED N. *Adventures of Ideas.* New York: New American Library, 1955.

WHYTE, WILLIAM H., JR. *The Organization Man.* New York: Simon and Schuster, 1956.

WILLIAMS, AMELIA W. and BARKER, EUGENE C. (eds.). *The Writings of Sam Houston, 1813–1836, Vol. V.* Austin: The University of Texas Press, 1941.

WILSON, RAY A. *Trails and Trials.* Creston, Iowa, 1959.

Wisconsin Magazine of History, V, No. 4, June, 1922.

WISCONSIN STATE HISTORICAL SOCIETY. *Dictionary of Wisconsin Biography.* Madison: Wisconsin State Historical Society, 1960.

Newspapers, Periodicals, Encyclopedias

Colliers Encyclopedia, Vol 17.

Current: Sept., 1961.

Denver Post: Oct. 6, 1959; Nov. 1, 1959.

Encyclopedia Americana, Vol. XXII, 1962.

Idaho Statesman, Holiday Number, Jan. 1, 1890.

New Bedford Mercury, One Hundredth Anniversary Supplement, Aug. 7, 1907.

New York Sunday Times Magazine, Aug. 5, 1962.

New York Times, Nov. 8, 1959; April 10, 1962; April 30, 1962; Dec. 4, 1962; Feb. 28, 1963; May 5, 1963; May 7, 1963; May 9, 1963; June 13, 1963; June 15, 1963; June 19, 1963; July 1, 1963; July 22, 1963; Aug. 29, 1963.

Reporter, Dec. 19, 1963.

Rocky Mountain News, Oct. 9, 1959.

Santa Fe New Mexican, New Year's Edition, Jan., 1910.

Seattle Daily Times, Anniversary Number, Feb. 14, 1909.

Sports Illustrated, April 16, 1962.

Sunday Denver Post, Dec. 13, 1959.

This Week Magazine, Sept. 13, 1959.

Time, Sept. 8, 1961.

Index